LIVE & BE WELL

LIVE&BEWELL

A CELEBRATION OF YIDDISH CULTURE IN AMERICA
FROM THE FIRST IMMIGRANTS TO THE SECOND WORLD WAR

by Richard
F. Shepard

and Vicki
Gold Levi

With Research
Assistance

by Moishe
Rosenfeld

Design by   Louise Fili

Ballantine Books • New York

A Hilltown Press Book

Copyright © 1982 by Hilltown Press, Inc.

All rights reserved under International and Pan-American Copyright
Conventions. Published in the United States by Ballantine Books,
a division of Random House, Inc., New York, and simultaneously in
Canada by Random House of Canada Limited, Toronto, Canada

Library of Congress Catalog Card Number: 82-90353

ISBN 0-345-29435-1

This book was prepared for publication by Hilltown Press, Inc., Worthington, Massachusetts.

Manufactured in the United States of America

First Edition: November 1982

10 9 8 7 6 5 4 3 2 1

Library of Congress Cataloging in Publication Data
Shepard, Richard F., 1922-
Live & be well.

Bibliography: p.191
1. Jews, East European—New York (N.Y.)—Social life
and customs—Addresses, essays, lectures. 2. New York
(N.Y.)—Popular culture—Adresses, essays, lectures.
I. Levi, Vicki Gold. II. Title. III. Title: Live and be
well. IV. Title: Yiddish culture in America
F128.9.J5s53 1982   305.8'924073   82-90353
ISBN 0-345-29435-1 (trd. pbk.)
ISBN 0-345-30752-6 (hard)

To YIVO, the iceberg of East European Jewish life, of which we represent the tiniest tip
RFS

To my great-grandmother Esther, who encouraged me to love this country; to my Grandmom Rose, who encouraged me to love books; and to my mother Beverly, who encouraged me to love
VGL

קאָנסטיטוציע

פֿון דער

בּרעזינער

קראַנקען אונטערשטיצונגס

סאָסיאיישאָן, אינק.

געגרינדעט דעם 30סטן מערץ, 1896

This book was, in every sense, a collaborative effort, calling upon the energies and knowledge and passions of scores of people. We wish especially to acknowledge our deepest debts to Moishe Rosenfeld, our research associate, who was as indefatigable as he was creative in tracking down hundreds of little known facts, and who translated much of the material we have taken directly from the original Yiddish; and Jack Noskowitz of the Workmen's Circle, who helped point us in the right directions, and then offered wise and constructive criticism of the finished text. It must further be acknowledged that the final text, and any errors therein, however, are our responsibility alone, and we trust Jack—and all those listed below—will forgive us if we have decided to stick with one interpretation rather than another.

Further special thanks go to Marek Web, head archivist at the YIVO Institute for Jewish Research, whose endless patience and guidance, as well as his astonishing knowledge of Jewish culture and history, were invaluable; to Diane Cypkin, archivist of the Yiddish Theatre Collection of the Museum of the City of New York, whose mastery of that particular archive has enriched our various discussions of the Yiddish stage immeasurably; and to Esther Brumberg of the Photo Library of the same museum, who helped us unearth scores of images of the old Lower East Side.

A number of people shared memories of their own, and those of their families', experiences: Fraydele Oysher and Arthur Tracy recalled the entertainment world in which they both performed so memorably; Hy Anzel offered details of Second Avenue's heyday, information to be presented in its full richness in his forthcoming book, *Moskowitz and Lupowitz: Stories and Recipes;* Herb Danska introduced us to the poems of his father, Lazar Dinsky; Victoria Secunda shared with us stories of her father-in-law, Sholem Secunda (further elaborated upon in her recent book, *Bei Mir Bist Du Schön: The Life of Sholem Secunda*); and Louise Levitas Henriksen made available insights about and memories of her mother, Anzia Yezierska, who is the subject of a forthcoming book by Mrs. Henriksen.

Thanks go as well to Zachry Baker, Fruma Mohrer, Rosaline Schwartz, Jack Weinstein, and the entire staff at YIVO; Douglas Bakken and David Crippen of the Henry Ford Museum, Edison Institute, in Dearborn, Michigan; Leroy Bellamy and Ann Wallmark of the Library of Congress; Nathan C. Belth of the Hebrew Free Loan Society of New York; Lillian Berger of Yonah Schimmel's Knish Bakery; Dr. Roderick Bladel and Daniel C. Patri of the Theatre Collection of the New York Public Library; Helene Blieberg of Grossinger's; Jennifer Bright of the Museum of the City of New York; Rick Camp of Lender's Bagels; Gary Canter of Canter's Deli in Los Angeles; Florence Cohen of the Jewish Labor Committee; the late Harvey Dixon of the Statue of Liberty National Monument; Rosemary Eakins and Ann Novotny of Research Reports; Mark Russ Federman and Sydney Berger of Russ and Daughters; Dan Field of Field's Exclusive Service; Rick Foster, manager of The Klezmorim; Harry Gold of the American Beverage Co.; Harold Harmatz of Ratner's; Norma Harrob and her staff at the Federation of Jewish Philanthropies; Morris Harth, associate director of corporate information, CBS, Inc.; Cyma M. Horowitz, library director of the American Jewish Committee; Fannie Jacobson of the *Jewish Daily Forward;* Leonard Katz of Katz's Deli; Milton Kutsher of Kutsher's Country Club; Robert Lazar, ILGWU archivist; Lorene Mayo of the Collection of Business Americana at the Smithsonian Institution; Frankie McCormick of the Songwriters' Hall of Fame; Jack Rechzeit and Seymour Rexsite of the Hebrew Actors Union; Norman Schapiro of Schapiro's Wine Co.; Bernice Selden, archivist of the YIVO Slide Bank; Bea Shustko of the Educational Alliance; Steven Siegel, archivist of the 92nd Street Y in New York; Fannie Zelcer of the American Jewish Archives; and the staffs of the Bronx Historical Society, the Chicago Historical Society, the Free Library of Philadelphia, the History and Genealogy Division and the Jewish Division of the New York Public Library, the National Council of Jewish Women, the National Parks Service, the Institute of Texan Cultures, and the Wisconsin Historical Society.

For their assistance in picture research we thank Meredith and Harry Collins of Brown Brothers; Robert Jackson and the staff of Culver Pictures; Irving Perton of Frederic Lewis, Inc.; Manny Kean of Kean Archives; and Stan Friedman of UPI.

For their help, good will, encouragement and friendship we thank Bill Aron, Linda Arking, Jay Bende, Sabell Bender-Molotnik, Anna Burak, Marilyn and Alvin Cooperman, Marc and Zosia Gold, Michele Gold, Irene Heskes, Trudy Kaplan, Jacob Katzman, Alex Robin, Richard and Estelle Rogers Levi, Ellen Levine, Ricki Rosen, Max Rosey, Nahma Sandrow, Zvee Scooler, and Sheldon Secunda.

For their professional skills, applied to making this book a reality, we thank agent Liz Darhansoff; copy editor Chris Jerome; proofreader Barbara Wood; art director Louise Fili; and our editor and publisher, Daniel Okrent.

Finally, our thanks to Annette Harchik Rosenfeld, who intervened for us in numerous ways; Alex Levi for contributing his photographic skills, his home, and his wife; and Trudy Shepard, whose eye for detail saved us many an error.   —R.F.S., V.G.L.

May 1982

Another book on Jewish life? Already there are mountains of books about Jewish life in America, books that study it, books that laugh at it, books that reminisce about it, books that analyze it. And films, and television shows. So much, and yet so much more to tell about. In this brief volume we are not studying, analyzing, laughing, or reminiscing, at least not particularly so, although maybe we are doing a little of each.

This is a book that is designed to create an appetite, to re-create an appetite, if you will, to offer a flavor of the people who landed in America with little more than heroic perseverance, strong passions, and a Yiddish language that expressed a culture unique to the world. They and their children were molded by the American experience, and in turn they molded that American experience. Yet, for all that has been written and collected about them, it is striking how quickly it all fades into the past, how the romantic aftertaste distorts the original flavor.

Theirs was an experience that needs remembering. Hester Street is no less seminal than Plymouth Rock in the lives of many of us. We make no pretensions here to unearthing the Yiddish-American history archeologically, or in any other way scientifically; others have done that. Our goal is to spur the interest, to inspire the reader to delve further, to look back in order to learn how our forebears looked ahead. We have found new things and we have embraced old things; above all, we have tried to give a sense of flavor, of variety, of a richness that merits celebration, honor, and not a little wistfulness. So much of what we write here is gone forever, relic of a world past. More, we hope, stays with us, in perhaps invisible ways.

This is a selective book. Just as it is not a reminiscence or a history, so it is neither an almanac nor an encyclopedia. We have, by in-

tent, focused our attentions here on a brief historical moment, one that begins roughly with the great waves of Jewish emigration from eastern Europe that began with the assassination of Czar Alexander II in 1881, and ends with the first guns of the Second World War. Too, we have concentrated—the subject demands it—primarily on Yiddish life in New York City, although the book ranges as far afield as Fairfax Avenue in Los Angeles and The Main in Montreal. Within these limits, this is a poking-around in a grandfather's attic, a selective and idiosyncratic tour of the treasures and sadnesses found there. Mostly, we have decided to include one person and not another because of some indefinable sense of Yiddishness; to evoke one event or institution and not another because of some inherent, indelible emblem of a bygone culture. Irving Berlin, who wrote songs called "Yiddle on Your Fiddle" and "Goodbye Becky Cohen" long before he gave us "White Christmas," is here; George Gershwin is not. Cream cheese, an Americanization of an eastern European staple, is here; chicken soup, unadorned and uncorrupted for centuries, is not. Y. L. Peretz, whose influence on Yiddish literature was unmatched, never came to America. He appears in these pages only in relation to those he influenced, writers who were not only Yiddish but American, too. We've also included many German Jews, and some non-Jews whose interaction with the eastern Europeans was profound or merely provocative. This is a book about Yiddish culture and its intersection with America. Where that intersection seemed clearest, most vital, or utterly singular, we have directed our attention.

So many sources and references were used in preparing this book that it would be futile to try to name them all, although a brief bibliography is included. We wish here to single out a few of the books that sum up the immigrant era according to their own perspectives, books we have found most valuable in our own work. *World of Our Fathers* is a skilled and entertainingly crafted work by Irving Howe, certainly the master interpreter of Yiddish-American life. *The Promised City* by Moses Rischin, another formidable volume, deals with immigrant life in New York at flood tide. In *Poor Cousins* Ande Manners chronicles in delightful fashion the touchy contacts, full of compassion and distaste, between the uptown German Jews and the newly arrived downtown Yiddish-speaking Jews. Our list, as you will see, numbers many more; each has something special to say, slicing the salami of historical record to one or another taste. We, for out part, have sliced the salami to serve you a lip-smacking sample. Anywhere else, we'd call it an hors d'oeuvre, but here we'll call it a *nosh*, a *lek un a shmek*. May it be good for you.

Note on Spelling: *By and large, we have sought in this book to follow the rules of transliteration from Yiddish to English characters as set forth by the scholars of the YIVO Institute for Jewish Research. In some very few instances, however, where the word in question has entered the English language intact, we have used the common "Yinglish" spelling.*

Adler, Jacob P. (1855–1926) He was one of the titanic figures in the history of the Yiddish theater in America, and founder as well of a theatrical dynasty that numbered, among his children, Celia, Stella (herself one of the most influential acting teachers of her generation), and Luther Adler.

The founder of this extraordinary family was born in Odessa and joined Abraham Goldfadn's pioneering troupe in 1879. When the czars suppressed the Yiddish theater in Russia, Adler moved to London, where he soon acquired a retinue of admirers despite the imaginative insults he aimed at sycophants and other nuisances in both Yiddish and Russian. For all his grandiose manner (Harold Clurman called him "the romance of the Yiddish theater"), Adler was a serious artist who avoided the *shund*, or trash, that was the primary element of so many of the Yiddish productions of his time. Adler's favorite part was as "The Jewish King Lear," but he was probably most celebrated as Shylock in *The Merchant of Venice*, in which he appeared speaking Yiddish with an English-speaking supporting cast in 1903 at the American Theater. When Adler died, 200,000 mourners lined Second Avenue for his funeral.

Aleichem, Sholem. See SHOLEM ALEICHEM.

Allen Street Prostitution on the Lower East Side flourished on the Bowery, on Chrystie, Forsyth, and Stanton streets, but nowhere with the vitality it displayed on Allen Street. Red lamps shone in apartments up and down the thoroughfare, where immigrant girls plied their trade in the service of notorious Jewish pimps called "lighthouses" because of their dominance over the red-lamped brothels. From the

New York Tribune, 1900: "When an objectionable tenant moves into a 'stoop' [a tenement building with a high stoop in front], puts up lace curtains and other decorations too expensive for and not in harmony with the surroundings, a tenant or possibly several tenants usually make objection and protest. But the 'stoop' pays at least twice as much rent when occupied by the objectionable tenant."

Although prostitution was well established in the neighborhood long before the arrival of the Jews, by 1900 Jewish prostitution and white slavery (promoted by such groups as the notorious Max Hochstim Association) were common. In 1899 the Year Book of the University Settlement of New York declared, "The greatest evil the Eighth Assembly District has to face is the evil of prostitution, which seems to exist to an appalling extent, and to be on the increase." In 1904 the Baron de Hirsch Fund, alarmed by the problem, founded the Clara de Hirsch Home for Immigrant Girls and two years later the National Council of Jewish Women opened the Lakeview Home for women on Staten Island. The situation also drew the attention of the New York Kehillah, whose investigations brought about the closing of many of the brothels. One particularly enterprising madam whose business attracted the attention of the reformers was "Mother"

(L), Jacob Adler in full declaim; (R), Stella Adler, Jacob's daughter, 1933

Jacob Epstein, alumnus of the Alliance Art School

Rosie Hertz; a mere streetwalker in 1892, by 1909 she operated eight houses scattered through the Lower East Side.

The reasons for Jewish prostitution were no different from those for other ethnic groups: poverty, weakened family ties, alienation, loneliness, and naivete. The remedy came with the rise in economic and social status of the immigrants and their children.

Alliance Art School At three cents a lesson, the Educational Alliance's art school was the Ecole des Beaux Arts of the Lower East Side, training ground for such artists as Jacob (later Sir Jacob) Epstein, Abraham Walkowitz, Chaim Gross, and Jo Davidson. Founded by Henry McBride, the art critic of the *New York Sun*, it flourished from the 1880s to 1905, then was reopened with the support of the needle trade unions in 1917. Among other students who passed through this East Broadway school of art, including some who later came back to teach, were Ben Shahn, Leonard Baskin, Moses Soyer, Louise Nevelson, Barnett Newman, and Mark Rothko.

Alrightnik One of the first phrases learned by immigrants who sought quick assimilation was "All right, all right." It indicated that all was under control and no further explanation was needed. Adorned with the all-purpose Slavic suffix, it became "al-

rightnik," one who was either a success or wished to create the illusion of success. Deborah Dash Moore quotes New York Judge Jonah Goldstein defining the path to "alrightnik" success that so many of his friends followed: each "once lived on East Broadway or Madison Street, went to school on Norfolk or Henry, learned the facts of life on Allen Street, was in business on Seventh Avenue, and lived on Central Park West."

Am Olam The dream of intellectuals, Jewish and non-Jewish, in the nineteenth century often had to do with a return to the land, a reversion that would let man enjoy the products of his own labor and avoid the hierarchical, industrial, capitalist society that so brutalized the masses. Among the Jews of eastern Europe, for whom farming—if permitted at all—was a decidedly un-Jewish pursuit, the promise of productive activity in a communal setting fired young imaginations in the same way the American utopian schemes of Brook Farm and the like appealed to young people of rather different background.

Some Yiddish-speaking Jews became early Zionists determined to renew the Palestinian desert, while others joined Am Olam ("Eternal People"), their eyes set on America and its cheap, virgin land. In the early 1880s the Am Olam movement saw the transportation of eastern European Jewish intellectuals and Socialists to distant North American farmlands. One such Canadian settlement, now Edenbridge, began life as Yiddenbridge. The Am Olam colonies, scattered in such distant locales as Louisiana and Oregon, did not last long, variously suffering the ravages of flood, yellow fever, intolerable climate, and ideological dispute.

Apart from Am Olam, other Jewish farming settlements appeared now and again. The Baron de Hirsch Fund supported the southern New Jersey village of Woodbine, which in 1903 became the first all-Jewish municipality in the nation. The Jewish Agricultural Society was chartered in 1900 in New York, also under subsidy of the Baron de Hirsch Fund, and issued a bilingual journal entitled *The Jewish Farmer*.

Amalgamated Clothing Workers
Founded in 1914, the Amalgamated is among the longest-running progressive labor unions in America.

The men's clothing industry's analog to the ILGWU, the Amalgamated established Sidney Hillman's eminence in the American labor movement and on the left flank of the Democratic Party. As concerned with its membership's at-home welfare as with its well-being at work, the union opened the Amalgamated Bank (which is still granting loans slightly below the going rate today) and pioneered worker housing with its enormous Workers Cooperative Colony in the northern reaches of the Bronx. Apartments in this immense development were sold to the union's predominantly immigrant Jewish membership at extremely low prices. Wrote Calvin Trillin, "In the late twenties, a Jewish garment worker who wanted to move his family from the squalor of the Lower East Side to the relatively sylvan

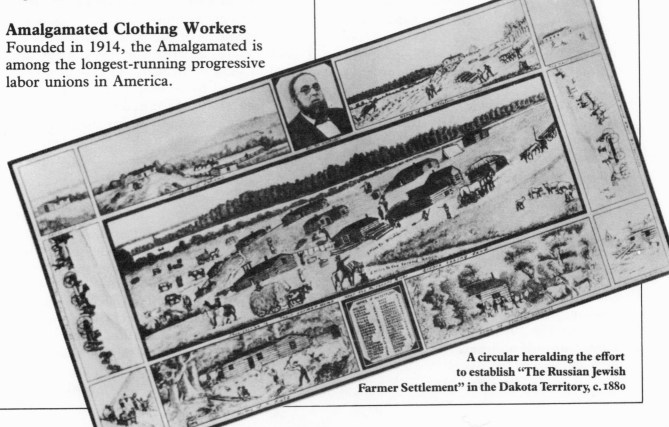

A circular heralding the effort to establish "The Russian Jewish Farmer Settlement" in the Dakota Territory, c. 1880

The 1911 Chicago garment workers' strike, which led directly to the founding of the Amalgamated

north Bronx could select an apartment on the basis of ideology."

In the 1970s, the Amalgamated merged with the Textile Workers Union, and soon thereafter led the successful nationwide boycott of the J. P. Stevens Company.

American, Sadie (1862–1944) As president of the New York chapter of the National Council of Jewish Women, Sadie American—whose surname reflected her immigrant father's regard for his new home—played a prominent role in aid programs, particularly those for women, directed toward the downtown immigrants by uptown Jews. Under her leadership, the council provided Yiddish-speaking women workers at Ellis Island in 1904 to meet immigrant girls and steer them away from the Allen Street flesh peddlers; established

homes for financially troubled Jewish women; and in 1906 took over a home for wayward girls, called Lakeview, on Staten Island.

In 1910 the council, the only American Jewish group to be represented, sent Miss American to London for a Jewish International Conference on the Suppression of Traffic in Girls and Women and to a similar conference in Madrid. So well known did she become that she was invited to advise the Italian government's immigration secretary on measures to protect Italian emigrants to the United States.

American Jewish Committee Assuming the role of the *hofjud* or *shtadlan* (court Jew) who historically interceded on behalf of the Jews before high authority, the AJC was founded in 1906, the creation of the German-Jewish, wealthier, and more assimilated elements of the American Jewish community. Membership was initially limited to sixty individuals, an elite group spearheaded by an even more elite executive leadership; the initial organization was directly influenced by a fear that more radical elements might seize the initiative when Socialist activism was running strong on Delancey Street.

Once established, the AJC fought discrimination, both ethnic and economic, with vigor. It defeated requirements for literacy tests for immigrants and led the effort to have Yiddish and Hebrew recognized as acceptable languages by immigration authorities.

Louis Marshall, who succeeded the committee's first president, Mayer Sulzberger, held office from 1912 to 1929 and became the consummate spokesman for American Jews. Some of the issues the AJC pursued under Marshall's leadership included the creation of the American Jewish Relief Committee for victims of World War I, which sought to secure rights for Jews in various European nations; and the battle to refute Henry Ford's bogus *Protocols of the Elders of Zion* in the late 1920s. For many years firmly anti-Zionist, the AJC has since become a staunch supporter of Israel.

Anarchism Since the advent of the Chassidim in the 1700s, squabbling over religious divergencies had riven the Jewish community in Europe. In the late nineteenth century, this contentious quality blossomed among modern, secular Jews, who substi-

tuted ideology for theology and proceeded to differ no less passionately about what was right and what was wrong. The anarchist movement displayed its initial strength among Russian intellectuals, and found a hero in the German Johann Most (author in 1881 of a diatribe on the assassination of the czar, entitled "At Last!"). Of Most, who arrived in America in 1882, Irving Howe wrote, "In the Jewish radical milieu of the eighties, where fervor counted at least as much as sense, he gained a following." The anarchist belief in the subordination, even eradication, of any form of governmental or political system was as anathematic to Marxist Jews as to their conservative, religious brethren. Still, the Jewish anarchists made their mark, holding Yom Kippur balls, publishing the *Freie Ar-*

A 1911 delegation of AJC leaders (Louis Marshall extreme L, Mayer Sulzberger third from L), in Washington to testify on American relations with Russia

beiter Shtimme (which survived well into the 1970s), and adopting such vivid heroes as Emma Goldman and Alexander Berkman.

Artef Players The tide of socialism that swept through large segments of the underpaid, exploited working class of the Yiddish community broke into schematic rivulets as distinct in the arts as they were in the labor movement. The Artef Players was created as the theatrical expression of the Jewish Communists, but so remarkable was its stagecraft that it drew acclaim from every quarter, including the established English-language press. Artef delivered agit-prop, to be sure, but it also brought reality to the theater, as did its English-language col-

leagues in such institutions as the Group Theater in the 1930s. Artef was founded in 1925, in the tradition of the Moscow Art Theater, and survived more than sixteen years. It did Gorki, and it did plays about impoverished sweatshop workers. Among Artef alumni who went on to renown elsewhere were the director Benno Schneider and actor-director Jules Dassin.

Asch, Sholem (1880–1957) Few Yiddish writers were as controversial among the Jews as Sholem Asch, once the most popular of Yiddish novelists, in English translation, among American readers. Unlike the man who later assumed this mantle, I. B. Singer, who is occasionally criticized by the

An Artef appeal for funds (L and R), and a scene from the troupe's production of Kulback's *The Outlaw.* At R in photograph is David Opatashu.

THE ARTEF MUST BE SAVED

ARTEF PLAYERS SPONSORS
••••

LUTHER ADLER
S. ALMAZOFF
FANNIE BRICE
JOSEPH BULOFF
N. BUCHWALD
MORRIS CARNOVSKY
HAROLD CLURMAN
OSSIP DYMOW
WILLIAM EDLIN
MENDEL ELKIN
FLORENCE ELDRIDGE
FRANCES FARMER
BEN GOLD
B. Z. GOLDBERG
MIKE GOLD
ALEXANDER GRANACH
BEN HECHT
LILLIAN HELLMAN
PERETZ HIRSHBEIN
SIDNEY HOWARD
MOSS HART
SAM JAFFE
M. KATZ
ARTHUR KOBER

FRITZ LANG
H. LEIVICK
B. LINDER
FREDERICK MARCH
K. MARMOR
WORTHINGTON MINER
DR. A. MUKDOINI
PAUL MUNI
P. NOVICK
CLIFFORD ODETS
A. OLKIN
M. J. OLGIN
JOSEPH OPATOSHU
SAMUEL ORNITZ
ELMER RICE
R. SALTZMAN
IRWIN SHAW
HERMAN SHUMLIN
SYLVIA SIDNEY
LILLIAN TAIZ
ERNST TOLLER
Z. WEINPER
JAMES W. WISE
WILLIAM WYLER
BENJAMIN ZEMACH

490

Yiddish literati but nonetheless commands universal respect, Asch became anathema in the Yiddish world because of the Christological themes in his three novels, *The Nazarene* (1939, although not published in its original Yiddish until 1943), *The Apostle* (1943, and not published in the original Yiddish at all), and *Mary* (1939). Asch was accused by critics and community spokesmen of being an apostate, a missionary who was trying to convince Jews of the acceptability of Jesus and Christianity. Abraham Cahan, in whose *Daily Forward* the writings of Asch had been a staple, not only rejected a serialization of *The Nazarene* but severed relations with Asch entirely. The writer's detractors looked for, and thought they found, indications of Christian missionary zeal in later books and even "discovered" the virus in earlier works.

The writer who so inflamed his own community was a proud, vain man of whom his own secretary and editor, the writer Shlomo Rosenberg, wrote, "Asch had a weakness for titles, the rich, and . . . gentiles." Once, as a young man, he was hailed by the Yiddish classicists Bialik and Mendele as a Yiddish writer. "I am not a Yiddish writer," Asch retorted, "I am a universal artist."

Asch was born in Kutno, Poland, and the first book he encountered was the Bible. At sixteen years of age he discovered secular literature and learned German, reading Moses Mendelsohn's translation of the Psalms and horrifying his devout parents. He left home, taught in another town, wrote some poems in Hebrew, and went to Warsaw to show them to Y. L. Peretz. The older man, the foremost Jewish writer of his time, urged Asch to write in Yiddish. The result was a career that stretched from short story to mammoth trilogy, from his first Yiddish publication (a story, "Moyshele," published in 1900) to novels about immigrant life in New York (to which he moved in 1914), the Polish underworld, the persecution of the Jews in the seventeenth century, even about a Jewish banker sentenced to death for the killing of a Kentucky colonel. Stung by the criticism of his Christian trilogy—he maintained he had written the novels to put their protagonists in the framework of Jewish life, to show how they were innately Jews themselves—he withdrew from the Yiddish literary circles of New York, eventually settling in Israel in 1955, where he was warmly welcomed. Asch suffered a stroke two years later, went to London for an operation, and died there.

Athletes As among all ethnic groups at the lower end of the economic scale, the children of the immigrant Jews saw success in athletics—particularly boxing—as a means of escape from the ghetto. When Benny Leonard became world champion, he car-

The champion wrestlers of the Chicago Hebrew Institute, 1919

ried with him the dreams of thousands who would do as he did (even if their mothers, like his own, cringed at the thought). Leonard carried his followers into the arenas in such large numbers that promoters and managers frantically scoured the streets of Philadelphia, Chicago, and every other city with a large Yiddish-speaking population for other Jewish contenders to place in the ring. Harold Ribalow wrote, "Whenever a likely-looking Jewish boy made a mark as a boxer, he was called . . . 'the new Benny Leonard.'" Maxie Rosenbloom, Barney Ross (born Barnett Rasovsky), and Al Singer successfully emulated Leonard's rise to the championship, and others who were not Jewish—notably Max Baer, who even wore a Star of David on his trunks—claimed they were, hoping to capture part of the immense following certain to rally to a Great Jewish Hope.

It wasn't only boxing that inflamed the partisanship of the Jews, who at some level recognized that acceptance in athletics was perhaps the swiftest means of assimilation (a writer for *The Day* mournfully suggested that "the grandfather studies the Torah, the father the business section, the son the sports page"). In 1923 the New York Giants uncovered a long-ball hitter named Moses Solomon whom they immediately started calling "The Rabbi of Swat" and touting as the Jewish Babe Ruth. Solomon didn't pan out, but in 1941 the Giants did connive to have four Jews in their lineup at one time, a gesture not lost on the enormous Jewish population of the city. Young boys' hearts stirred when Hank Greenberg

became a huge star with the Detroit Tigers, and their mothers clucked approvingly when Greenberg declined to play on Yom Kippur. Basketball, which required little equipment and only a small piece of land, became immensely popular as well. City slums that would later produce phalanxes of black basketball stars yielded, from the 1920s through the 1950s, Jewish players and coaches—men like Nat Holman, Menchy Goldblatt, Red Holzman, and Dolph Schayes—who were among the best in the nation.

But it wasn't only ethnic pride, and the desire to assimilate, that enabled sports to play such a large role in the lives of the immigrants. There was, undeniably, also a certain *frisson* of amazement—that Jews, by stereotype frail and bookish, could actually do these things, perform great feats of strength and coordination. In 1923 an athlete of a different sort, a circus strongman named Zisha Breitbart, traveled the country billed as "the pride of the Yidn," packing Yiddish vaudeville houses wherever he went. He would drive nails with his fists, lift huge weights, and otherwise perform the usual run of sideshow feats of strength. And before each performance, he would, wrote Stanley Feldstein, "pledge always to avenge the honor of the Jew, and illustrated the point with tales of his encounters with anti-Semites who spoke disparagingly of Jews . . . When [the anti-Semites] disbelieved and would not desist, 'I broke them like a match.' . . . At this, the crowd would jump to its feet, stamping and roaring in jubilation."

B

Badkhn The *badkhn* was a merrymaker, a laugh-provoker most commonly found at Jewish weddings. More than a stand-up comic, the *badkhn* was steeped in Jewish wit and humor, which is to say that he also knew suffering and anguish, and was able to compound all of this in a particularly Yiddish way that made the mouth laugh and the eyes tear. A great *badkhn* like Elyokum Zunser (1840–1913) knew Hebrew, the Bible, the Talmud, and the folklore of his religion, wrote poems and songs, and could even improvise at length about whoever might be paying him to play a particular party. Abraham Cahan remembered, as a child in Europe, attending a wedding reception at which Zunser presided, greeting the bride "with eloquent salutes fashioned around her name and the names of her groom and their parents."

Most *badkhonim* did not make their entire livings from this ill-rewarded line, but supplemented their incomes with such compatible trades as matchmaking. (After arriving in America, Zunser supported himself by running a printing shop on East Broadway.) There are still *badkhonim* who make the scene at Orthodox or Chassidic weddings in America, but even they have largely abandoned the distinctive style of their craft for the electronically amplified routines of those professional "Yankee" comics called emcees.

Bagel Perhaps the best-known symbol of the eastern European Jew in America, the bagel—from the German word for "ring"—has been transformed, across the ocean and the years, from a luxury borne only rarely on *shtetl* tables more accustomed to cheap brown bread, to a virtual cliché. The historiography of bageldom covers a full 350 years, but it was not until 1951 that the bagel's status as a staple was fully recognized. In that year, New York's bagel bakers went out on strike, and the *Times* headlined its front-page story, "BAGEL FAMINE THREATENS IN CITY/LABOR DISPUTE PUTS HOLE IN SUPPLY."

Baron de Hirsch Fund Baron Maurice de Hirsch (1831–1896) was a wealthy and aristocratic Bavarian Jew, a man worth an estimated $100 million in 1890, a friend of the Prince of Wales. Espousing assimilation of the Russian Jews, de Hirsch tried unsuccessfully to persuade the czarist regime to allow him to provide material support to his Russian coreligionists. He soon realized that only emigration could ameliorate their distressed condition, and he and his wife, Clara, devoted substantial

Badkhn Elyokum Zunser, 1895

time, effort, and money to the settlement of Jews in the Western Hemisphere. In 1889 de Hirsch directed that the proceeds of a $2.4 million endowment be used to establish farm colonies and vocational schools for immigrant Jews in the United States. In 1891 this endowment was incorporated as the Baron de Hirsch Fund, administered for decades after de Hirsch's death by prominent American Jews. Among its other activities, the fund established a rural Jewish community, Woodbine, in southern New Jersey.

Baron de Hirsch Trade School, Class of '95

Barondess, Joseph (1867–1928) His was a life perhaps unusual in the ordinary run of lives but in a way typical of many immigrant stories. Barondess, his wife, and their baby arrived in New York in steerage, the final stop on a long trek from their native Ukraine, during the blizzard of 1888. He lived in a Ludlow Street basement in the usual squalor that beset newcomers, worked as a cloakmaker, and soon became a union organizer and a leader in the great 1890 Cloakmakers' Strike, the first major labor action in the needle trades. "The King of the Cloakmakers," according to Moses Rischin, "spoke in homilectical Yid-

dish, studded with Talmudic allusions, alternated wit with pathos, and was as able to scold his followers into line as to debate a rabbi's right to kosher boycotted bread." Active in the moderate wing of the Socialist Party, he soon abandoned union battles altogether and went into the insurance business. As his station in life changed, Barondess's views moderate further; what had, for Barondess and so many others, been a brutish existence became a secure and comfortable one. Nonetheless, he remained an activist, though of a more establishment sort, as a founder of the American Jewish Congress, as an appointee to the New York City Board of Education, and as a vigorous champion of the Zionist Organization of America.

Ben-Ami, Jacob (1890–1977) The career of this fine, resonant, and dynamic actor spanned the most animated years of Yiddish theater in America and extended well beyond them. Born in Minsk, he played organ in a circus in his early teens, sang in a synagogue choir, and was retained to sing in a theater. By 1906 he had begun acting—albeit for no salary—in his hometown, then became a prompter for a Yiddish troupe, and before he turned twenty met Peretz Hirshbein and helped the poet-dramatist establish his company in Odessa. (Years later, Ben-Ami directed the great Yiddish film, *Green Fields*, based on the Hirshbein comedy.) Ben-Ami came to America with Sarah Adler's group in 1912, joined Thomashevsky, and toured with the popular Keni Liptzin. He also directed three one-act plays by Peretz at the Neighborhood Playhouse, a theater established on the Lower East Side to bring the performing arts in Yiddish to the immigrants and their children.

Jacob Ben-Ami in *The Miracle of the Warsaw Ghetto*

In 1918 Ben-Ami was hired by Maurice Schwartz for seventy-five dollars a week at the Irving Place Theater, where he was soon hailed as "the initiator and driving force to start a Yiddish Art Theater." It was here that Ben-Ami staged Hirshbein's lovely rural play *Farvorfn Vinkel*, a critical success and commercial failure launched on one of the company's "literary Wednesdays." Soon, however, Ben-Ami fell out with Schwartz and in 1919 founded his own Jewish Art Theater in America, dedicated to loftier ideals than mere entertainment.

Benefis The theater benefit, or *benefis*, to this day one of Broadway's fundamental supports, was as it is today a boon to producers and a bane to actors in the earliest days of Yiddish theater in America. Eighty years ago, the benefit filled the house on the first four nights of the week, when organized groups—clubs, unions, *landsmanshaftn*, federations—purchased blocks of tickets. *Benefis* audiences, who paid full price for the tickets the sponsoring organization bought at up to seventy-five percent discount (the difference, of course, supporting the organization and its efforts), wanted—as they do today—light, musical, escapist stuff. Producers who could sell out their houses on weekends with serious fare would occasionally try to slip substantial work past *benefis* audiences, but they didn't dare try it with any frequency (Maurice Schwartz warned of turning away

such trade with a *baykhl,* as a literary drama was somewhat contemptuously called). Most difficult of all was simply getting the audience to pay attention to whatever might be onstage. *Benefis* audiences, usually composed of people who knew each other, were often impossible to quiet down at the start of the show, occupied as they were with waving to friends across the house and greeting others in the row behind them. Producers, directors, and actors would accommodate such behavior by opening plays with throwaway lines and delaying the entrance of the stars until the audience subsided into at least a facsimile of order.

Benefis **night at the Grand Theatre**

Berg, Gertrude (1899–1966) Harlem-born, Columbia-educated, Gertrude Berg spent nearly thirty years in millions of American homes on radio and later television as star of a show that began as "The Rise of the Goldbergs." When the show started out in 1929, Goldberg's broadcasting experience consisted of little more than having translated a radio ad for gasoline into Yiddish. She was nonetheless able to persuade NBC to air the show, which she wrote as well as starred in, and it immediately became a national hit, running for forty-five hundred separate broadcasts over the next seventeen years.

The concept was simple enough, concerned as it was with the life of Molly Goldberg, her husband, Jake, and their two children in a working-class tenement. It was a New York story replete with rising Yiddish inflections, but without the actual Yiddish accents and dialect employed by stage comics. Mrs. Berg was a keen-eyed and sharp-eared observer of the way people lived, and the veracity of her presentation struck a chord. After her signature shout to a neighbor—"Yoo-hoo, Mrs. Bloom!"—became a national catch-phrase in the thirties, the show by 1941 enjoyed the widest dissemination of any American radio program, with a listening audience of ten million people daily.

In 1949 "The Goldbergs" was translated to television, still starring Gertrude Berg, expiring, finally, in 1955. Among the actors who passed through its orbit were John Garfield, Marjorie Main, Joseph Cotten, and Van Heflin, as well as the unfor-gettably weary Philip Loeb in the role of Jake. Loeb's own life ended tragically, a suicide as a result of the anti-Communist blacklisting during the McCarthy era.

Berkman, Alexander (1870–1936) A Russian-born anarchist, Berkman was an ascetic whose goal was utter self-discipline on behalf of his cause. His family was a prosperous one, but an uncle who was a nihilist had been sentenced to death by the czar, an event that surely changed Berkman's life. Living in America by the time of the bitter Homestead Strike in 1892, Berkman shot and stabbed Henry Clay Frick of the Carnegie Steel Corporation; although Frick did not die, Berkman served fourteen years in prison. Upon his release, he resumed his close relationship with Emma Goldman, and was deported with her to Russia following the Palmer Raids of 1919. In 1936 he committed suicide in the south of France.

Alexander Berkman after one of his periodic indictments, this one in 1918

Irving Berlin (R), in a re-creation of
Nigger Mike's Bowery Bar, at the Astor Hotel, 1940

Berlin, Irving (1888–　　) The Siberian-
born Jew who was to become to popular
songwriting what Heinz was to pickles arrived on the Lower East Side before his
fifth birthday. Four years later his father, a
part-time cantor, died, and the boy went to
work on the streets, singing for pennies.
He became a song plugger and singing
waiter at a Bowery cafe, where the newspaperman Herbert Bayard Swope gave him
his first public notice: a feature story about
the teenaged waiter who refused a tip from
a prince. By 1907, when he published his
first song, "Marie from Sunny Italy," he
had Americanized his name from the original Isidore Baline; by 1911 he had Berlin-
ized the entire country with his first enor-

mous success, "Alexander's Ragtime
Band."

Despite his use of a transposing piano,
which enabled the technically illiterate Berlin to write in more than one key, his feelings for melody and rhythm were unerring.
Berlin's prodigious output ranged from
such well-assimilated standards as "White
Christmas," "Easter Parade," and "God
Bless America" to earlier, less catholic
numbers like "Yiddle on Your Fiddle,"
"Yiddisha Nightingale," "That Kassatsky
Dance," and "Goodbye Becky Cohen."

Bintel Brief The "bundle of letters" became a staple in the *Jewish Daily Forward* in
1906, when editor Abraham Cahan saw the
need for his readers to have a place to air
their problems. Not so much advice to the
lovelorn (although it was often that, too),
"Bintel Brief" was instead a sort of primer
on life in America for the perplexed immigrant.

In his memoirs, Cahan (who wrote the
answers personally when the column began)
said, "People often need the opportunity to
be able to pour out their heavy-laden
hearts. Among our immigrant masses this
need was very marked. Hundreds of thousands of people, torn from their homes and
their dear ones, were lonely souls who
thirsted for expression, who wanted to hear
an opinion, who wanted advice in solving
their weighty problems. The 'Bintel Brief'
created just this opportunity for them."
And thus did the letters pour in, even from
those who had to pay others to write them.

Isaac Metzker, who studied sixty years'
worth of "Bintel Brief" letters, noted how
the problems of the *Forward*'s readers
changed as they progressed from poverty to
relative comfort, from the sweatshop to
better lives. Still, a selection from across

the years indicates that the problems were, if nothing else, singular:

"My son is already 26 years old and doesn't want to get married. He says he is a Socialist and he is too busy. Socialism is Socialism but getting married is important too."

From a man who needed money for his desperately ill wife, and was compelled to go back to work in a shop then on strike: "Now my conscience bothers me because I am a scab. I am working now. I bring home $15 a week, sometimes $16. But I am not happy, because I was a scab and left the union. . . . Dear editor, how can I go back now in the union and salve my conscience?" The editor replied that neither the writer nor the union was guilty, but the union should look into it; if it were found that the man's recital of circumstance measured up, "they will certainly forgive him and he can again become a good union man."

A woman wrote to tell how she had fallen into an intimate affair with a businessman, a dominating man who ordered her to move in with him, which she did. "Dear editor, it's possible I should be scolded for my actions, but believe me, I can't explain myself why I obeyed him. . . . Save me and advise me what to do."

And on and on, the full panoply of human problems. A father asks whether his son should continue studying chemistry, which the boy loves, because Jews can't get jobs in chemical firms. A mother wants advice about how to wean her daughter away from the Christian Science doctrine her son-in-law brought into the family. The president of a

"society" writes that a member, a widow, had committed suicide because of poverty and troubles, "not for silly reasons," and now the president is being attacked by members for allowing her to have a regular burial rather than interring her by the cemetery fence, as custom dictates.

Most representative of all, perhaps, was this letter: "I read the troubles in your 'Bintel Brief' each day very attentively. But my own troubles are so great, so enormous, that I will not even ask your permission to print my few words in your paper, as others do, but simply, I ask you right on the spot: 'Help!' "

Boarders The boarder was an economic fact of life on the Lower East Side, one who soon became a social fact of life as well. At a time when many young, male immigrants were arriving in New York, having left family behind with the promise that all would soon be brought over with the riches earned in the New World, the need for lodging was urgent. While Jewish husbands worked in factories and shops, Jewish wives supplemented the family income by taking in boarders. In Anzia

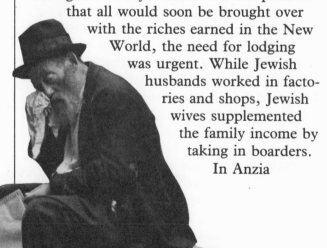

Borscht Belt queen Jennie Grossinger, with Eddie Fisher

Yezierska's novel *Bread Givers,* one such woman explains how this source of revenue can be tapped: "Do as I have done. Put the spring over four empty herring barrels and you'll have a bed fit for the president. Now put a board over the potato barrel and a clean newspaper over that and you'll have a table. All you need yet is a soapbox for a chair and you'll have a furnished room complete." The boarder was completely absorbed into the family, even going so far as to coddle and scold the children. The institution of the boarder also provided an endless source of plots for novels and plays, and was equally valuable to stage comics, who could delight and scandalize audiences from Chrystie Street to the Catskills with ribald tales of intimacies between boarders and their landladies.

Borscht Belt It was *Variety* editor Abel Green who conceived of the term "Borscht Belt" to describe the Jewish vacation resorts of the Catskills. It has since been universally understood to explain the origins of the hordes of comics who nurtured their talents in those hospitable hills before finding their ways onto "The Ed Sullivan Show." The term, of course, derived from the cold beet soup that served as an inevitable preamble to *milkhik,* or dairy, meals in the kosher hotels and inns. Today it is an

appelation that the hotels and the local chambers of commerce are trying to live down as they attempt to lure non-Jewish trade into the area (they've even tried calling it the "Champagne Circuit"). But the Borscht Belt was a distinctly Jewish phenomenon, where the prettiest lakes and hills played second fiddle to the endless food and entertainment. (See CATSKILLS for a sense of the countryside; here, we're talking about what went on indoors.)

Although the area was—and is—dotted by innumerable modest cottage colonies and the like, the big hotels were the luxury liners of the mountains, places where infinite care was taken to keep guests busy from reveille to taps. Dining room seating was carefully supervised, with families, elderly couples, young singles, and children all sorted by table. And the entertainment —well, the entertainment is what made the area famous. This was the proving ground for comics, the sounding board for singers, the testing place for generations of performers who often as not began their careers as waiters. They ranged from Danny Kaye to Lenny Bruce, from Milton Berle to Mel Brooks, from Buddy Hackett to Joey Adams. They performed at all the big houses in the area, some doing the early show at one place and then the closer at the competitor's hotel over the mountain.

Athletes were big Catskill draws as well, particularly at Grossinger's, which set aside space for such as Joe Louis and Barney Ross to train for their fights, and for the attendant press to dine at Grossinger's tables, golf on Grossinger's course, and mention the name in every dispatch from the boxers' camps. Still, comedy—unbridled, often uncensored, but inevitably very Jewish—was the staple of the Borscht Belt, the product that made it famous. And if Yiddish was the language of the Borscht Belt, and the Borscht Belt supplied television with an ungodly number of comedians, and if television became the most effective cultural medium in the country, then it was no surprise that they knew what a *yenta* was in Peoria. Soon a Jackie Mason could begin to believe the whole world was Jewish. Wallace Markfield, writing about the energetic comic with a Yiddish accent as thick as sour cream, described how Mason "would start from a basic absurdity, work around, over and alongside it like a good Talmudist, all the while insisting not only upon his own Jewishness, but the Jewishness of the entire universe. 'If I'm not Jewish,' he has Richard Nixon speculate, 'so how come I'm talking with this accent?' " How come, indeed?

Boston Perhaps it was Bostonian in a way, in this city of well-born Yankees who looked down on the immigrant Irish, that the established German Jews actually rejected the first Yiddish-speaking *Ostjuden* when they arrived in 1882. Scorned from synagogue pulpits and in the local Jewish press, the eastern Europeans found Boston effectively closed to them. When those first 415 immigrants reached Boston that year,

they were promptly sent on to New York by the newly organized Boston Emigrant Aid Society. When eighteen of these families asked instead to be shipped back to Russia and the society did not have the money to comply, the supplicants turned to a general aid society which agreed to pay passage for those recommended by the president of the United Hebrew Benevolent Association. The scandal that resulted finally shamed the established Boston Jews into helpful acceptance of their Yiddish-speaking cousins.

Not that any attitude would have deterred the immigrants, who brought Boston's Jewish population from three thousand in 1875 to eighty thousand by 1907.

Bostonian Mary Antin with immigrant students, 1916

Almost all settled west of Hanover Street and the enormous Italian immigrant quarter in the North End. Zvi Hirsh Masliansky said the area reminded him of Vilna: "Large synagogues, with truly Orthodox rabbis, Talmudic study groups, almost all the stores closed on Saturday." To Mary Antin, author of the classic immigrant memoir *The Promised Land*, the area was a sad and hopeful mix, "pitiful in the eyes of social missionaries, the despair of boards of health, the hope of ward politicians, the touchstone of American democracy."

Proper Yankee Boston, which had even less use for the immigrants than did the city's German Jews, may have agreed to help the eighteen families who wished to return to Russia for particularly ignoble reasons. Senator Henry Cabot Lodge called the immigrants "inferior" people, and historian Henry Adams wrote of the "furtive

Ysaac or Jacob still reeking of the Ghetto, snarling a weird Yiddish. . . . The Jew makes me creep."

Still, the Yiddish-speaking Jews established themselves in Boston, much as they did in the other great port cities. On Arlington Street in Chelsea, Mary Antin's father set up a store in a tenement basement. "He put in a few barrels of flour and of sugar, a few boxes of crackers, a few gallons of kerosene, an assortment of soap of the 'save the coupons' brands," his daughter wrote. "He put out his sign, with a gilt-lettered warning of 'Strictly Cash,' and proceeded to give credit indiscriminately." Eventually the immigrant Jews moved from their old neighborhoods to Blue Hill Avenue in Dorchester (anchored by the celebrated G&G Deli), on to Mattapan and Roxbury, and eventually to Brookline and Newton.

Louis D. Brandeis, c. 1915

Brandeis, Louis Dembitz (1856–1941)
This Kentucky-born, Harvard-trained, German-Jewish lawyer, who would become the first Jew appointed to the United States Supreme Court, was not particularly active in Jewish affairs until he was summoned to New York from his prosperous Boston legal office in 1910. The epochal garment industry strike of that year had created a state of war between the Jews who managed the industry and those who toiled in it, and Brandeis was seen as the ideal mediator. His study of the conditions and lives of the workers led not only to a settlement, but also awakened in Brandeis, for the first time, a strong sense of his own Jewishness. He soon became a leader of the American Zionist movement and a strong influence on Woodrow Wilson's acceptance of Britain's Balfour Declaration.

Brice, Fanny (1891–1951) Fanny Borach began her career mimicking immigrant accents in her father's saloon on Forsyth Street. Soon stagestruck, she Americanized her name and began performing wherever she could find work, trying at first to abandon her ghetto style to find wider acceptance. In 1910, however, while playing vaudeville in a burlesque house, Irving Berlin instructed her to sing his "Sadie Salome" with a Yiddish accent. She became a hit, and Florenz Ziegfeld signed her for his "Follies," in which she would appear as a headliner through 1923. In the 1921 edition of "The Ziegfeld Follies," she established herself as a straight singer with her performance of "My Man," a French song with English lyrics by Channing Pollock. It became her trademark. In the mid-thirties Brice launched a new career, this time as radio's Baby Snooks, an annoying little girl who eternally exasperated her father with

Fanny Brice in *The Ziegfeld Follies of 1910*

her innocent whine, "Why, Daddy?"—a line soon repeated in households throughout the country. Among her three husbands were the gambler Nicky Arnstein and the showman Billy Rose. Barbra Streisand was the logical choice to play Brice in the stage and film musical *Funny Girl*, but the Egyptian actor Omar Sharif was a rather bizarre Arnstein, a small-time hood played here

**Fanny Brice as "Baby Snooks,"
George Burns as George Burns**

with the looks and style of some strange, foreign princeling.

The Bronx The only borough of New York attached to the North American mainland was, at its zenith, home to a thriving collection of Yiddish-origin communities whose residents considered themselves somewhat better than those products of the intracity Jewish diaspora who found their way to Brooklyn. This wasn't especially accurate, but it evidenced the Bronx Jews' perception of themselves as working-class people interested in theater, books, and current events, folks who were not terribly far up the social or economic scale but who had risen to steady wages and broadened their horizons when the subway to the Bronx opened in 1904 and led them to their promised land. Deborah Dash Moore cites one advertisement encouraging readers to "Buy where the kiddies grow husky in the open air."

Although the opening of the subway to the borough made the great migration from the Lower East Side possible, the movement of Jews to the Bronx began in the late 1890s, when the Baron de Hirsch Fund bought a tract at 137th Street and Willis Avenue, initiating an ultimately unsuccessful project intended to bring modern, better tenements and clothing factories to a relatively uncrowded area. Eventually the Amalgamated's Workers' Cooperative Colony near Van Cortlandt Park, complete with worker-mandated open areas, was glorious enough contrast to the dingy tenements of the Lower East Side. But the pinnacle of the Bronx-Jewish dream was attained along the lordly Grand Concourse, a handsome boulevard that the WPA's *New York City Guide*, published in 1939, considered "the Park Avenue of middle-class

Roosevelt Gardens on the Bronx's Grand Concourse, in the 1920s

Bronx residents.'' The Bronx Jewish population peaked at 585,000 in 1930, fully one-third the city's total Jewish population. But accelerating Jewish economic success and the flow of blacks and Hispanics into the borough sent most of the Bronx Jews to the suburbs; by 1970 only 143,000 remained (less than twelve percent of the city's Jewish population by then), many in the immense Co-Op City project and in the upper-middle-class Riverdale section, an area once beyond Jewish aspirations.

The Bronx Jews were romanticized in such entertainments as Gertrude Berg's radio series "The Rise of the Goldbergs" and in the hilarious stories of Arthur Kober, author of *Thunder over the Bronx*. These adventures of Bella, the working girl, and her family were immortalized in the play and movie *Wish You Were Here*.

Bronx Express This landmark play, written by Ossip Dymov, who had been brought to America by Boris Thomashevsky, was first performed in the 1920s and became an immediate hit, even though it ignored the temptation to pander to Moishe (the Yiddish theater's term for what was termed uptown John Q. Public). This comic story of a buttonmaker who is seduced by an alrightnik friend into becoming a wheeler-dealer is predictable enough: our hero makes the grade in the usual ruthless way and then regrets his renunciation of the virtuous ways in which he was reared. Happily, it's not too late: it was all a dream. The play was revived by the Folksbiene company in an adaptation called *Bronx Express 1968*, when perhaps the notion "to quit schlepping on the subway"—the words of the *Daily News* critic who reviewed the revival—had an even more convincing appeal.

Brooklyn Until it became a borough of New York City in 1898, Brooklyn was the third-largest city in the United States and the Jewish community was even then one of its largest components. German Jews had begun settling in Williamsburg, just across the river from Manhattan, as early as the 1830s, and had achieved commercial and political success in Brooklyn life. In the 1880s eastern European Jews found haven in distant Brownsville when a clothing manufacturer moved his factory there. When an elevated line opened soon thereafter, sweatshop operators and their workers transformed the neighborhood from farmland into sweltering tenement territory equivalent to the Lower East Side itself. The completion of the Williamsburg and Manhattan bridges shortly after the turn of the century brought another surge of immigration across the East River. Boro Park, which had begun as a literal *judenrein* by decree of an anti-Semitic politician at the turn of the century, became a virtual Jewish village when the pres-

sure of demand opened the area up. By the early 1920s nearly three-quarters of a million Jews called the "Borough of Churches" home—more, in fact, than lived in Manhattan.

Brooklyn has inspired more literary creation than perhaps any other eastern European–Jewish enclave in the country, perhaps because it became the primary locus of city life for the Americanized children of the immigrants. Alfred Kazin, Chaim Potok, Arthur Miller, Harold Robbins (his excellent *A Stone for Danny Fisher* was rather different from the steamy best-selling puddings he would serve up later in his career), Daniel Fuchs, and perhaps a score of others farmed Brooklyn for literary material. Murder, Inc., created the bloody record and extraordinary mythology of the Jewish gangster from the streets of Brownsville and East New York, and for years the Brooklyn Dodgers—situated right in the middle of Brooklyn's Jewish population in the Flatbush section—catered to their fans by keeping a Jewish coach, Jake Pitler, on the baselines. Despite several decades of suburban flight,

Jake Pitler, the Jewish fixture in the Ebbets Field coaching box

Burns and Allen, from *The Big Broadcast of 1932*

largely to intensely Jewish suburbs in Nassau County, Brooklyn has remained a goal for immigrant Jews. Williamsburg and Crown Heights today are the centers of America's Chassidic community, having burgeoned in the years immediately after World War II; nearly twenty thousand Syrian Jews have settled in Flatbush; and an influx of Soviet Jewish émigrés in the Brighton Beach area has earned that neighborhood the nickname "The New Odessa." These ethnic concentrations, especially of the Chassidim in Williamsburg and Crown Heights, mean that leading rabbis can deliver blocks of votes and have thus developed enormous political power in New York.

Burns, George (1896–   ) The professional merger in 1923 of George Burns (born Nathan Birnbaum on the Lower East Side) and Gracie Allen (alumna of San Francisco's Star of the Sea Convent School) prefaced their marriage by three

years and began the tenure of one of the great male-female comedy teams of our time. Burns began his performing career at age seven as the tenor in a street singing group called the Peewee Quartet, which performed in virtually every Lower East Side bar and cafe, and on occasion on the decks of the Staten Island ferry (in his memoirs, Burns notes that the other Peewees—Moishe Friedman, Heshy and Mortzy Weinberger—went on to honest careers outside show business). Burns left school at thirteen and was successively a trick roller skater, a dance instructor, and a vaudevillian before he met Allen, who had already "retired" from the stage and enrolled in a secretarial school.

Their success as supporting players in Eddie Cantor's vaudeville show, as stars of their own long-running radio and television shows, and as featured players in more than twenty films in no way depended on Burns's New York ghetto background, but his tolerant suffering in the face of Allen's incalculable dizziness was not without immigrant Jewish roots. From his memoir *The Third Time Around:* "I came from a very large family. There were seven sisters, five brothers, and no mother or father. We were so poor we couldn't afford parents." Or, "We had gaslight but very little of it, because about once a week when the gas ran out you had to put a quarter in the meter. My mother always kept the flame turned down very low to make the quarter last as long as possible. In fact, the light was turned down so low I was eight years old before I knew what my sisters looked like. Then one night my mother turned up the light, I got a look at my sisters and blew it out." His sardonicism was gentler with Gracie, but Burns was forever put upon, even if forever tolerant.

C

Cafe Royal Perhaps somewhere in the world the cafe tradition lingers, but it can't hold a candle to the style that prevailed from 1911 to 1953 at Second Avenue and East Twelfth Street at the Cafe Royal. The cafes of the area probably arrived with the Germans who preceded the Jews on Second Avenue and who used them as forums for debates on life, literature, and ideology. With the coming of Yiddish to the avenue—soon to be known as "knish alley"—the Royal became both an intellectual haven and a Jewish Sardi's.

The man who opened the Royal soon lost it to his headwaiter, Oscar Szatmarie, in a game of Hungarian klabyash. Oscar also won, legend has it, busboy Herman Tantzer. Herman waxed rich as party to the confidences of the customers, who often paid extra to have him page them—loudly. A *glezele tey*—a glass of tea—was the sine qua non at the Cafe Royal, its clientele primarily literary and theatrical (from Jacob Adler and Boris Thomashevsky to such uptown drop-ins as Alexander Woollcott, Theodore Dreiser, Charlie Chaplin, Fannie Hurst, and, from rather farther afield, Leon Trotsky). The Royal's richness was so celebrated that in 1942 Elia Kazan staged a play, *Cafe Crown*, starring Sam Jaffe in the Herman Tantzer role. By that time, Herman had become a banker as well as a busboy, and while he continued to accept nickel tips, he had a brisk moneylending business (actors had credit with him, writers did not), invested in shows, and managed a sizable portfolio. Herman did better than the show about him did.

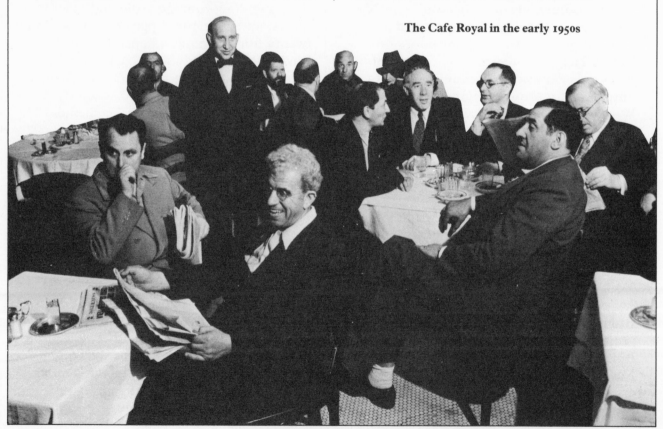

The Cafe Royal in the early 1950s

Cahan, Abraham (1860–1951) The brilliant, autocratic, controversial Abe Cahan dominated the Yiddish newspaper world for almost half a century and in the process became the single most influential figure in the nation's entire Yiddish-speaking community. As editor of the *Jewish Daily Forward*, he was a man with one foot in the Jewish community and the other in the life of America beyond it, yet both were always planted (with firmness early in his career, later less so) in an idealistic socialism. Nevertheless Cahan's keen sense of his audience kept the *Forward* remarkably free of dialectic and filled with news and commentary of more general interest. His was a dual mission: informing and Americanizing the Yiddish public while at the same time—through his own writings, as well as through his friendships with such as Lincoln Steffens, Hutchins Hapgood, and William Dean Howells—explaining the Yiddish-speaking Jews to the rest of the country. That he had his detractors—those who disliked his politics, his occasional imperiousness, his promotion of what they considered a "debased" New York Yiddish—was of little consequence to Cahan.

Born in Vilna, he was a twenty-two-year-old revolutionary when he fled to America after the assassination of Alexander II. His first years in America aroused mixed emotions in him: the thrill of freedom on one hand, a displeasure with America's shortcomings as a utopia on the other. Despite his leftist zeal, he harbored deep sentiments for old-country *Yiddishkeit* and even retained a soft spot for the religious ways of his fathers (though not to the extent that he would actively practice or otherwise perpetuate them). He also harbored a certain awe for the American aristocracy. New York's new immigrant Jewish

Abe Cahan and his newspaper

quarter was tiny when Cahan arrived; in his autobiography he wrote that the houses the Jews occupied on East Broadway had only a few years earlier been a native American neighborhood uplifted by the residence there of William Vanderbilt.

Cahan was both dreamer and passionate onlooker. Nothing escaped his notice, neither the customs of Americans (who peculiarly cooled their coffee by adding water) nor the growing divergence between the Yiddish spoken by the immigrants and that written in the press or declaimed from the stage (he was appalled by the degradation of the language, but did not hesitate to mimic it when he took over the *Forward*).

Cahan first worked in a tobacco factory, at night studying *Appleton's Grammar*, which was designed to teach English to Germans. He achieved fluency in the new tongue and later taught it, both in a yeshiva and, for twelve years, at a public school. At the same time, he immersed himself in

New York's Socialist circles, where German was the semiofficial language. He questioned whether this was suitable for the Jewish immigrants among whom the Socialists campaigned, and soon delivered what he said was the first Socialist speech in Yiddish, in a German saloon on East Sixth Street. In 1886 Cahan and an associate published *Di Naye Tsayt (The New Era)*, a Socialist newspaper "written in the simplest Yiddish so that even the most uneducated worker could understand it." It was a bold stroke, and despite the criticism that Cahan received from linguistic purists, it was a formula he would remember.

In 1897 Cahan participated in the founding of the *Forward* but soon left in a dispute with his colleagues. He had by this time already written for many Yiddish papers, as well as for the *New York Sun* and other English-language journals. He made the acquaintance of William Dean Howells, who encouraged him to write about life on the Lower East Side for a wider public, and he met Lincoln Steffens, who had read his novel *Yekl, A Tale of the Ghetto* (the product of Howells's entreaties), and who hired him as a reporter for the *Commercial Advertiser*, of which Steffens was city editor. Here Cahan quickly learned the newspaper business, American-style, and contributed enormously to the education of intellectually alert journalists such as Hutchins Hapgood and Jacob Riis. Cahan became the guide for both men when they sought to explore and write about the life of the ghetto.

In 1902, by now a prominent figure both within and outside the Lower East Side, Cahan returned to the *Forward* on his own terms and proceeded to fashion it into a creature of his own design. He instituted many features that endured for decades, paid his writers more than most other newspapers did, and remained active until just a few years before his death at age ninety-one. Throughout his career as editor and activist, Cahan remained a writer as well. His greatest work was *The Rise of David Levinsky*, written in English in 1917, an unromanticized

THE RISE OF DAVID LEVINSKY

A NOVEL BY ABRAHAM CAHAN

GROSSET & DUNLAP, *Publishers*
by arrangement with HARPER and BROTHERS

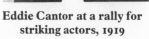

story of a young immigrant getting ahead in New York, a man who found fortune but not happiness. Curiously, it was not translated into Yiddish until 1950, when the *Forward* serialized it. In the 1970s the film *Hester Street*, adapted from a Cahan story, achieved both critical and commercial success.

Cantor, Eddie (1892–1964) He was a lithe, nervous-looking man whose brown eyes popped and rolled and earned him the sobriquet "Banjo Eyes." When he skip-danced sideways across the stage, clapping his hands and singing "If You Knew Susie," he brought the house down. His was the classic route to stardom from the streets of the Lower East Side, and in his heyday, Eddie Cantor was among the most popular entertainers in the country.

Born Edward Iskowitz, Cantor was orphaned at two and raised by his grandmother. He recalled an early life of street performing, rolling his eyes for a laugh from his youngest days, and distracting the attention of passersby with his antics while fellow members of his street gang—named for its leader, a lad called "Pork-Faced Sam"—picked pockets. While his friends went on to more serious crimes and to working as scabs during strikes, Cantor moved from the streets to amateur nights (including one stand as a blonde-wigged Little Lord Fauntleroy at the Educational Alliance) to Broadway and "The Ziegfeld Follies." His big hit was "Whoopee" in 1929; he was the lead act when the Palace put on its last vaudeville show in 1930; and he appeared in several movies and on his own radio show for more than a decade. Throughout his career, Cantor relied on the quick ad-lib and on a certain bathetic sentimentality that ensured his hold on his pub-

lic. If his days on the Lower East Side could be recalled with effect, Cantor would—and did—summon them instantly.

Eddie Cantor at a rally for striking actors, 1919

Castle Garden

Today a National Park Service landmark in Manhattan's Battery Park overlooking New York Harbor, Castle Garden became the nation's first formal immigrant receiving station in 1855. Before it closed in 1889, a total of 8,280,917 immigrants had entered America through its doors. A distinctive, round stone structure, it looked like what it had been designed to be, a fort protecting the harbor (its original name was Castle Clinton). Opened in 1811 on a small artificial island two hundred feet into New York Bay and later joined to the Battery by landfill, it was renamed Castle Garden in 1822 when it became a concert hall. Here P. T. Barnum introduced Jenny Lind to the American public, and here Samuel F. B. Morse demonstrated his telegraph.

When Castle Garden first began receiving eastern and southern European immigrants (under the aegis of the State of New York, since this was before the federal government took control of immigration), it had the virtue of being within walking distance of the Lower East Side, where relatives, friends, or simply people who spoke

Castle Garden when it was the "State Emigrant Landing Depot"

the same language could be found. However, its adjacency to those teeming streets could be a problem, too, for one had to avoid the depredations of the con men and crooks who congregated outside, aiming to swindle the newcomers out of whatever pitiful savings they had amassed to start their new lives in America.

Catskills In 1900 the Jewish Agricultural Society initiated financial support for Jewish farmers in Sullivan County, New York, in an effort to encourage truck or dairy farming. But farming ran second in this area, as it always would, to another source of income. According to a 1911 Immigration Commission report, "Along the line of the New York, Western and Ontario Railroad, traversing Sullivan and Ulster Counties, numerous Russian hebrews have settled in recent years and have engaged in farming and other pursuits." The other pursuits were boardinghouses, first as healthful restoratives for tubercular city

slum dwellers and sweatshop workers, and later for everyone who could afford to escape the Lower East Side or Brownsville or the Bronx for several days each summer.

The first Jewish settlements in the area were in the upper tier of the Catskills, around the towns of Hunter, Fleischmanns, and Tannersville. While such organizations as the Jewish Agricultural and Industrialization Society and the Jewish Colonization Association encouraged farmers to take in boarders to help provide cash for seed and equipment, the eventual result was the virtual disappearance of farming as a way of life for the Jews already in the area. The times, the locale, and probably the farmers themselves were simply better suited to the resort business. Grandview House, the earliest boardinghouse in the mountains to cater to Jewish business, opened in the early 1890s. As the Jewish resort business grew, so did resistance to it; newspaper advertisements noted which resorts refused to allow Jewish guests (one, Laurel-in-the-Pines, would later become a strictly kosher resort when it could no longer resist history), and civic figures spoke of "pollution" from the proliferation of Jewish hotels.

In the earliest days, accommodations were the least of it. The city dwellers poured off the trains into rooms almost as crowded as those of the tenements they were fleeing. One did nothing but sleep in the rooms, anyway, and the proprietors preferred to create grand impressions with spacious lobbies and sumptuous dining rooms. One early entrepreneur, Jacob A. Sussman, opened his boardinghouse at Woodbridge in 1898, and spent his winters calling on potential clients in the city with chunks of pressed cheese he had made in his own kitchen. It couldn't have been a better calling card for East Siders looking for an alternative to their urban gloom. The big potatoes in the Catskills were such institutions as Grossinger's, the Concord, Kutsher's Country Club, the Nevele, and Brown's, among others. The best known of the lot is Grossinger's, today a huge pleasure-palace on twelve hundred acres. It began life in 1914 when Selig Grossinger, a pants-presser in the city, bought a run-down farm in Ferndale, hoping to improve his life. Grossinger, his wife, his daughter Jennie, and Jennie's husband, Harry, took in boarders at their seven-room farmhouse for eight dollars a week.

When the automobile era arrived, Grossinger's and the other Catskill resorts (and the summer camps for religious

groups, *landsmanshaftn*, and various Marxist sects) were served by Route 17, a seasonal Eternal Road with Jewish traffic backed up to the Jersey border on weekends. Highlights on Route 17 included the stopover at the Red Apple for refreshments and the drive up the steep Wurtsboro Hill, where many voyagers learned that their old cars, adequate for the city's flatness, could not make the grade. In the years after World War II, the so-called Kwikway replaced old Route 17, bypassed the Red Apple, and shortened the entire trek to less than two hours.

Sullivan County, the keystone of the Catskills, has long been known jocularly as "Solomon County," but in recent years many of the smaller resorts have become decidedly ecumenical or have been bought by Christian religious sects. Curiously, the

Catskill frolics: a mock (cross-sexual) wedding at Kutsher's, 1916

The headline of this World War I charity appeal poster reads "Don't worry, he's all right"

northern Catskills, where it all began, became in the thirties and forties the vacation retreat for Jewish refugees from Hitler's Germany. Particularly around Fleischmanns, these resorts featured hotels and cafes that provided European-style outdoor tables for coffee and tortes. All this, too, is gone, and the area has now become non-denominational ski country.

Charity A burly Texan, showing off, squeezes an orange so dry that he offers $500 to anyone who can get a drop of juice from the wizened rind he has left on the table. A frail-looking fellow ventures to try and, wonder of wonders, manages to get half a glass of juice from the shreds in front of him. "How did you do it?" asks the Texan. "Easy," the little fellow says, "I'm a fund-raiser for the UJA."

It's not entirely hyperbole. Probably no people in history have been as adept at charitable works as have the Jews. This appeal to conscience, which has its roots in earliest Jewish teachings, has united different classes of Jews from the most diverse origins even in moments of mutual detestation. Those who came to America and established themselves found a few decades later a "greenhorn" generation of Yiddish-speaking Jews that was an embarrassment and threat to their status as Americans. Even though some of the early views of charity were rather peculiar (see HEBREW EMIGRANT AID SOCIETY), and Theodore Herzl could say to Baron Maurice de Hirsch, "The character of a people may be ruined by charity," Jewish philanthropic groups swiftly institutionalized themselves and dispensed funds and energy in staggering proportions to help the immigrants. The Hebrew Sheltering and Guardian Society took shape in 1879; even earlier, nine groups in

Chicago had formed the United Hebrew Relief Association in 1859. Boston had the first Federated Jewish Charities in 1895, and the first Jewish Welfare Fund was established in Oakland, California, in 1925.

Chicago More than a quarter of a million Jews live in Chicago and its suburbs today, not appreciably more than the city boasted sixty years ago; indeed, by the time the first eastern European Jews arrived in the city in the 1870s, there was already a German-Jewish population sufficient to raise a complete company of Jewish volunteers in the 82nd Regiment of Illinois during the Civil War. The easterners immediately found their way to the West Side, a neighborhood strikingly similar to New York's Lower East Side. According to Ira Berkow's *Maxwell Street*, by 1891 a survey indicated that sixteen thousand Jews were living around Maxwell Street in the heart of the area, with its wooden-slat sidewalks, unpaved, muddy streets, piled-up garbage, dearth of toilets, plethora of sweatshops, and booming crime. The West Side also boasted the Maxwell Street Settlement, established in 1892 by Jane Addams, founder of Hull House. The acrimony in the city's Jewish community at the time led Addams to remark, "It seems to me there is more ill-feeling between the Reform and Orthodox Jews than between Jews and Gentiles."

Among the indigenous institutions of the area were such notable gathering places as Lyon's Delicatessen and Gold's restaurant. The Yiddish theater thrived at Glickman's Palace, the Metropolitan, and the Empire, and the celebrated Joseph Buloff was brought directly from Vilna to Chicago to direct and star in Dramatishe Gezelshaft reproductions. Still, the city was a way station on the Yiddish theater circuit, as it

Chicago's Maxwell Street, 1906

was in the English-language theater. In 1935 Paul Muni and others organized *Mir Shikager* ("We Chicagoans"), later called Yiddish Arts and Friends, to help Yiddish actors who had been abandoned on the road by their managers find their way home. The *Daily Forward* had a Chicago office and ran special pages of Chicago news.

As the city grew, the Jewish population spread throughout the West Side, into such enclaves as Albany Park and North Lawndale and eventually, years later, to the Rogers Park neighborhood on the North Side, and certain of the suburbs yet farther north on Lake Michigan.

Cohen, Morris Raphael (1880–1947) Cohen was one of the countless pearls to emerge from the unprepossessing oyster that was the Lower East Side. He arrived from Minsk at age twelve, and tended his father's cigar and soda stand at the Othello Poolroom on the Bowery. Like so many of similar background, Cohen emerged from the ghetto through the classrooms of City College, then at Twenty-third Street and Lexington Avenue, graduating in the class of 1900. His primary benefactor was Thomas Davidson, the Scottish educator who devoted himself to teaching the poor

children of the ghetto; it was at Davidson's summer camp in the Adirondacks that Cohen, then nineteen, read Plato and studied Dante.

From CCNY, Cohen went to Harvard, where he received his doctorate in 1906, having studied philosophy under William James, Ralph Barton Perry, and Josiah Royce. He returned to New York, taught at the Educational Alliance, and then began a celebrated professorial career at City College that stretched from 1912 to 1938. Throughout that period, he was the brightest star on City's faculty, a stern and acid-tongued pedagogue who left an indelible mark on the countless students—largely Jewish boys from the same East Side streets from which he had sprung—who passed through his classroom. After leaving City College, Cohen taught at the University of Chicago.

Communism Just as one wing of the young, idealistic Russian youth movement that engaged either actively or intellectually in revolution against the czars turned toward anarchism, so did an extremely large number turn toward communism. Most of these Marxists, after arriving in America, found intellectual homes in the various so-

cial democratic parties and unions that proliferated in this country, but the Bolshevik
Revolution of 1917 forced everyone to take
sides. There followed two decades of internecine battle on the Jewish left, as among
leftists of all backgrounds; still, in 1917,
when the choice was between the Bolshe-
viks and the counterrevolutionary "whites,"
the violent anti-Semitism of the "whites"
kept otherwise skeptical Socialists in the
Bolshevik camp.

By 1919 the Jewish Socialist Federation had split in two, and a Jewish Federation of the Communist Party was formed.
Three years later *Freiheit*, a Communist
daily published in Yiddish, appeared; the
Workmen's Circle had a strong Communist
faction in the twenties; and men like Morris Winchevsky, hopeful of a thriving Yid-

dish culture in Russia under the Bolshe-
viks, supported the Communists. One
source estimates that the American Communist Party was fifteen percent Yiddish-
speaking in the 1920s. Through the Trade
Union Educational League, the Communists were able to gain control of a number
of unions, particularly the Cigarmakers and
the Furriers; for a while, they called the
shots in the mighty ILGWU during the
1926 Cloakmakers' Strike. Their cultural
activities included a children's camp, Kin-
derland, where the bunks were called "the
36 Soviet Republics"; adult camps called
"Nit Gedayget," or "No Worries" (Mel
Lasky, a teacher from New Jersey, remembered, "I went there because I heard everyone believed in free love. This, I must say,
proved to be untrue"); and the Freiheit

Communist rally, Union Square,
May 1, 1934

Singing Society and Mandolin Orchestra.

Three events—other than the periodic purges of Communists in various unions and other organizations—led to the weakening of the appeal of Soviet-led Communism in Yiddish-speaking America. In 1929, when news of the Arab slaughter of Jewish settlers in Palestine reached the United States, the *Freiheit* condemned the act. But when the party line dictated that the Arabs were part of a war of "national liberation," the *Freiheit* changed its position. The *Forward* led a boycott of the paper, and it was a call widely heeded. The Stalin purge trials of the 1930s further weakened the Communists among Jewish intellectuals, and the Hitler-Stalin pact dealt a withering blow throughout the American Jewish community.

Cream Cheese A bagel without it seems impossible, but a bagel with it was awfully difficult until 1920, when the Breakstone Company introduced this spread in its mass-produced form to the New York market. Called "Breakstone's Downsville Cream Cheese" after the upstate community in which it was produced, it soon outdistanced farmer's cheese, pot cheese, and the other delicacies traditionally applied to bagels. Incidentally, the fussy entrepreneur you see on television, Sam Breakstone, had nothing to do with this product. The founders of the company were Isaac and Joseph Breakstone; Sam never existed.

Czernowitz Yiddish Language Conference On August 30, 1908, an extraordinary five-day conclave, called to discuss the role and future of the Yiddish language, convened in the city of Czernowitz, then in the Bukovina region of Austria-Hungary (it

is now Cernovtsy, in the Soviet Union). Forty of the seventy people who attended had voting rights, and their views and actions delineated for the first time in one place the multiplicity of viewpoints toward Yiddish, or *mame-loshn*—"mother tongue." Among the writers and editors who appeared were Y. L. Peretz, Sholem Asch, and M. L. Halpern. Other delegates represented Zionist and Socialist organizations, while yet others ranged from Yiddish nationalists to proponents of Hebrew. They came from Russia (particularly the area that now comprises Poland), Galicia, Bukovina, and one each from Rumania, Switzerland, and the United States.

The conference was the idea of Nathan Birnbaum, a Viennese who learned Yiddish late in life and was at a disadvantage at the meeting because of his lack of fluency in the language. Birnbaum enlisted support for the conference during an American tour early that year, when he sold the idea to Chaim Zhitlowsky, David Pinski, Jacob Gordin, and A. M. Evalenko.

Zhitlowsky prepared the invitation, which outlined the need and purpose. "In the past several decades," he wrote, "the Yiddish language has made great progress. Its literature has achieved a level of which no one had imagined it capable. Yiddish newspapers are distributed in hundreds of copies daily and weekly. Yiddish poets write songs which are sung by the people, stories which are read by the people, plays which the people eagerly flock to see. Every day the language itself becomes more refined and richer.

"But it continues to lack one thing which older tongues possess. The latter are not permitted to roam about freely and widely in the linguistic world to attract all sorts of diseases, defects and perhaps even

Conferees at Czernowitz (L to R) Abraham Reisen, Y. L. Peretz, Sholem Asch, Chaim Zhitlowsky, H. D. Nomberg

death. . . . No one, however, pays heed to the Yiddish language. Thousands of Yiddish words are replaced by German, Russian and English words which are completely unnecessary. The live rules of the language which are born and develop with it in the mouths of the people go unrecorded and it appears not to possess any such rules. Each person writes it in another way with his own spelling because no standard, authoritative Yiddish orthography has thus far been established. True, the disgrace attached to Yiddish in the past has been diminished. People are less and less ashamed of the contemporary language of our people. . . . But it is still an object of ridicule and contempt. People are still ashamed of it. And is this not because of the faults noted above?"

The invitation said that the conference would deal with Yiddish grammar and orthography, a Yiddish dictionary, Jewish youth and Yiddish, and with the Yiddish press, stage, and the economic situations of writers and actors. It called for the establishment of an authority that would arbitrate matters of Yiddish usage. The one thing, according to the invitation, the conference did not plan on considering was the dispute between those who favored Yiddish as the national language of the Jews and those who looked to Hebrew to fulfill that role. And yet this became a central, certainly the most heated, topic of the sessions. Charges and countercharges reverberated in the debate. Those who saw Yiddish as the language of the moment, but asserted the inevitability of Hebrew as the language of the Jews in their own land, were particularly subject to verbal assault. Peretz, who loved both Yiddish and Hebrew, was torn, eventually favoring the recognition of Hebrew as the national tongue and of Yiddish as the "folk tongue" of the Jews. The Socialists advocated the elimination of Hebrew as a Jewish tongue altogether because it tied, they claimed, the people to religion.

Yet, out of the conference's welter of emotion and words arose a consciousness of Yiddish literature as a modern institution and increased confidence of, and respect for, those who spoke Yiddish. On the other hand, the injection of the Hebrew-Yiddish question deepened the rift, by rigidifying the positions each side held. This rift would be settled—for most Jews, anyway—only with the founding of the State of Israel and the designation of Hebrew as the national tongue.

Davidson, Thomas (1840–1900) Davidson was a wandering scholar, a Presbyterian idealist who lived in London, Boston, Italy, and Greece before he discovered the Lower East Side and the Educational Alliance. The area and the institution well suited his dream to help people find strength and to develop democratic ideals through education. He organized the Breadwinners' College (later, as a memorial, called the Davidson Club) at the Alliance to help provide working people with a liberal education, and sponsored a summer camp in the Adirondacks where young people studied the classics. In his autobiography, Morris Cohen called Davidson "the light of my life."

The Day Second to the *Forward* in popularity and prestige, *The Day (Der Tog)* began as a liberal paper with Zionist tendencies. It published such a breadth of viewpoints, such a wealth of literary selection and objective journalism, that it became, as Irving Howe wrote, "by American standards, the most satisfactory Yiddish newspaper." Among its unique journalistic achievements was its serialization between 1922 and 1927 of the Yiddish translation of the Bible by the poet Yehoash.

But *The Day* was down-to-earth, too;

it had an ace crime reporter, Joel Slonim (who also covered city politics and wrote poetry on the side), and perhaps its star attraction was Sarah Bronstein Smith, whose soapy tales of domestic strife and melodrama riveted the paper's readers. Other contributors to *The Day* included Sholem Aleichem, David Pinski, Jacob Gordin, Sholem Asch, and the playwright and travel writer Peretz Hirshbein, a man of dramatic style and appearance who entertained friends by tearing telephone books in half.

In his memoir *Sons and Natives*, Judd L. Teller recalled that "*The Day*'s editorial domain was run somewhat like a Central American Republic. There were frequent coups d'etat by persons aspiring for the editor's post, assisted by 'outside intervention' from one or another of the contending Zi-

The staff of *The Day*, c. 1925

onist factions or contentious unions then engaged in internecine warfare."

Among the editors of *The Day* was Herman Bernstein, an American newspaperman who could not read the paper he edited, claimed Teller, "because he did not know a word of Yiddish." When Bernstein was appointed United States minister to Albania, the appointment was hailed on the East Side as a victory for "our Jews" because until then only uptown *Yahudim* had held such high posts.

Detroit There were fewer than one thousand Jews in Detroit in 1880, and nearly half of these were the German-Jewish members of Temple Beth El, the city's first synagogue. Soon enough the great wave of immigration began, and the members of Beth El offered two rather misguided charities before the next decade was out: the Hebrew Ladies' Sewing Society, and the Self-Help Circle. In fact, self-help was required by the turn of the century; harassment of the city's immigrant Jewish peddlers had reached such proportions that they were compelled to organize the Jewish Peddlers Protective Union.

The Hastings Street area on the city's east side harbored most of the Yiddish-speaking population, which would, over the next eighty years, move virtually in lock-step on an almost perfect forty-five-degree vector through the heart of the city to its northwest side, to the close-in suburbs, and, today, to the far reaches of Oakland County. Some institutions, carried along in the northwesterly migration, retained their identity of origin if not location of origin: the Dexter-Davison market, for decades the community's primary source of lox, herring, and the Sunday *New York Times*, occupied two different locations after leaving

the intersection of Dexter and Davison avenues two decades (and ten miles) ago.

Fearful of anti-Semitism in the automobile industry, and particularly in the plants of Henry Ford, Detroit's Jews did not flock to the area's occupational mainstay. Instead, small businesses—greengroceries, tailor shops, laundries—became the economic bulwark of the city's Yiddish population. Many entrepreneurs spent much of their energy attempting to evade the depredations of the Purple Gang, the notorious Jewish criminal mob that preyed on the city's Yiddish-speaking small businessmen.

Dr. Brown's Cel-Ray Tonic The *Washington Post* recently called its taste "inexpressibly exotic." Generations of New York Jews—not to mention those living elsewhere with the same cultural longings—have searched desperately for the beverage when separated from their trusted supplier. Marketing executives at the American Beverage Company of Queens, planning to go national with it, have decided to junk plans to disguise its provenance, choosing instead

David Dubinsky takes the inaugural chest x-ray at the Union Health Center, 1949.
At left is Herbert Lehman, New York governor and U.S. senator

"to bite the bullet and put 'celery soda' on its label." It is, indeed, made from celery seeds. And there never was, not even back in 1869 when it was first bottled, a Dr. Brown.

Dubinsky, David (1892–   ) Dubinsky was elected president of the International Ladies' Garment Workers' Union in 1932, soon after the wars between the Communists and the Socialists had virtually brought the ILGWU to its knees. Wrote Dubinsky's colleague Gus Tyler, "To bring anarchists and socialists together was not too hard because they both agreed that they disliked the communists more than they disliked each other. The communists, how-

ever, were still a problem, because they had quite a following of people whose backs had felt the Czarist knout." When Stalin issued an order to all Communists to leave their old unions and form new ones, Dubinsky, who had been a leader of the ILGWU's right wing in the twenties, gladly embraced those who questioned the wisdom of Moscow—if they questioned, they were not the sort of Communists he should fear, and he would need them to help rebuild the ILGWU. His union united and Roosevelt in office, Dubinsky led a series of general strikes all over the country and saw membership increase from forty thousand to two hundred thousand in the space of two years.

An active member of the revolutionary Jewish Labor Bund in Russia by the time he was fourteen, first arrested for political activity at fifteen, jailed for eighteen months at sixteen, exiled to Siberia at seventeen, Dubinsky emigrated to the United States in 1911. He would become one of the nation's most powerful labor leaders, both inside the labor movement and in the wider world of politics. He founded the American Labor Party so unionists who despised the Tammany Democrats could find a ticket on which to vote for Roosevelt; when he suspected the ALP had fallen into the hands of the Communists, he

A San Francisco production of
The Dybbuk, 1925

helped found the Liberal Party. He joined with Sidney Hillman and John L. Lewis to create the CIO, and after twenty years' effort saw that organization merge with the AFL.

The Dybbuk *The Dybbuk* has no specific connection to America. It was written in 1914 in Russia—in Russian—by S. Ansky (Shloyme Zanvi Rappoport) and was first presented in Yiddish in Vilna six years later, after the author's death. But it is undoubtedly the best-known, most-revived play in the Yiddish theatrical repertoire, and for this reason alone deserves inclusion in this volume.

Ansky was a Jewish folklorist who apparently got the inspiration for the play on a tour of Ukrainian cities in 1911. Based on the author's feeling that physical strength was alien to the Jews, who believed that faith would be ever triumphant, it is the story of the spirit of a dead youth which enters the body of the girl he loved, and of the efforts to exorcise it.

The Dybbuk received its first American production in 1922 at Maurice Schwartz's Yiddish Art Theater and was so rapturously received that Schwartz constantly restaged it to make up for losses from other productions. It was presented in English for the first time by the Neighborhood Playhouse in 1925; a revival in 1954 included in its cast Jack Gilford and Theodore Bikel. Its most recent performance in New York was in 1980, as the first production of a new national Yiddish theater. *The Dybbuk* is also the basis for Paddy Chayefsky's successful Broadway play *The Tenth Man*, which Chayefsky set in contemporary Mineola, Long Island.

Edelstadt, David (1866–1892) In his brief but eventful ten years in this country, Edelstadt became a romantic spokesman of the labor movement. Having emigrated to the United States with a group of comrades to found an agricultural colony, he instead found himself working as a buttonhole maker in a Cincinnati tailor shop. In the process he learned of the exploitation of American working people, and he also learned Yiddish (Russian was his mother tongue). A poet from boyhood, he wrote only in Yiddish for the last four years of his life, penning poems of fiery protest and indignation, and editing the Yiddish anarchist journal *Di Freie Arbeiter Shtimme*. Struck down by tuberculosis—"the sweatshop disease"—Edelstadt was mourned by Jewish workers as both son and leader. Edelstadt's poems were later set to music as hymns and as marching songs, and his collected works were published in London in 1910 and in Moscow in 1935.

The Educational Alliance Founded in 1889 by a group of German Jews that included Jacob Schiff, Isidor Straus, and Judge Samuel Greenbaum, the "Palace of Immigrants" on East Broadway served as academy, social hall, library, etiquette class, religious center, bathhouse, and in a host of other capacities for the entire Lower East Side, as many as thirty-seven thousand people using its main building and two branches in one week in the first decade of this century.

Its express purpose was "Americanization," beginning with day classes for newly arrived children, where enough English was taught so they could enter the public schools at not too great a disadvantage, and evening classes for their parents, focusing on civics as well as English. Every Ameri-

can holiday was celebrated at the Alliance (complete with lessons on the particular personage or event being honored), lectures on American history and social customs were delivered, Yiddish translations of the Declaration of Independence were distributed, and virtually everything else that could be done to "dissolve the ghetto" was conducted under the Alliance's roof (one early measure, the barring of spoken Yiddish from the premises, was later discarded).

But many of the Alliance's activities encompassed parts of its constituents' lives that had little to do with Americanization. There were social clubs for young people, sports in the gymnasium, religious services,

shower baths for whoever wished them, lectures on physiology and hygiene, lessons in sewing, music, cooking, dancing, art. Its library served from five hundred to one thousand people a day at a time when New York had no public libraries. A Children's Educational Theatre presented plays

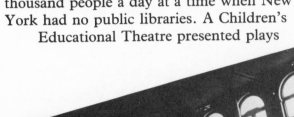

Facets of the Educational Alliance: above, a girls' gymnastics group; at R, a citizenship class; below, the Alliance's Camp Salomon for Mothers and Children

as disparate as *The Tempest* and *Little Lord Fauntleroy* (which must have been pretty remarkable in the accents of the Lower East Side). Classes were taught in virtually every academic subject and in a variety of trades, ranging from typing to telegraphy. On one evening in the late nineties, young men listened to a physician lecture on "The Marriage Question: Its Physical and Moral Sides." The Alliance also sponsored vacation camps for boys, for girls, and one for mothers and their young children; it provided free legal aid (staffed by Yiddish-speaking attorneys) and a "desertion bureau," which attempted to track down errant husbands and provided a rent check when the tracking was fruitless.

The main reception center at Ellis Island

The Alliance continues to operate on the Lower East Side, now with expanded staff and facilities to provide services in Chinese and Spanish as well as English and Yiddish.

Ellis Island On these twenty-seven acres, where the Dutch once went to find oysters, where pirates and mutineers were hanged, where the federal government picked up a piece of land in 1800 from the children of a New Jersey farmer named Samuel Ellis (and took ninety years to figure out how best to make use of it)—on this sandspit in New York Harbor, between twelve million and sixteen million immigrants between 1890 and 1954 began the process of becoming Americans.

Castle Garden had been active, though small; Ellis Island was hyperactive and enormous. In 1907 more than one million immigrants passed through its waiting rooms, its interview lines, its medical inspections. A forbidding, official-looking establishment in its early days (later, red spires and green cupolas gave it a strangely Byzantine appearance), it could be avoided only by those who crossed the ocean in cabin class—and it was not rare to find that a family had saved money for an extra year or two to buy cabin tickets for relatives who might otherwise have had difficulty passing the rigorous health examinations given steerage passengers. Those who did not pass the physical, or the various other tests, were turned back. When the Israeli Nobelist S. Y. Agnon first saw Ellis Island on a visit to New York in the 1960s, he was moved to recall that in Europe it was known as the "island of tears," tears shed by those who were not allowed to set foot on the mainland. Jacob Riis, in 1903, wrote, "Behind the carefully guarded doors wait the 'outs,' the detained immigrants, for the word that will let down the bars or fix them in place immovably. The guard is for a double purpose: that no one shall enter or leave the detention room. . . . Here are the old, the stricken, waiting for friends able to keep them; the pitiful colony of women without the shield of a man's name in the hour of their greatest need; the young and the pretty and thoughtless, for whom one sends up a silent prayer of thanksgiving at the thought of the mob at that other gate, yonder in Battery Park, beyond which Uncle Sam's strong hand reaches not to guide or guard. And the hopelessly bewildered are there, often enough exasperated at the restraint, which they cannot understand." As many as six hundred detainees were turned away each

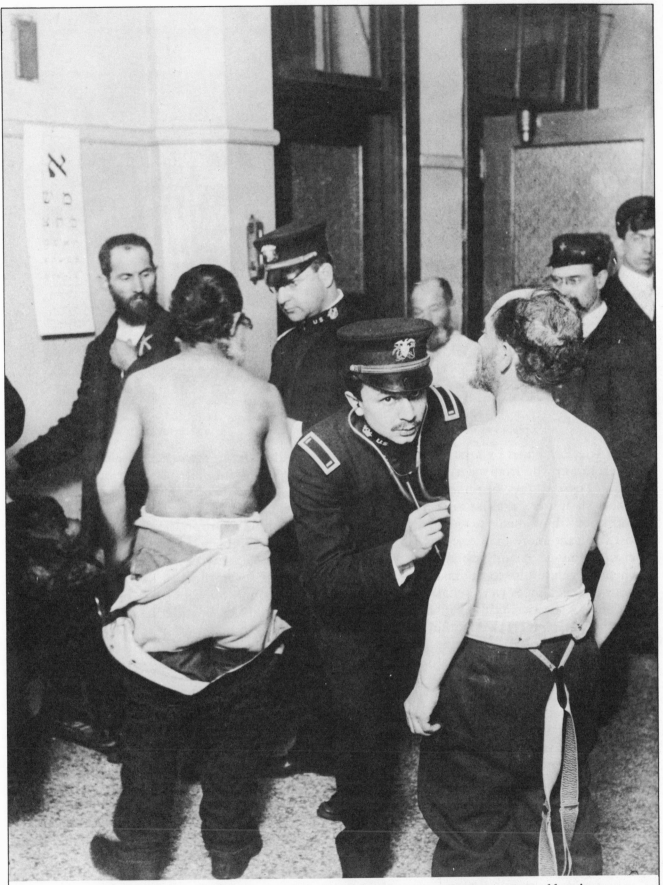

Medical detainees, 1907. The man at left bears a "K" on his collar, indicating a suspected hernia

Ellis Island's Registry Hall, 1916. The Ukrainian choir recital taking place was one of a series of Sunday concerts introduced during World War I

day. A letter signed by a hundred such, which ran on the front page of the *Forward*, said, "Tuesday they begin again to lead us to the 'slaughter,' that is, to the boat. And God knows how many Jewish lives this will cost, because more than one mind dwells on the thought of jumping into the water when they take him to the boat." These particular detainees were refused entry for not having the twenty-five dollars required to enter the country, a rule they had not been informed of as they departed European shores, and one that was unevenly applied. (It was finally repealed in 1914.)

For those who did come through, there were seemingly endless entrance formalities. From the "observation deck" of Ellis's great hall, where distinguished visitors could watch the admission process, one could see detention areas, kitchens (including one kosher facility), baggage areas, money-changing offices, railroad ticket offices. One of the supposed virtues off the island, as compared with the earlier Castle Garden facility, was its isolation from corrupt outside elements that preyed on the

immigrants; however, some elements inside were little more altruistic. Bribe solicitations weren't uncommon. Sometimes even solicitation was dispensed with in favor of the simple expropriation of whatever money the immigrant had on his person.

In the early years, as in 1907, when as many as seven thousand arrived in one day, those bound for Ellis were picked up from the various harborside berths where the liners docked, and were ferried to the island, sometimes remaining on the ferry barges for hours. Doctors could take the time to look only for the most obvious physical defects, marking these unfortunates with chalk for further examination. Inspectors checked for tuberculosis, for apparent mental defects, for deafness; they asked questions to determine, in Irving Howe's list, "character, anarchism, polygamy, insanity, crime, money, relatives, work." Then, finally, the ferries that traveled around the clock from Ellis Island to Manhattan would take the newly admitted immigrant to his promised land—as likely as not a room in a tenement on the Lower East Side.

Federation of Jewish Philanthropies

"Federation," as it is commonly called by those associated with it, was established in New York in 1917 and is today the largest local philanthropic organization in the world. It was born of two urges: first, to aid European and Palestinian Jews affected by World War I; and more enduringly, to create order out of the chaos of Jewish philanthropic agencies that had sprung up in New York by that time, agencies in constant competition with one another for both contributions and good deeds. Founded by German Jews, it became a more widely based organization; in 1974, when it joined its annual fund-raising campaign with that of the United Jewish Appeal, the primary fund-raiser for Zionist activities, the breach between at least the monied sector of the eastern European Jewish community and the German Jewish community was formally healed.

Today, Federation supports more than 130 organizations in the New York area, from hospitals and child-care centers to that old, established wonder of East Broadway, the Educational Alliance, which relies on Federation for thirty percent of its annual budget.

Feigenbaum, Benjamin (1860–1932) For

decades associate editor of the *Daily Forward* and a leader of the Workmen's Circle, Feigenbaum was as prominent a public speaker as he was a journalist, a Warsaw-born, Orthodox-reared man who became a fervently antireligious Socialist. He somehow found a way to merge the morality and ethics of the faith in which he was raised with his political beliefs, and managed the

A Federation-sponsored orphan home, 1916

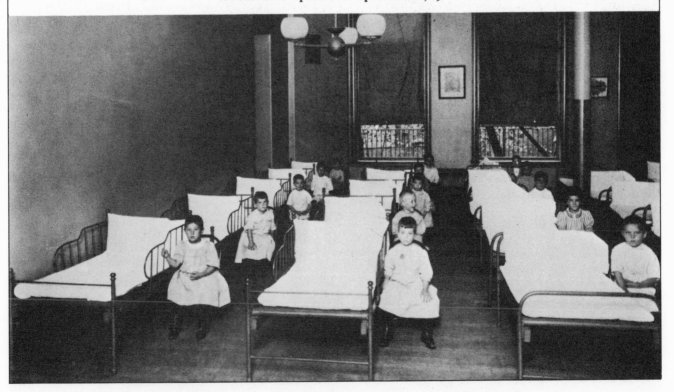

synthesis in, among other books, *The Labor Laws of the Talmud*. An immensely popular lecturer, his particular upbringing and orientation toward Jewish life struck a chord with many of his generation. He was a practical man, too; as Irving Howe affirms, when Feigenbaum made it a rule that every organization that could afford it should be charged a flat fee of five dollars by a lecturer, it was an innovation that "constituted a major step forward in the profession."

Folksbiene This highly competent theater group emerged from the literary and theater societies of decades past that involved themselves in serious amateur theatricals. In *Vagabond Stars*, Nahma Sandrow lists a random sampling of the amateur societies that proliferated in this country early in the century—Jacob Gordin Circle, Goldfadn Club, Y. L. Peretz Club, Mendele Literary-Dramatic Association, Literary Art Corner, United Dramatic and Musical

Club, and in New Jersey, the Newark Intimate Theater Group of the Young Men's and Young Women's Hebrew Association Yiddish Lyceum.

Folksbiene is the survivor. Organized in 1915—which probably makes it New York's oldest theater company, English or Yiddish, commercial or not—Folksbiene has operated since that time under the aegis of the Workmen's Circle, allowing not a single season to pass without at least one production. While the Folksbiene is in fact amateur, its standards of production, casting, and direction have always been highly professional; among the directors it has brought in for its productions are such as Joseph Buloff and Jacob Ben-Ami. It has developed further renown for the purity of its Yiddish, eschewing as it does all Americanisms and other linguistic intrusions.

Ford, Henry (1863–1947) From 1920 to 1927, the automobile magnate published in his newspaper, the *Dearborn Independent*

A 1944 production of Sholem Aleichem's *200,000*

(which enjoyed a peak circulation of 500,000), almost one hundred viciously anti-Semitic articles, ranging from the "revelation" of the discredited *Protocols of the Elders of Zion,* to charges that well-established American Jews of German origin had "ordered" the immigration of Orthodox eastern European Jews to stimulate Judaism in America. The paper's attacks on Jews in general and Jews in particular brought a lawsuit and a community-wide boycott of Ford cars, which in turn led Ford to execute an abrupt about-face and issue a retraction and an apology in 1927. This document was drafted by Louis Marshall, and Ford evidently signed it unread. Still, it drew much notice in the press; songwriter and impresario Billy Rose celebrated it with "Since Henry Ford Apologized to Me." Some of the lyrics:

I was sad and I was blue
But now I'm just as good as you
Since Henry Ford a-pol-o-gized to me . . .

My mother says she'll feed him if he calls
'Ge-fil-te fish' and matzo balls . . .

Still, a poll commissioned by Ford Motor Company in 1940, at the direction of Henry's son Edsel, showed that seventy-eight percent of the American male public had heard that Ford was anti-Semitic. In 1943 the company spent $83,000 advertising Ford cars in Jewish publications—and this was a year in which the company wasn't even making cars. It was the first step in a campaign to try to win back Jewish buyers to the Ford line, a campaign proven necessary by a 1944 Elmo Roper study which showed that Ford had so offended American Jews that they had virtually stopped buying the company's vehicles by the late 1930s.

The Ford International Weekly

THE DEARBORN INDEPENDENT

Ten Cents

Dearborn, Michigan, August 6, 1921

$1.50

Jewish Jazz—Moron Music—Becomes Our National Music

Story of "Popular Song" Control in the United States

Henry Ford and his newspaper

Forward, Jewish Daily Of all the lively Yiddish papers that have come and gone within the last century, the *Jewish Daily Forward* was the most vibrant, the most provocative, the best adapted to journalism in the new land. It is still alive today, somewhat diminished by dwindling numbers of Yiddish-speaking readers, the sole survivor among daily papers of the constant linguistic attrition in its community. It had a circulation of nearly 250,000 during World War I and was the wealthiest and most widely read Yiddish newspaper in the country, with eleven local and regional editions.

The *Forward* was founded in 1897 as a Socialist organ, more moderate than the other Socialist publications of its time. At the organizational meeting in New York's Valhalla Hall where it became a reality, Jewish Socialist workmen contributed not only money but pocket watches, watch chains, and other jewelry to finance the new undertaking. Abraham Cahan, who left the *Forward* briefly but returned to become the dominant force in the paper's life, later remarked, "If there was a paper supported by a holy spirit—upon holy inspiration—it was ours."

The *Forward*'s promise was not immediately realized. Cahan's ideas of news coverage conflicted with the concepts of those who favored a doctrinaire, even arid, posture for the paper's readers. Cahan quit, but returned to the editor's desk in 1902. His impress was immediately felt with his first issue. Large headlines, in the manner of the sensational press of the day, were introduced. The colloquial Yiddish heard on the streets of New York appeared in its columns (even though this was a Yiddish that Cahan himself had detested when he arrived in America years earlier). Encountering sentences that seemed to him pompously unintelligible, Cahan would try them out on the elevator man, who served as the "average reader" Cahan was trying to reach.

Although Cahan was a devout Socialist, he was not a sectarian one, and the *Forward* urgently trumpeted the labor cause, campaigned for the freeing of Eugene V.

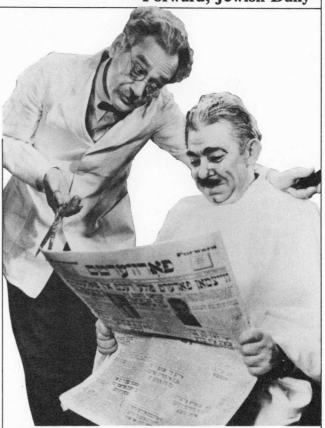

Forward **readers, from a Yiddish production of** *Awake and Sing* **by Clifford Odets**

Debs from prison (later, when it established a radio station, the call letters—WEVD—were selected in Debs's honor), and argued, however unavailingly, the cause of the anarchists Sacco and Vanzetti, calling their trial "the American Dreyfus case."

However much and however perilously the *Forward* stuck out its neck, it was not the paper's political coloration that accounted for its popularity. Cahan insisted on bringing the wider America into the homes of Yiddish readers, and he also brought their own situations home to them. Though the *Forward* was certainly Socialist and harbored one or two ideologically strict writers, it did not go out of its way to attack religion and remained ever conscious of its Jewish nature. It may have tried to be all things to all readers, but read it was, the living word for many hundreds of thousands of people. "The *Forverts* is read most assiduously not only by the proletariat," read an article in H. L. Mencken's *American Mercury* in 1927, "but also by that part of the Yiddish intelligentsia which criticizes it most severely. None can resist the lively, human appeal of Cahan's paper, even though one may condemn it ever so often as yellow."

The innovations in Yiddish newspapering introduced by Cahan included such articles as "The Fundamentals of Baseball Explained to Non-Sports," with a diagram of the Polo Grounds; pieces by Cahan on proper American etiquette; notes on how American fathers went fishing with their children; and, most popular of all, "A Bintel Brief," the extraordinary letters column that for decades aired the everyday problems of the paper's readers. It was very much in the tone of the *Forward* to tell mothers to give their children handkerchiefs, and to reply to Socialists who wondered what this had to do with socialism, "And since when has socialism been opposed to clean noses?" Among the more celebrated writers whose work appeared in the *Forward* were Sholem Asch (later dropped because of what Cahan called the "missionary" trends in Asch's novel *The Nazarene*), Abraham Reisen, and Zalman Shneour; later, I. B. Singer and Chaim Grade would become regular contributors.

In 1908 the *Forward* moved into a new ten-story building at 175 East Broadway, a proud structure that towered over the low-lying tenements and later boasted the largest Yiddish neon sign in history, an enormous "*Forverts*." "When they tear down No. 175," Cahan once said, "the East Side will go the way of all Jewish ghettos—kaput." The *Forward* has long since moved to more modest quarters uptown, but No. 175 stands today, occupied now by a Chinese religious organization, yet still bearing engraved likenesses of Marx, Engels, Liebknecht, and LaSalle on its facade.

Freie Arbeiter Shtimme *Di Freie Arbeiter Shtimme* (*The Free Workers' Voice*) was an anarchist paper founded in 1890 and edited until his early death by the poet David Edelstadt. It died with him, and was then reborn under the aegis of Saul Yanowsky, a severe critic whose pen could inflict deep wounds. For his part, Edelstadt set the tone a few days before Yom Kippur in

Workers at *Di Freie Arbeiter Shtimme*

1890 with a poem entitled "To the Defenders of Obscurantism": "Why complain, you orthod-oxen? . . . Do you want us to bow down to your archaic god, lower our heads before every pious idiot? Each era has its new Torah. . . . We also have our new prophets—Borne, LaSalle, Karl Marx; They will deliver us from exile, but not with fasts and prayers!" Despite its strident politics, *Di Freie Arbeiter Shtimme* under Yanowsky was welcoming to short story writers, poets, and essayists of literary quality and indeterminate ideology.

Freiheit The *Freiheit* (*Freedom*) was founded in 1922 by the Jewish arm of the American Communist Party. For most of the more than half-century of its existence, this daily paper espoused the party line and was vilified by its detractors as "the organ of the New York diocese of the Moscow Papacy." Its justification of the Arab riots in Hebron in 1929 and of the Hitler-Stalin pact of 1939 hurt its credibility, and justified much of the criticism hurled at it. Nonetheless, despite its political orthodoxy and its unrelenting opposition to Jewish nationalism and Zionism, it remained an important Yiddish cultural institution. Under the editorship of Moissaye Olgin, who with others quit the staff of the *Forward* following the Menshevik-Bolshevik split after the Russian Revolution, *Freiheit* was notable for the literary quality of its writers, among them H. Leivick, Abraham Reisen, Mani Leib, and M. L. Halpern. Olgin remained editor until he died in 1939, his paper constantly buffeted by the consequences of his fealty to the party line.

After the Hebron riots, the boycott organized by the *Forward* hurt the paper badly. As with other large-circulation Yiddish papers, it had carried a good deal of consumer advertising from non-Jewish businesses ignorant of its politics. Recalled Jacob Schwartz, a merchant who helped organize the boycott, "We organized a campaign to deprive the *Freiheit* of the revenue produced by these big companies. I myself went uptown to the advertising agencies, and told them, in no uncertain terms, that the Jewish community was betrayed by the paper's editorial policy on Palestine. . . . We don't care how good your products are," Schwartz told the advertisers, "if it appears in the pages of the *Freiheit*, we will make your soap, your hats, your anything, look anti-Semitic."

Today, the *Freiheit* generally departs from the party line on Jewish questions, and maintains positions closer to the Eurocommunists than to Moscow.

Fuchs, Daniel (1909–   ) Fuchs's "Williamsburg Trilogy," about Jewish life in that part of Brooklyn, brought him and his neighborhood wide attention when he was still in his twenties. The first of the books, *Summer in Williamsburg*, was a story reflected through the eyes of a boy in his last year at City College whose father is an elderly news dealer and whose brother has become a gangster. It is peopled by philosophers and racketeers, by hard-hearted, vituperative types and earnest idealists. The subsequent novels in the trilogy were *Homage to Blenholt* (1936) and *Low Company* (1937). Fuchs went to Hollywood as a scriptwriter in 1937, and in 1956 earned an Oscar for *Love Me or Leave Me*.

Fur Workers Union The ode "To a Worker," by the Furrier poet Lazar Dinsky, reads,

Whether you sew silk, or I sew furs
Your needle thrusts, my scissors cut, are now
in our bones.
A glance from the boss, and the shop rushes on
And from our fingers ooze our crimson tears.

The poem's delicacy runs counter to the
commoner image of a Furrier in the
1930s—member of the most radical, and
the toughest, union in the garment trade.

The Furriers were the longest-lived
Communist-led union in the industry, a
strong and well-organized group led by the
fiery Ben Gold. Assistant leader of the
union shop of Pike and Rabinowitz when
he was only fourteen, Gold was a flamboyant, proud, exceedingly energetic leader
who retained control over the Furriers for
nearly thirty years, resigning from the
Communist Party only when the Taft-Hart-
ley Act required union leaders to swear
they did not belong to it. Gold's union was
composed largely of highly skilled crafts-
men who worked in the four-block fur district between Twenty-sixth and Thirtieth
streets along Seventh Avenue, a primarily
Jewish union spiced by the distinctive flavor of several hundred Greek furriers fully
as militant as their Jewish coworkers.

Gold and the Furriers were in a virtually constant state of siege—at war with
the anti-Communist unions within the CIO,
with the New York City police, and with
the fur manufacturers and the gangsters
they employed, fundamentally, to "break
heads." The Protective Fur Dressers' Association, representing employers who dealt
primarily in rabbit furs, and the Fur Dressers' Factor Corporation, representing those
who manufactured higher-grade fur garments, originally made pacts with the notorious Lepke Buchalter and Jake "Gurrah"
Shapiro to help control the market, creating
a manufacturers' cartel that benefited employers and workers alike. (Not to mention

A Furriers union banquet, 1937

Fusgeyer aboard the S.S. *Breslau*, 1912

the mobsters themselves. Philip Foner, official historian of the union, estimates that the fees collected by the mob—a penny for every skin produced, plus a flat fee from every firm in the industry—amounted to nearly $10 million annually.)

But when the Protectives precipitated a strike in 1933 by refusing to honor contractual commitments to the unions, they enlisted the mobsters to back up their intimidation techniques with violence. Gold put together a Furrier paramilitary group to defend the unionists, and the streets of the fur district ran red. On April 24, 1933, the mob invaded union headquarters; one worker and one mobster were killed, and scores on both sides (and not a few New York policemen) were injured. Gold himself, in the company of S. J. Zuckerman, labor writer for *The Day*, were once backed up to a restaurant wall by a cadre of Lepke's goons and saved only when several hundred fur workers came running from both ends of the block, routing the mobsters. Although the Furriers eventually fought the Protective Associations and their hired thugs to a draw, terror and violence

were epidemic in the fur district for months at a time. During the 1933 strike, iron pipes and vials of acid were commonplace in the area, the hideous tools of Lepke's trade.

Fusgeyer Yiddish emigration to America more often than not started with a pogrom, a terror that persuaded people there was no future in the *alte heim*, and that life in a land that held the promise of freedom was worth the pain of exile and journey. In 1899, when pogroms erupted in Rumania, hordes of *fusgeyer*—wayfarers—left on foot to make their way to the German ports, particularly Hamburg. They were generally young, healthy, skilled workers who understood the value of organization for mutual aid, and each *fusgeyer* group sold possessions and pooled its money to ensure that every member of the group would arrive in America. Their emigration resembled a procession of trade and community groups: Painters and Dyers of Bucharest; Wayfarers of Barlad; Students, Workers, and Clerks of Golatz. Some *fusgeyer* groups were composed exclusively of women.

Gallery of Missing Husbands By 1910, when Jewish immigration was reaching its peak, a new problem emerged: the increasing instance of men deserting their wives and children. Many younger immigrants, rooted in the overpowering family traditions of the *shtetl* and suddenly plunged into the alienating industrial process and the looser "American way of life," became disenchanted with the women they had taken as wives, as likely as not through the offices of a marriage broker. Others simply could not bear the crushing weight of family support in the face of grinding poverty and despair.

Soon, letters from deserted wives began to fill the newspapers. One Boston paper collected them in a column, "Farshvundene Mentshn" ("Missing Persons"); the *Forward* went a step further with its "Gallery of Missing Husbands," complete with photographs of the wayward. The paper worked closely with the National Desertion Bureau, founded in 1911 by the Jewish Social Service, in pursuit of the vanished men.

Galveston Plan By the early 1900s Jewish leaders were daunted by the concentration of new immigrants in New York and other eastern ports. Jacob Schiff,

ever attuned to the shifting tides of need among the immigrants, in 1907 launched a plan that would divert this migration to other parts of the country. Schiff approached Israel Zangwill, a founder of the Jewish Territorial Organization, and after rejecting Zangwill's suggestion that Schiff buy large tracts of land in the Southwest for a "National Jewish Home," secured Zangwill's aid in directing newcomers to the Texas port of Galveston.

The plan was effected under the aegis of the Jewish Immigrants' Information Bureau, headed by Morris D. Waldman, and abetted by Galveston's Rabbi Henry Cohen, the leader of that city's sizable German-Jewish community. Although many other immigrant aid associations

Immigrants arriving in Galveston, 1907

declined to cooperate, the program succeeded in settling ten thousand immigrants in the Southwest by the time World War I started.

Gangsters There seems a special fascination for modern American Jews in the stories of Jewish gangsters. This interest is almost as puzzling as the Jewish gangster phenomenon itself, as though one needed reassurance—in terms of the Zionist credo, the normalization of the Jew—that there were Jewish strong-arm men, vicious murderers, ruthless mobsters to compensate for the generalization that Jews specialize in don't-hit crime.

No question: the Jewish gangster was a fact, and in the first forty years of the century as much a fact in this country as his Italian counterpart; in New York, perhaps more so. In the era in which Jews grew up in slums, experiencing the disintegration of family authority, there were renowned gangsters just as there were (and now no longer are) famous Jewish boxers. One escaped the poverty of the ghetto by the same means employed by every other ethnic group.

"It is not until they have become Americanized, have adapted themselves to the environment of the district and adopted its ways and vices, that they become full-fledged wretches," a contemporary observer said. Until the 1880s, according to Moses Rischin in *The Promised City*, there had been only one Jewish murder case in New York, in which Pesach Rubinstein was sentenced to death for killing his girl cousin. Rubinstein committed suicide in prison, but his unique crime so titillated everyone that a popular street song went "My name is Pesach Rubinstein . . ."

By the turn of the century Jews were moving in on Lower East Side crime, formerly the preserve of the Irish, and word spread of Michael "Sheeny Mike" Kurtz, the so-called champion burglar of America. In 1909 three thousand Jewish children were brought to juvenile court, and newspaper readers found the Jewish criminal a front-page commonplace. As their criminal activities grew, so of course did their renown, enhanced by their euphonious nicknames: "Bugsy" Siegel, Jake "Greasy Thumb" Guzik, Arthur "Dutch Schultz" Flegenheimer, "Kid Twist" Reles, Nathan

"Kid Dropper" Kaplan   **"Greasy Thumb" Guzik**   **"Kid Twist" Reles**

The military funeral of Monk Eastman, complete with floral garlands sent by his fellow mobsters

"Kid Dropper" Kaplan—the list goes on and on. One of the earliest and most deadly of Jewish gangsters was Monk Eastman, the very model of the modern thug, with his short build, bullet-shaped head, cauliflower ears, and ferocious expression. Eastman operated brothels and commanded pimps and gambling houses. He extorted protection money from merchants, sold strong-arm services to the higher bidding side of labor strikes, worked to fix elections for Tammany Hall—and all the while used as his headquarters a Broome Street pet shop. When Eastman went to prison, gang power passed to Big Jack Zelig, a merciless killer who was one of the prime inaugurators of big-time racketeering in New York. Zelig sold protection to gamblers and other crooks who, upon becoming clients, saw him plague the competiton with knives, brass knuckles, murder, and torture.

In July 1912, gambler Herman Rosenthal gave a story to the *New York World* in which he fingered his partner, Lieutenant Charles Becker of the police department antigambling squad, for double-crossing him. Three days before Rosenthal was to appear before a grand jury, he was murdered on Forty-fifth Street. Within four weeks, three of the assassins—one Italian and two Jews—were arrested, and they along with Becker were indicted, convicted, and executed. Harry Hopkins, then a worker in a Lower East Side settlement house, recalled how the boys in attendance at the settlement observed a moment of silence at the scheduled time of execution.

By the 1920s the proliferation of Jewish gangsters had reached such proportions that the following roll call of Yiddish-reared immigrants and children of immigrants only indicates the outlines of the problem:

In Chicago, Jake "Greasy Thumb" Guzik rose to become the business manager of the Capone mob, the apparent inventor of the nationwide "crime syndicate," a man

"Bugsy" Siegel, 1940

who never carried a gun but who never ventured out with less than $10,000 cash in his pocket (a sufficient ransom to buy off kidnappers on three occasions). Guzik served federal time for income tax invasion; in 1928 he filed a tax return for $18,000 when his actual liability, according to the IRS, was $642,000.

In Detroit, the notorious Purple Gang of Samuel "Sammie Purple" Cohen and the three Bernstein brothers bootlegged Canadian whiskey for the Capone mob, ran protection rackets, strong-armed businessmen, and hired themselves out for murders and kidnappings. They entered their decline in the early 1930s when three members received life terms for first-degree murder and the rest were systematically picked off by a rival Italian mob.

In New York, the gunsels of Murder, Inc., off the streets of Brownsville and East New York, plied their trade in the garment industry, in the gambling syndicates, and in virtually every criminal endeavor available as the unofficial enforcers of the syndicate's internal rules. Lepke Buchalter, perhaps the most feared of all the Jewish mobsters, made his name and his fortune as a strongman in labor-management wars. Lucky Luciano said, "With the rest of us,

it was booze, gambling, whores, like that. But Lepke took the bread out of the workers' mouths." His control over various city industries was pervasive in the middle thirties, his "schlammers" collecting millions in protection money throughout the New York industrial sector. Buchalter was executed at Sing Sing in 1944 for first-degree murder. Arnold Rothstein, son of an honored member of New York's Jewish community, sat atop the New York syndicate and was personally responsible for acts as varied as fixing the 1919 World Series and settling, through some well-placed threats, the 1926 garment industry strike.

The list went on and on, down through the years, scores disappearing in violent death, hundreds dropping out as they moved their criminal gains into legitimate business. After World War II, "Bugsy" Siegel, the stylish, too-independent gambling entrepreneur, was killed by rival mobsters when he defied syndicate orders, and Meyer Lansky prevailed over his worldwide gambling empire up to and beyond the day in the 1970s when he was denied permission, as an undesirable, to settle in Israel. Just as Lansky attempted to cleanse his image with charitable contributions to any number of Jewish causes, so did many of his unsavory predecessors manage to keep reputations clean in at least part of the Jewish community. As noted by Robert A. Rockaway, the relatives of Longie Zwillman, the New Jersey syndicate boss, heard him eulogized at his 1959 funeral by Dr. Joachim Prinz, president of the American Jewish Congress. And three years earlier, when Jake Guzik died, an Orthodox rabbi described him as a man who "never lost faith in his God. Hundreds benefited by his kindness and generosity. His charities were performed quietly."

Garment Industry The "needle trade," the "rag business," or simply "*shmattes*" (as in, "I'm in *shmattes*") has always been the most prominent Jewish industry in America, both in the executive suites and, until World War II, in the sweatshops and factories. (One ILGWU official points out, to keep the record straight, "The garment industry is *not* a Jewish industry, but a Jewish-*influenced* industry. The *mezuzah* industry is a Jewish industry.")

Many German-Jewish fortunes were started in the garment business back in the 1850s. A hundred years later a commentator would note that "the transition from cloak maker to cloak manufacturer is comparatively short": by the mid-twentieth century, eastern Europeans were as prominent in the business as their German-Jewish predecessors had been, and the garment district of New York, centered since the early 1930s along Seventh Avenue, remained one of the last redoubts of Yiddish culture and language. The invention of the sewing machine and the cutting knife

Garment industry strikers, 1910

(which could slice through several pieces of fabric at once) made the mass production of garments economical, but not more so than the sudden arrival in America of thousands upon thousands of artisans and unskilled laborers in desperate need of employment. In 1890 the Baron de Hirsch Fund conducted a survey which found that sixty per-

Tenement pieceworkers

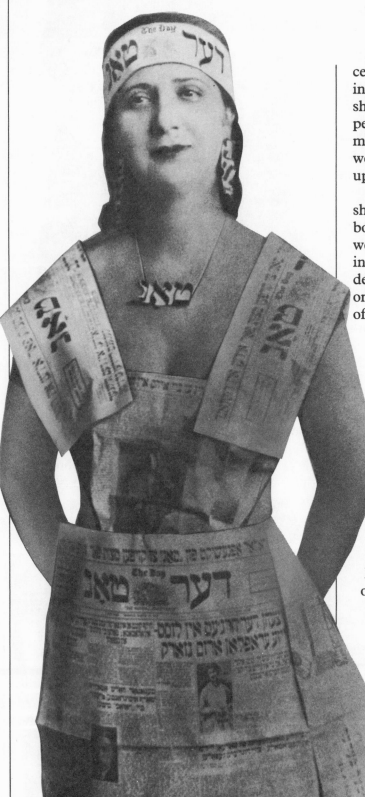

cent of employed immigrant Jews worked in the garment industry, usually in sweatshops or at home doing piecework. Eleven percent of all eastern European immigrant males were tailors, and thousands more were "Columbus tailors," people who took up the trade after arriving in America.

As the labor history of the industry shows, relations between the immigrant laborers and the established manufacturers were dreadful. The business was centered in New York, Boston, Chicago, and Philadelphia, and in every one of those cities the omnipresence of *shleppers* carrying bundles of material and bags of finished garments, the grimy tenement sweatshops and young girls pouring into factories, marked the Yiddish immigrant quarter. Jacob Riis wrote in 1890, "Every open window of the big tenements . . . gives you a glimpse of . . . men and women bending over their machines. Morning, noon or night, it makes no difference."

Gersten, Berta (1894–1972) Sophie Tucker's mother on Broadway, Benny Goodman's mother in the filmed story of the clarinetist's life, this actress's best-known role was, again as a mother, in one of the few American-produced Yiddish-language films of enduring quality, Gordin's *Mirele Efros*, also known as *The Jewish Queen Lear*. A veteran of Maurice Schwartz's Irving Place Theater, Gersten was leading lady (and lover) to Jacob Ben-Ami for nearly half a century, and the original Esther in the Broadway production of Odets's *The Flowering Peach*.

Gersten at a costume ball, garbed in *The Day*

Brooks Atkinson, in his review of the Odets play in the *New York Times*, wrote, "Although Miss Gersten is comic, she acts with a magnificence that pulls the whole play together."

Glatstein, Jacob (1896–1971) As described by the critic and translator Ruth Whitman, Glatstein's poetry was "caustic, lyrical, technically remarkable, extending from the lost world of the East European Jew and the catastrophe of Nazi genocide to his experience as a private human being, a contemporary man caught in the dilemmas of 20th century America." With Aaron Glanz-Leyeles and N. B. Minkoff, he was one of the poets who inaugurated the intellectually self-searching *Inzichist*, or introspective, school of Yiddish poetry.

An immigrant from Lublin in 1914, Glatstein was well read, familiar with the great writers of America and Europe, and especially with the leading Yiddish poets, particularly his beloved Peretz. Although he entered New York University Law School, his life's wish was to write poetry, in whatever language he could. When he met Minkoff, he opted for Yiddish. His work paralleled—and sometimes led—the course of Yiddish poetry in America following the generation of the "sweatshop poets": it moved from an early internalized self-expression to a palpable concern with the fate of the Jews. Glatstein was a coiner of words and usages, a brilliant manipulator of the language. He also wrote fiction, notably a trilogy about his return to Poland in the 1930s: *When Yash Started Out*, *When Yash Arrived*, and *Homecoming at Twilight*.

Gold, Michael (1893–1967) With one book, *Jews Without Money*, Michael Gold established himself as an American author.

This autobiographical work depicted not the lives of those on the Lower East Side who rose from rags to riches on the traditional American staircase of success, but rather the world of the losers, the proletarian mass drowning in an exploitative sea. The book is not so much an integrated narrative as it is a panoramic view—didactic, perhaps, but powerfully so—of the ghetto and its prostitutes, its criminals, its filth and despair. Yet, as Lewis Gannett observed in his review, "Sometimes—not very often in this book—he falls into the bathos of Messianic prayers for deliverance by the dreamy road of romantic revolution." Published originally by Liveright, *Jews Without Money* became a perennial reissue from International Publishers, the Marxist publishing house, and standard reading in leftist Jewish homes throughout the country. In 1965 it was issued in paperback by Avon Books and proceeded through five printings. In his introduction to that edition, Michael Harrington wrote, "As he later told it, [Gold] had 'no politics . . . except hunger' until he was 19. Then, during the unemployment crisis of 1914, he strayed into a Union Square demonstration, bought a copy of *The Masses*, and was knocked down by a cop when he resisted a police charge on

Jacob Glatstein

the crowd. It was, like the sudden conversion of the narrator on the final page of the novel, an epiphany, a revelation." Gold was a journalist and playwright as well as a novelist, a Communist who succeeded Max Eastman as editor of *The New Masses* in 1928. Seven years earlier he wrote an essay, "Towards Proletarian Art," which was to be an influential work among Communists who asserted that the sole merit of artistic creation was determined by its social and political content.

Golden, Harry (1902–1981) This son of an editor of the *Forward,* raised on the streets of the Lower East Side, somehow found his way to fame and fortune publishing an idiosyncratic English-language paper, improbably called *The Carolina Israelite,* in Charlotte, North Carolina. The paper was fundamentally a sounding board for whatever interested Golden (articles ranged from "Cato's Hangover Cure" to "A Plan to Solve the Problems of the White Citizens' Council") and was circulated through the mails, in terribly small numbers, across the country. Among its readers were William Faulkner, Carl Sandburg, and Earl Warren. The only thing that made Golden, and his paper, Yiddish was that he was utterly incapable of writing in anything but a tone filled with the irony, fatefulness, and immense shrug of the shoulders that so characterized a particular American-Jewish essay style. Golden, in fact, might have been its leading practitioner, sort of a Borscht Belt political philosopher stranded in the foothills of the Blue Ridge Mountains.

Golden became a well-known figure with publication of his collection of essays *Only in America,* which was an immense national best-seller in 1958. Soon after the book's publication, it became known that Golden, under the name Harry L. Goldhurst, had served a five-year term in a federal prison during the 1930s for mail fraud. Immediately after that news surfaced, he returned to the best-seller lists with another collection, *For 2 Cents Plain,* surely the only best-seller that took its title from a description of a glass of seltzer water. He wrote several other books over the next few years, including a paean to his native New York, *The Greatest Jewish City in the World.*

Goldene Medine The "Golden Land"—it was the catchall phrase that defined the dream harbored by America-bound Jews pouring out of the cities and *shtetlekh* of eastern Europe in the late nineteenth and early twentieth centuries. Dream and reality, however, differed greatly. One story told by thousands of immigrants to their children and grandchildren summarized the disparity precisely: "When I left for America, I was told the streets were paved with gold. When I got here, I found that not only were they not paved with gold, they weren't paved at all. And not only weren't they paved, but I was expected to pave them!"

Goldfadn, Abraham (1840–1908) The man who "invented" Yiddish theater was an unlikely candidate for the task: a Rumanian newspaperman, a member of the Jewish middle class. His inspiration provided the mouthpiece through which the national and folk ethos of the Yiddish-speaking masses would find expression. His style of theater was in the tradition of commedia dell'arte, built around a plot, some songs, and the improvisational speeches of the actors. Goldfadn specialized in historical dramas such as *Bar Kokhba* and *Shulamis,* both of which became long-lasting hits, as did his *Shmendrik,* which gave this word to the Yiddish language. This last work employed the devices that were Goldfadn's trademark: speech defects, physical deformities, and eccentric motions. Although such theater caught the public fancy right from the start, it had little appeal for the Yiddish intelligentsia; years later his work had to be "rehabilitated" by the Artef Players.

Goldfadn followed the Yiddish theater to New York in 1887, but

he failed there; the form had moved faster

Visions of the *goldene medine.*
The map below details the agricultural and industrial produce of the various states

Songsheet from Goldfadn's *The Curse of the Daughters of Zion*

Emma Goldman, 1917

than he had. He returned to Rumania, then came back to America in 1902, living on a stipend of ten dollars a week provided by Jacob Adler and Boris Thomashevsky. Still, he was at first unable to persuade them to produce one of his plays. Goldfadn had become a virtual object of ridicule in his last years. He was accused of senility by a member of Adler's company, which had had the rights to, and then rejected, *Ben Ami*, his last play; the Adler actors tittered and winked at each other as they read through it. But Thomashevsky's company felt otherwise, and agreed to produce it. On Christmas night, 1907, Goldfadn attended the opening of *Ben Ami*, and went back each of the next four nights, feeling a vindicated man. On the fifth night, he fell ill and died. His funeral, according to the *New York World*, attracted seventy-five thousand people to the streets; the paper's reporter wrote, "He was no more than a modest poet and dramatist, 'the Jewish Shakespeare.' There is great doubt that his name was known in even one Fifth Avenue home, yet he is known in each and every tenement."

Goldman, Emma (1869–1940) The most notorious American anarchist of her era, "Red Emma" Goldman was born in Lithuania, spent her childhood in St. Petersburg, and came to Rochester, New York, at seventeen. Her conscience was aroused by the execution of anarchists in Chicago after the Haymarket explosion of 1886, and after a short, unhappy marriage she went to New York, where she met the anarchists Johann Most and, on the very day she arrived in the city, Alexander Berkman, who would be closely involved in her life for forty years. In 1893 Goldman was jailed for inciting to riot in Union Square; while in prison, she devoted herself to nursing and the study of American literature. In 1901 she was arrested when President McKinley's assassin said he had been influenced by her speeches and writings. Released soon thereafter, she gave a newspaper interview in which she expressed sympathy with the assassin's motives, and in the next breath offered to nurse McKinley—still struggling for his life—back to health; he was, she said, "a human being."

Goldman's life in the years following

consisted largely of speechmaking, writing (she edited two journals, *The Blast* and *Mother Earth*, the latter the first American showcase for the works of Ibsen and Strindberg), and maintaining an apartment known as "the home for lost dogs." Located at 210 East Thirteenth Street, it was a one-room flat she shared with Berkman and an endless train of homeless and penniless radicals and intellectuals for whom sleeping space was always available.

In 1919 Goldman and Berkman were among 247 aliens ordered deported by Attorney General Mitchell Palmer, architect of the antiradical "Red Raids." As the ship departed, she said, "We expect to be called back to Soviet America." In fact, she soon became disillusioned with the Revolution, particularly its refusal to grant political liberties to Soviet citizens. In 1921 Goldman and Berkman fled, eventually to Berlin; in 1924 she published *My Disillusionment in Russia,* and in the next year, *My Further Disillusionment in Russia.* She lived thereafter in England, France, and Canada, returning for a brief American visit in 1934. Although she remained an opponent of Soviet Marxism the rest of her life, she never abandoned her belief in an ideal anarchistic society. Her autobiography, *Living My Life,* is a classic of its genre.

Gordin, Jacob (1853–1909) "The distinctive thing about the intellectual and artistic life of the Russian Jews of the New York Ghetto, the spirit of realism, is noticeable even on the popular stage," wrote Hutchins Hapgood. He went on to identify the two men of the Yiddish stage who best exemplified this quality—Jacob Adler, the actor, and Jacob Gordin, the playwright. Gordin was a mighty force for quality in a field that too often looked only to the box office.

He had come to manhood as a Russian writer, worked on a farm, and believed at first that the Jews had earned "Russian scorn by their orthodoxy and their un-peasantlike life." He arrived in America in his late thirties with a group that hoped to establish a farm commune, but when that failed, Gordin forsook his beloved Russian-language writing to work on a Lower East Side Yiddish newspaper. He had never seen a Yiddish play in Russia, and knew little of Yiddish theater until he met Adler in a restaurant. He soon found himself writing for the Yiddish theater, and in short order became its leading author, with Adler the star of many of his plays. (Keni Liptzin, a particularly well-married actress known as the "Yiddish Duse," often financed—and also starred in—Gordin's works.) Gordin, some said, brought the Russian touch to the Yiddish theater, but in the process made certain that the situations were Jewish and thoroughly familiar to his audience. His *The Jewish King Lear,* which took Shakespeare's tragedy and placed it in a Jewish home, was wildly successful. His other plays included *Siberia, Mirele Efros* (also known as *The Jewish Queen Lear*), *Sappho, God, Man and Devil* (a reworking of both the story of Job and the Faust legend), and *Kreutzer Sonata.* Nahma Sandrow, in *Vagabond Stars,* tells of the effect of *Mirele Efros* and *The Jewish King Lear,* with their stories of ungrateful children, on the audience. A Lower East Side banker, she wrote, could tell when these plays were running because the next morning conscience-stricken customers would stream into his bank to send money orders to their parents back in the old country.

Gordin deplored the tendency of Jewish intellectuals to overlook the need to build a serious, literary theater. "The Yiddish theater," he once said, "cannot hope for the arrival of a powerful, talented writer so long as the majority of its authors will, like me, be men who take to dramatic writing through accident, who write pieces only because they are forced to do so in order to make a living."

Greenhorn One of the immigrant community's favored Americanisms, "greenhorn" —*griner* in Yiddish—was the all-purpose description for one just off the boat, fresh from the old country. Abraham Cahan, in his novel *The Rise of David Levinsky*, has his hero muse upon the word during his first day in New York: " 'Green one' or 'greenhorn' is one of the many English words and phrases which my mother tongue has appropriated in England and America. Thanks to the many millions of letters that pass annually between the Jews of Russia and their relatives in the United States, a number of these words have by now come to be generally known among our people at home as well as here. . . . As I went along I heard it again and again. Some the passers-by would call me 'greenhorn' in a tone of blighting gaiety, but these were an exception. For the most part it was 'green one' and in a spirit of sympathetic interest.

It hurt me all the same. . . . 'Poor fellow! He is a green one' these people seemed to say. 'We are not, of course. We are Americanized.' "

In 1912 the Immigrant Publication Society published a Yiddish-language *Guide to the United States for the Jewish Immigrant* filled with the sort of advice greenhorns needed to protect themselves: "BEWARE of swindling expressmen, cabmen, guides, agents of steamships and hotels, solicitors, porters, men who say they are journalists or lawyers. BEWARE OF NOTARIES . . . Many notaries are ignorant men, and do not know how to draw up the documents that pass through their office to be witnessed. BEWARE of people whose friendship is too easily made. Swindlers abound on ship and shore. Do not trust strangers who offer to change your money for you, to buy your tickets, or to put your property together with theirs. . . . Those who call themselves bankers are often adventurers. Ask in New York how many Jews who have lost money in such ways. GIRLS and YOUNG WOMEN SHOULD BE AWARE of strange men who offer them well-paid positions or who propose marriage to them. . . . " And on and on. No wonder Levinsky felt uncomfortable.

Greenhorns at the golden door, 1909

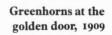

Halpern, Moshe Leib (1886–1932) The poet M. L. Halpern found his calling by a strange route: unlike most of the other New York Yiddish literati, who came from the Russian domain, Halpern was a Galician from the old Austro-Hungarian Empire, his education attained in cosmopolitan, and western, Vienna. Arriving in that city as a twelve-year-old, he first studied painting, then developed a fascination for the German writers, particularly Nietzsche. He began to write in German, and switched to Yiddish only when his friends, Jewish writers themselves, prevailed upon him.

In 1908 Halpern emigrated to the United States, wandered through various American cities and Montreal (where he helped edit a weekly that failed), and finally settled in New York. There, he was affiliated (at least in the minds of critics and historians) with the school known as *Di Yunge*, those younger poets who in 1907 declared their determination to write in a more personal vein than the older, cause-oriented poets. But Halpern, though an exceedingly personal poet, became annoyed with the group's insistence on clinical poetic technique; a born ec-

Jacob Epstein's cover illustration for the first edition of Hapgood's book

centric, he could not fit himself to any particular category. Halpern's style was forceful, even coarse, but he evinced a powerful, sardonic, entirely effective delivery. He disliked God, the people, and himself, in no particular order, but was forever unable to abandon any of these. He joined the Communists in 1921, writing for the *Freiheit*, a prestigious catch for both the party and the paper. But by 1924 he was through with them, his bitterness too individualistic to be institutionally channeled. His most popular book, a collection called *The Golden Peacock* (a popular poetic metaphor for "the wandering Jew"), was published in 1924.

Hapgood, Hutchins (1869–1944) This Chicago-born, Harvard-educated newspaperman was in 1902 the author of *The Spirit of the Ghetto*, the first book to describe the Jews of the Lower East Side as other than exotic specimens of unfortunate, perhaps unredeemable, immigrants washed up on the shores of Manhattan. It remains, arguably, the single best book about the time and place written by an outsider—by the man Abraham Cahan called "the only gentile who knows and

Samuel Ornitz, author of *Haunch, Paunch and Jowl*,
testifying before HUAC, 1947

understands the spirit of the ghetto."

At the time Hapgood worked on the book, he was a writer for the New York *Commercial Advertiser*, his editor Lincoln Steffens, his colleagues Jacob Riis and Abe Cahan. It was Cahan who led him through the cultural mazes of the East Side, and who put him in touch with the young artist Jacob (later Sir Jacob) Epstein, who would illustrate Hapgood's book. The writer's great affection for and understanding of what he saw enabled him to capture the teeming life of the ghetto as it was. Unlike Riis, who only saw the degradation of people in such conditions, Hapgood found the strengths and values of the Yiddish settlement. His book never received wide circulation, but portions of it have been frequently anthologized in the eighty years since its original publication.

Later, Hapgood would become one of the founding members of the Provincetown Players, and beyond that, little else. From 1914 until the end of his life, he did not hold a job, writing prose of wildly uneven quality, devoting much of his life to libertinism and the squandering of what money he had. He did write the introduction to Alexander Berkman's prison memoirs, and late in life a self-serving and somewhat embittered autobiography.

Harkavy, Alexander (1863–1939) It was often an uphill struggle, even among Yiddish-speaking Jews, to demonstrate that Yiddish was a language in its own right and not simply a bastard dialect, somehow inferior. Harkavy, Russian-born descendant of a family of scholars, was one of those who got the message across in America, where he arrived in the early 1880s. This author and lexicographer was best known, perhaps, for his trailblazing dictionaries, Yid-

dish-to-English and English-to-Yiddish, which went through two dozen editions and were based on forty thousand Yiddish words. It was the logical enterprise of a man who, when still in his twenties, wrote the first Yiddishist paper, establishing the language's niche in linguistics. He later wrote a textbook, *Englisher Lerer*, which taught English to Yiddish-speakers and sold more than one hundred thousand copies. Harkavy was also HIAS's first full-time representative on Ellis Island.

Haunch, Paunch and Jowl This novel of the rise of an East Side figure was published anonymously in 1923, and caused an immediate commotion. Its first-person narrator, Meyer Hirsch, was born into the corruption of his neighborhood, and spent his time alternately studying and stealing, doing so well that he was able to rise from street urchin to shyster lawyer to superior court judge. It is a sensational, lurid novel that achieved critical as well as commercial success.

The author, eventually identified, was Samuel Ornitz, later a screenwriter and one of the Hollywood Ten who were sentenced to jail for contempt of Congress during the McCarthy era.

Hearst, William Randolph (1863–1951) This unlikely candidate for inclusion in a book of this sort arrived here, as he did at the pinnacle of yellow journalism in the United States, through his own ambition. Aware of the anti-Tammany sentiments that coursed through the Lower East Side, Hearst attended assiduously to New York's burgeoning Jewish vote in his putatively "reform" mayoral campaign shortly after the turn of the century, and again when he ran for governor of New York in 1906. In both campaigns he carried the East Side, employing special Yiddish sections of his papers to make it clear that, even more than he disliked Tammany Hall, he despised the Russian czar. In 1904 Hearst went so far as to found a Yiddish daily paper, much in the tone of his English-language papers; it foundered and died in a matter of weeks.

Hebrew Actors Union Organized during the theatrical season of 1887–88, this was the first actors' union in America, preceding Actors' Equity by a full thirty years. The Yiddish theater, with its fanatical *patryotn*, its larger-than-life leading figures, was firmly predicated on the star system, and in the nineteenth century this system meant the great mass of actors were paid barely subsistence wages. The union was able to redress this problem, and grew stronger as its successes grew more frequent; it was also a leader in the movement to establish the United Hebrew Trades. It was a difficult union to join, as Maurice Schwartz learned when he was rejected and had to actively enlist support to be admitted. The union had a rule that an actor had

Executive committee of the Hebrew
Actors Union, 1935

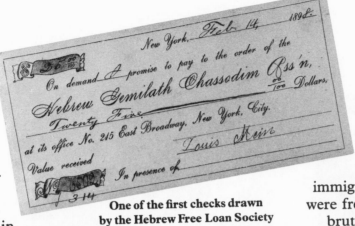

**One of the first checks drawn
by the Hebrew Free Loan Society**

to serve in the "provinces" (outside New York) before being admitted to membership, a rule that proved a boon to theater companies in cities west of the Hudson. The union had jurisdiction over all Yiddish shows in New York, and over many that toured. An actor who did not belong found himself without roles.

The Hebrew Actors Union remains active today, occupying its own building on East Seventh Street, where members continue to gather for a *kibitz*, a glass of tea, and perhaps news of a casting call. What has changed, of necessity, is the intensity of the union's adversary relationship with producers and theater owners; now, the union devotes much of its energies to fostering the medium of Yiddish theater itself. In 1980, in concert with other Jewish cultural and labor groups, it launched an effort to establish a Jewish National Theater with a well-received production of *The Dybbuk* in the auditorium of a West Side temple. The union and its associates hope eventually to move into permanent quarters in a small new theater on West Forty-second Street.

Hebrew Emigrant Aid Society Probably the least admirable of the multitude of charities established by uptown German Jews for their immigrant brethren, HEAS grew out of the Russian Emigrant Relief Society, established in 1881. The organization's rules were handed down imperiously, never discussed with those they were designed to benefit (or, as some insisted, control). One HEAS officer, Moritz Ellinger, in 1882 declared, "America is not a poor-

house, an asylum for the paupers of Europe." HEAS actually lobbied to put limits on immigration and its agents were frequently accused of brutal mistreatment of detainees at Castle Garden. The group ceased functioning by 1884, and should not be confused with HIAS, a body of an entirely different character.

Hebrew Free Loan Society In 1892 eleven immigrant Jews met in the Wilner Synagogue on the Lower East Side to discuss the plight and poverty of their neighbors, and to put up the grand sum of $95 to be loaned to newcomers at no interest. This was the founding of the Hebrew Free Loan Society, rooted in the biblical injunction (from Exodus), "If thou loan money to my people, thou shalt not lay upon him interest." These interest-free loans—*gemilath chassodim*—amounted in that first year to $1,205; in 1976 the organization's trust in the financially distressed was expressed by loans of $1.5 million.

Word of the founding of the society traveled uptown quickly, and the ubiquitous Jacob H. Schiff was the first "outside" benefactor, contributing $100, and thus doubling the original fund, only months after the society was founded. In 1896 Schiff donated a further $1,000; then, over the next four years, $5,000 annually; in 1901, $11,000. Others followed Schiff's lead, including the Lewisohn, Straus, and Warburg families; among the most generous early donors were Baron Maurice and Baroness Clara de Hirsch.

In recent years the society has been working with groups of the aged, with new

Hebrew Orphan Asylum Band

immigrants, and with the Lubavitcher Chassidim, granting home loans to the sect's members in the Crown Heights section of Brooklyn.

Hebrew Orphan Asylum To Harry Roskolenko, the "immense" building on Amsterdam Avenue and 138th Street "was a place that I dreaded. It meant no parents, no relatives—just blue jumpers, a barracks of imagined terror." To the thousands of homeless Jewish children who passed through its doors from its opening in 1880 until it was shuttered in 1941, it was the only home available. Growing rapidly in the peak immigration years, when disease and desertion daily left children homeless on the Lower East Side, the asylum as often as not was a place of nurture for young people, many of whom passed almost directly from its halls to those of its uptown neighbor, City College.

Among its alumni was humorist Art Buchwald, who entered the asylum when he was six years old, and recalled that "for all its glory, it did not look exactly like the Fontainebleau." Buchwald, who expressed

gratitude to the institution, stayed only six weeks before moving into the home of foster parents; however, he reported there from time to time over the next eleven years "to get issued clothes or have my teeth fixed."

Hebrew Sheltering and Immigrant Aid Society The brief tenure of HEAS as protector of the immigrant Jews was scandalous; HIAS, by contrast, was—and is— every bit as good as its predecessor was malign. When the uptown-funded United Hebrew Charities took over HEAS's functions in 1884, its directors did what they could to stop the flow of immigration, going so far as to send an appeal to European Jewish agencies to, in effect, bar the gates. When this request was ignored, the spectacle of immigrants arriving and being forcibly turned back (returning to Europe on cattle boats, and earning their return passage by tending animals) spurred the then-tiny Russian-Jewish community in New York to step into the breach.

HIAS, as it would become known, was the result of the merger of two smaller agencies, both founded and, at the outset, supported by, the community in which the immigrants would soon live. As its good works became manifest, the more enlightened segments of the German-Jewish community began to support it, and soon it stood as the official welcoming hand offered by New York's Jews to those arriving at Ellis Island. It stationed translators and investigators at Ellis, it argued the status of detainees with the Immigration Service (with whose officials it enjoyed unusually good rapport), it sent representatives to investigate the conditions in steerage on the various transatlantic liners. The Hamburg-America Line, for one, was induced to police its own personnel, and to post various notices on board in Yiddish. The society placed new arrivals in contact with relatives who had immigrated earlier, it provided railroad tickets to those heading for other cities, it ran an employment service for those opting to stay in New York. And, in the building once occupied by the Astor Library, now by the Public Theater, it provided overnight shelter for those just arrived from Ellis Island.

Today, HIAS serves Russian Jews escaping from Soviet repression, and has relocated more than fifteen thousand Indochinese families in the past three years.

Herring It came from the waters of the Baltic back in the old country, it came from the Atlantic over here; it could be pickled, marinated, preserved in brine and its own fat *(shmalts)*, or *gehakt* into tiny pieces. It kept well, it tasted good, and best of all, it could be obtained from Russ & Daughters on Houston Street, which Calvin Trillin described as "a splendid refutation of the false teaching that a store selling pickled herring cannot have character and a

clean display case at the same time." The descendant of Russ's Cut Rate Appetizers on Orchard Street, which opened for business in 1911, Russ & Daughters has been at the present location for fifty years. The firm trades in caviar, smoked salmon, and sturgeon as well as in the homelier herring, but there is no archway inside the store dedicated to any of the fancier delicacies.

Hester Street The few blocks of Hester Street on either side of Ludlow was called the *Khazermark*, or Pig Market, even though pig was about the only thing not on sale there. The name derived from European

Beneath Russ and Daughters' celebrated "Arch de herring"

Hester Street at Norfolk, c. 1910

pig markets, crowded, noisy places where swine were sold and slaughtered. On Hester Street, the noise came from the press of humanity that jammed the neighborhood to buy from the stalls and the ubiquitous, traffic-blocking pushcarts. Jacob Riis, in *How the Other Half Lives*, wrote, "Thursday night and Friday morning are bargain days in the Pig Market. . . . There is scarcely anything else [other than pig] that can be hawked from a wagon that is not to be found, and at ridiculously low prices. Bandannas and tin cups at two cents, peaches at a cent a quart, 'damaged' eggs for a song, hats for a quarter, and spectacles, warranted to sit on the eye, at the optician's who has opened shop on a Hester Street doorstep, for 35 cents; frowsy-look-

ing chickens and half-plucked geese, hung by the neck and protesting with wildly strutting feet even in death against the outrage, are the staple of the market." Even human beings—the unemployed looking for day labor—were for sale on Hester Street.

Hillman, Sidney (1887–1946) In 1907 Sidney Hillman was a greenhorn working for six dollars a week in a Chicago clothing factory; in 1944 he was the center of a national political storm when Franklin Delano Roosevelt was supposed to have uttered, concerning the Democratic Convention's choice of a vice-presidential candidate, "Clear it with Sidney."

Only seven years after his arrival in the United States, Hillman was elected the first president of the new Amalgamated Clothing Workers union. He had attained such eminence by leading a successful strike in Chicago against the enormous Hart, Schaffner & Marx clothing company, resisting the efforts of the ineffectual United Garment Workers to take control of the strike effort. He built the Amalgamated virtually from scratch, and soon it dominated the men's clothing industry as the ILGWU dominated women's clothing. Once firmly established at the union's head, Hillman kept it independent, even purging its corrupt, mob-dominated Local 4 of the insidious influence of the gangster Lepke Buchalter, who had successfully infiltrated the union in his campaign to bring virtually every industry and union in the city under his control. Turning his attention to a larger arena in the 1930s, Hillman played an important role in drafting the National Industrial Recovery Act, and in the passage of the Social Security Act and the National Labor Relations Act.

Hillman headed the CIO's Political Action Committee, which became labor's most effective political group in the country, an effectively singleminded organ that could deliver votes to favored Democratic Party candidates on the basis of their support for the issues PAC cared about; he also joined with David Dubinsky to found the American Labor Party, and later the Liberal Party. It was in such roles that Hillman grew close to President Roosevelt. Although everyone around Roosevelt denied that he had ever said, "Clear it with Sidney," the Republicans in 1944 used the rumor as the virtual watchword of their campaign against FDR.

Hillquit, Morris (1869–1933) Like so many others, Riga-born Morris Hillquit

found his political faith as a result of the oppression he knew in Europe and, after emigrating, in the American shirt factory where he worked. After joining the Socialist Party, he became an editor of the *Arbeiter Shtimme*, attended New York University Law School, and began practicing law. In 1909 Hillquit played a leading role in the epochal garment strike and in 1914 served with Louis Brandeis on the board of arbi-

**Sidney Hillman
and friend**

tration that settled the next crippling strike in the industry. Although more a theoretician than a politician, in 1917 Hillquit was the Socialist candidate for mayor of New York, and received nearly 150,000 votes, until that time the largest vote for a Socialist in any American city. This was a feat all the more remarkable in that Hillquit and his party strenuously opposed American involvement in World War I, thus earning assaults from those who feared immigrant Jews would be seen as unpatriotic shirkers. Among those who attacked Hillquit directly were Louis Marshall and Joseph Barondess; further criticism came from those who condemned his longtime opposition to "Jewish nationalism." Hillquit ran once more for mayor in 1932, attracting a record 250,000 votes to the Socialist ticket.

Hurok, Solomon

(1890–1974) The celebrated impresario's career began in Brownsville, in Brooklyn; he had arrived there via Philadelphia after running away from home in Russia when he was fifteen.

Working in a hardware store, he spent spare hours organizing benefit concerts of neighborhood talent in behalf of the Socialist Party. His gift of persuasion displayed itself in 1911, when he induced violinist Efrem Zimbalist to play at one of his benefits—his first contact, Hurok would recall, "with a Big Name." Taking the first two letters of his name and those of a friend named Goldberg, he formed something called the Van Hugo Musical Society and presented Zimbalist in Carnegie Hall. He failed to bring the singer Feodor Chaliapin to New York from Paris, and took a job as director of a new Labor Lyceum, under whose roof unions held lectures, debates, and the like. In 1916 he went out on his own, and in the next sixty years rose to such preeminence in his field that it would have been reasonable to think his last name was "Presents," his middle "Hurok," his first merely "S." Throughout his life, however, Hurok kept a humble box of matzo on his dining room table; he thought it was a healthful food.

Morris Hillquit, 1920

S. Hurok presents himself

Industrial Removal Office Financed by the Baron de Hirsch Fund in collaboration with the B'nai B'rith, the Industrial Removal Office from 1900 to 1917 led a movement to alleviate the crowding on the Lower East Side by resettling immigrants in other cities. The program placed seventy-five thousand eastern European Jews in these smaller communities, including Cleveland, Los Angeles, Grand Rapids, and St. Louis.

International Ladies' Garment Workers' Union They organized the biggest Jewish-dominated industry in the country, they became one of the leading labor organizations in the world, they exerted a strong and progressive influence on the Democratic Party—they even got the apostrophes right in their name. They were the "International," a union like no other.

Founded in 1900 through the merger of seven small unions of cloakmakers and pressers in New York, Newark, Baltimore, and Philadelphia—with a grand total of only two thousand members—the International progressed slowly at first. As late as 1908 it needed a twenty-five-dollar donation from Socialist activist Meyer London to rent office space. But the next year, in what was first perceived as another ripple in the growing labor strife on the Lower East Side, more than twenty thousand shirtwaist makers, most of them immigrant girls and fewer than one percent of them members of the union, went on strike. This action would change the face of American management-labor relations.

The strike began at a packed, fiery meeting at the Cooper Union, when the leaders of the struggling International decided to call for a walkout throughout the industry. The risky maneuver succeeded when eighteen-year-old Clara Lemlich inspired the crowd with a speech in which she declared, "I am tired of listening to speakers who talk in generalities. . . . I move that we go on a general strike!" The meeting erupted in a pandemonium of approval, and a four-month walkout of historic proportions began. The entire East Side enlisted in the strike's support, as did sympathetic uptowners, some as far removed in background from the strikers as Anne Morgan, sister of J. P. Morgan. Strike funds were raised throughout the East, phalanxes of volunteer publicists got the cause mentioned in all the major newspapers of the day, and by the time the strike was settled, the ILGWU had twenty thousand well-organized members.

The next step occurred only months later. A mass rally announced for June 30, 1910, in Madison Square Garden, brought sixty thousand garment workers to what the *Forward* called "the greatest Jewish labor meeting the world had ever seen." Thus began the great Cloakmakers' Strike, an effort that dwarfed the previous year's shirtwaist makers' action. Said Meyer London, "We offer no apology for the [cloakmakers'] strike. If at all, we should apologize to the tens of thousands of the ex-

An early version of the world's most famous union label

Striking ILGWU cloakmakers, 1916

ploited men and wo-
men for not having
aroused them be-
fore." B. Hoffman,
the labor historian
known to his readers
as Tsivyon, pointed
out in 1929 the criti-
cal difference be-
tween the two
strikes: "The strike
of the girls in the
waist and dress in-
dustry was not re-
garded by the public
as an ordinary con-
flict between capital and labor. In the strike
of the girls, a great part was played by
what may be called the social conscience.
Ladies of the highest social circles threw
themselves into the strike; the League for
Woman's Suffrage was active in it; and the
press, at least a considerable part of it, was
outspokenly in sympathy with the girl strikers." By contrast, "the cloakmakers'
strike was a pure conflict between capital
and labor." Settlement was reached
through the intervention of A. Lincoln Fi-
lene, the Boston merchant, who enlisted
Louis Brandeis as the chief arbitrator.
Meyer London, representing the union,
said, "I, personally, would have liked to
see a state of affairs where mankind should
control everything in a co-operative effort,
but I realize in the year 1910 and in the
cloak trade it is hardly possible of realization." When Brandeis came up with a solu-
tion that recognized "the preferential union
shop," one of the last major obstacles to
settlement was hurdled. In September the
signing of the historic "protocol of peace"
ended the strike.

The International and its leaders—men
like London, Morris
Sigman, and Ben-
jamin Schlesinger—
repeatedly battled
over the same pieces
of turf, with varia-
tions, for years. In
1915 the union lead-
ership went to court
to block a manage-
ment union-busting
tactic predicated on
the creation of a
"rival"—that is, in-
dustry-controlled—
union called the
"International Ladies Garment Workers
Union of the World" (no apostrophes, and
three words tacked onto the end); they also
successfully resisted a criminal indictment
of twenty-four union officials on a variety
of trumped-up charges ranging from extortion to first-degree murder. The following
year, several employers attempted to renege
on the protocol of peace, and in 1926 Communist locals in the union led a cata-
strophic strike of thirty-five thousand workers without first calling a membership
referendum, an effort aimed more at taking
control of the union than at winning management concessions. Hasty settlements
with a number of employers threatened to
shatter the union, and the resulting internal
conflict came to be known as the International's "civil war." Only through a string
of tactical errors by the Communists was
the faction that would install David Dubinsky at its head able to prevail. The strike
had cost the workers and the union over $3
million, and Dubinsky's adroit leadership
alone preserved its effectiveness.

In the years following, the ILGWU re-
constituted itself, moving ever closer to the

mainstream of the American labor movement, and in the process changing its ethnic character markedly. It was once a virtually all-Jewish body, but by the 1960s changes in the nature of the work force, in the inner-city populations of the cities in which it was prominent, and in the socioeconomic status of the children of its original immigrant workers saw the union's Jewish membership dwindle to a mere fraction of its original size.

Inzikh The rapidity of change in fortunes among the immigrant Jews seems reflected nowhere more dramatically than it was in the productions of the community's poets. Within twenty years one new Yiddish school, the "sweatshop poets," gave way to another, *Di Yunge*, which was in turn antiquated by the *Inzikhistn*. (*Inzikh* means, roughly, "introspective.") The movement took root in 1919 when Aaron Glanz-Leyeles, Jacob Glatstein, and N. B. Minkoff established a common criterion for writing poetry and a journal, *In Zikh*, to spread the gospel.

Whereas the "sweatshop poets" built their work around themes of oppression and rebellion, and *Di Yunge* rebelled against collective concepts and wrote of their more personal perceptions of the world, the *Inzikhistn* looked only within themselves for the meaning of life. In their 1920

manifesto they declared, "The world exists for us only as it is mirrored within us, as it touches us. The world is a non-existent category, a fiction, if it does not relate to us. It becomes a reality only in us and through us." Often recipients of more formal (and American) education than their predecessors, the *Inzikhistn* in some respects paralleled similar movements in occidental poetry. They distrusted the regular metric and verbal constrictions of more traditional poetry, writing in free verse with free expression of diction and sounds. Still, they were by no means universalists who happened to write in Yiddish; they received inspiration from the Bible, from Jewish life, and after the Holocaust, from Jewish faith.

From the Labor Stage production of Harold Rome's *Pins and Needles*—the ILGWU's David Dubinsky (C) makes peace between actors portraying the AFL's William "Mama" Green and the CIO's John "Papa" Lewis.

(facing page) Jolson in *The Jazz Singer*, a la Hollywood;
(above) Jessel in a Yiddish poster for the
Broadway version

Jessel, George (1898–1981) "In his twenties and thirties," wrote Tony Hiss in his *New York Times Book Review* consideration of the last of Jessel's several autobiographies, "he palled around the New York speaks with the Hon. James J. Walker, invented the Bloody Mary one morning in Palm Beach to kill a hangover and get in shape for a volleyball date with Alfred Gwynne Vanderbilt, . . . pub-crawled in Berlin and encountered ex-World War I ace Col. Hermann Goering in drag pawing Ernest Roehm, and dined in Chicago with Al Capone. . . . His first wife left him for the great Christian Science craze that swept the country after World War I, he wasn't good enough for his second wife, Norma Talmadge, and he was too old for number three, a girl almost 30 years his junior [Lois Andrews was, in fact, sixteen when she married the forty-two-year-old Jessel]. In between he had flings with Helen Morgan, Lupe Velez, Rita Hayworth and (most recently) Xaviera Hollander."

This was the George Jessel who was born poor in Harlem and died the self-proclaimed "Toastmaster General" of the United States? This, and more. He was also a producer, a writer, the vaudeville partner at age ten of one Walter Winchell, the creator of the title role in the original Broadway version of *The Jazz Singer,* the "discoverer" of Mitzi Gaynor. Jessel was also a man who, said his *Times* obituary, "traded heavily throughout a career that spanned seven decades on his Jewish upbringing in New York." His podium style was such that, the *Times* continued, "no one could receive a proper burial without a eulogy from Mr. Jessel." He presided at several hundred funerals, by his own count, and raised more than $60 million in behalf of Israel Bonds alone, one of the several Jewish charities

for which he toiled. Fifteen years before his death, Jessel estimated he owned 600 thank-you plaques, 200 City of Hope torches, and 188 honorary synagogue memberships.

Jolson, Al (1886–1950) The role George Jessel created on Broadway—*The Jazz Singer*—became Al Jolson's greatest triumph when the film was released in 1927 as the first talking picture. It was little wonder that Jessel objected to changes made in the script's transition from the stage to film: the eventual product was closer in detail to the story of Jolson's own life than to anything a writer's imagination could have concocted.

Jolson (born Asa Yoelson), like so many other entertainers of his generation, arrived in the United States as a child, son (in this case) of a cantor, ran away from home, sang in saloons, entered the vaudeville circuit, and so on. He made his first stage appearance when he was eleven, at the Herald Square Theater, as part of the mob in Israel Zangwill's *Children of the Ghetto*. In 1909 he put on blackface in a San Francisco vaudeville show and ignited a national craze for mammy songs and his own particular way with them. His voice had a mellow roughness coupled with a sentimentality employed to great effect on such songs as "Sonny Boy" and "Bye Bye Blackbird." Jolson's distinctive style has been emulated by scores of performers ever since, for reasons that remain unclear.

K★a★p★l★a★n, H★y★m★a★n Hyman Kaplan, who spelled his name with stars between the letters to demonstrate his devotion to his adopted land, was born in the 1930s in the pages of *The New Yorker*, the fictional child of "Leonard Q. Ross" (actually Leo Rosten, thirty years later the author of *The Joys of Yiddish*). Rosten's stories, collected in 1937 in the best-selling *The Education of H★Y★M★A★N K★A★P★L★A★N*, centered around the English classes Hyman and other new Americans attended, conducted by their beloved Mr. Parkhill. Hyman was a cutter in a dress factory, no doubt far more capable—if infinitely less creative—with his cutter's tools than he was with his adopted language. A cheerful greenhorn, enthusiastic, blandly immune to correction or refinement of his speech, Hyman was completely confident in the progress he was not making with the new tongue. From Hyman's letter to his brother in Warsaw, written as a homework assignment: "Do you feeling fine? I suppose. Is all ok? You should begin right now learning about ok. Here you got to say ok. all the time. ok the wether, ok the potatos, ok the prazident Roosevelt." Or his patriotic dissertation on three great Americans, "Judge Vashington, Abram Lincohen, an' Jake Popper." The first "vas fightink for Friddom, against de Kink Ingland, Kink Jawdge Number Tree, dat tarrible autocarp who vas puddink stemps on tea even, so it tasted bed." "Lincohen" freed the slaves, of course, and Jake Popper was a delicatessen owner "mit a hot like gold," who got sick, had doctors "who insulted odder doctors" and gave him "blood confusions" but "efter a vhile, Honest Jake Popper pest away."

English for immigrants, in a New York City night school class—Harvard for the Hyman Kaplans

Harry Tarowsky of Katz's supports the war effort

Katz's Delicatessen Founded in 1888 by a Mr. Iceland, this venerable institution became Katz's in 1915. The "downtown Lindy's" was a favorite of the Yiddish theater crowd, and later earned wider notoriety for shipping salamis to American servicemen all over the world, popularizing the idea with its inimitable slogan "Send a salami to your boy in the Army." It has always been "strictly meat" at Katz's, the salami joined by celebrated pastrami, corned beef, and other deli specials. The original William Katz's son, Leonard, is one of the three partners who run the business today.

Kehillah As often happens, it was an anti-Semitic incident that sparked the move for communal unity in New York's Jewish community in 1908, when the idea of a Kehillah was advanced; as happens just as often, it was the fear of communal uniformity that led to its expiration a decade later. The seminal incident arose from a charge by New York City Police Commissioner Theodore Bingham that Jews accounted for half the city's criminals although they represented only a fifth of the city's population. In the ensuing uproar among the Jews—who acknowledged that crime was indeed a vexatious problem on the Lower East Side—came the realization there was no visible entity to defend the community's reputation. Judah Magnes, a thirty-one-year-old associate rabbi of the uptown Temple Emanu-El, but a maverick among his wealthy and assimilated congregants, immediately saw the need for a strong organization "to define the rights and liberties [of Jews]" and also to cope with the problem of criminality. The following year the New York Kehillah (the word means "community") was founded, headed by Magnes and representing more than two hundred organizations of both Yiddish-speaking Jews and their German coreligionists. The Kehillah leadership's strong ties to the American Jewish Committee heightened suspicions among downtowners that they were being manipulated for the benefit of uptown assimilationists.

Operationally, the Kehillah administration was fairly well insulated from factional politics, and it performed many services that had long been needed. Most notably, it established a Welfare Committee that worked with the police to expose and combat prostitution, fences, burglary rings, protection rackets, and illegal gambling in the Jewish areas of the city. Kehillah's virtually omniscient intelligence network was effective in breaking up Joseph "Yuski Nigger" Toblinsky's extortionist Yiddish Blackhand Association, which poisoned the horses of nonconforming businessmen. Kehillah's chief investigator, Abe Shoenfeld, helped police close 103 brothels as well. The Kehillah Bureau of Jewish Education published modern textbooks, issued teaching materials, and offered other aid to Hebrew teachers (this part of the program distressed many uptowners, who thought supporting Hebrew would only retard their assimilationist gains). Kehillah also organized a Board of Rabbis, with jurisdiction over marriage, divorce, and the kosher laws; this function, however, collapsed into the gaps of differing religious perspectives. More successful was its Bureau of Industry, which succeeded as a mediator in a number of labor-management crises, notably in helping to settle a strike in the fur industry. In all, it was a relative success, largely because of the efforts of Magnes, who enjoyed the admiration of the Yiddish-speaking populace. However, this respect cost Magnes. By 1918, when he had demonstrated such a sense of community with the downtowners that he even opposed World War I, the uptown Jews withdrew their support.

Kessler, David (1860–1920) He was of that first generation of Yiddish actors, an alumnus of Goldfadn's company who went to London in 1886 and from there to New York. He appeared with Jacob Adler in Jacob Gordin's first drama, *Siberia;* in Asch's controversial *God of Vengeance;* and was a huge success in Kobrin's *Yankl Boyle.* By 1913 Kessler had his own company, often ranked with Adler's and Thomashevsky's in New York's Yiddish theater pantheon. Admired for his portrayal of earthy, somewhat vulgar and powerful types, he was a key figure in the trend of realism that reached the Yiddish stage long before it penetrated English-speaking theater. Kessler's admirers—his *patryotn*—were no less fervid

than those of other stars. When Kessler played the title role of *Uriel Acosta,* a part long identified with Adler, Kessler fans drenched the Adler fans who picketed the theater with cold water and hot invective.

Kike This epithet has cloudy origins, but one prominent theory holds that German Jews bestowed it on the eastern Europeans with contempt, deriving it from the final *-ki* or *-ky* of so many Yiddish surnames. Moses Rischin maintains that Russian Jews "often were forced to Germanize their names in order to escape the stigma among German credit men" who were "embarrassed by Russian business competition [and] dismissed their rivals, whose names often ended with 'ki,' as 'kikes.' " Another theory holds that illiterate immigrant Jews, required to mark forms on Ellis Island with an *X,* declined to make the symbol they associated with the Christian cross and instead made a circle, called in Yiddish a *kaykl* or *kaykele;* immigration officials, this theory holds, called those who signed in such a manner "kikes," not with venom but out of convenience. A third theory also embraces the *kaykl* derivation but attributes it to the

David Kessler, 1916

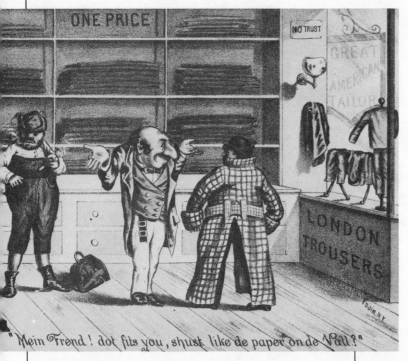

"Mein Frend! dot fits you, shust like de paper on de Vall?"

A newspaper characterization of the "kike" tailor, c. 1890

circle marking made by itinerant Jewish merchants who did not want to check accounts off with an *X*.

King, Edward (1848–1896) A Massachusetts-born gentile who had lived for many years as a journalist in Paris before he came to the Lower East Side, King was devoted to the ghetto, where he became a history teacher at the Educational Alliance, a labor movement activist, and the author of *Joseph Zalmonah*, a novel loosely based on Joseph Barondess's life. As a young boy, the scholar Maurice Hindus was one of the many East Siders who came under King's spell. Hindus recalled their first meeting: "Reaching out his hand, he greeted me with a hearty handshake and a word of welcome. Then I knew that, so far as he was concerned, my knee pants did not matter."

Kishinev Massacre On Easter Sunday, 1903, during Passover, church bells rang out at noon in the Russian town of Kishinev, signaling the onset of a brutal attack on the town's Jewish quarter. The resulting pogrom played a critical role in increasing the surge of Jewish immigration to America. The Kishinev pogrom was the most extreme of the anti-Semitic outrages perpetrated with the acquiescence—even support—of the czarist government, which in 1881 had determined to starve one-third of Russia's Jews, drive out another third, and convert the remainder to the Orthodox Church. As Russian troops stood by, drunken rioters armed with axes and clubs murdered forty-nine Kishinev Jews, injured five hundred more, and looted and destroyed fifteen hundred buildings, leaving nearly twenty thousand people homeless.

The Kishinev massacre was widely publicized and evoked expressions of horror and sympathy throughout the western world. In America, it served as a unifying point for the diverse and often quarreling elements of the Jewish community, rallying the wealthiest German Jews and the poorest of the new Yiddish-speaking immigrants in common cause. Rabbi Judah Magnes of Temple Emanu-El led a huge protest march in the city, the first Jewish parade in New York, and Jacob Schiff floated loans to help Japan in its war with Russia (one campaign briefly popular on the Lower East Side aimed to raise money to purchase a battleship, name it *The Kishinev*, and present it to the Japanese Navy). Relief organizations sent money to help victims of the pogroms, and to aid them in arming for self-protection. A petition signed by more than twelve thousand Americans, including a variety of politicians, three archbishops, and seven bishops, called upon the czar to end the

persecution of the Jews; Secretary of State John Hay, speaking for Theodore Roosevelt's administration, said, "No person of ordinary humanity can have heard without deep emotion the story of the cruel outrages inflicted upon the Jews of Kishinev."

Klezmer A *klezmer* is, literally, an itinerant musician; the term, however, refers to a particular kind of music, an amalgam of eastern and central European popular forms leavened by a distinctive "hot" improvisational style. In this country, the music's influence was such that Henry Ford's rabidly anti-Semitic *Dearborn Independent* would proclaim in a headline, "Jewish Jazz—Moron Music—Becomes Our National Music."

The European *klezmorim* were as likely to be found in the *shtetl* as in the big city, playing for weddings and other festivals. As they traveled, the musicians—generally regarded as wild, somewhat disreputable sorts—would pick up local melodies and transform them to fit the instrumentation and talents of the particular *klezmer* group. In America, versions of *klezmer* music remained audible after World War II largely at weddings and bar mitzvahs, and at resort functions in Miami and the Catskills. Earlier, though, *klezmer* was notable as the Jewish contribution to the growth of big band jazz. In New York, large, sophisticated *klezmer* ensembles, theater orchestras, and concert bands emerged—among them Jo-

The Max Leibowitz Orchestra, purveyors of *klezmer*

seph Charniavski's Yiddish-American Jazz Band, the Abe Schwartz Orchestra, and the Max Leibowitz Orchestra. "Mainstream" jazz musicians such as Artie Shaw and Ziggy Elman came straight from the *klezmer* tradition, and the Benny Goodman Band's epochal performance of "Sing, Sing, Sing," in the famous 1938 Carnegie Hall jazz concert, was in many parts an expression of *klezmer* music at its best, particularly in Elman's raucous trumpet passages.

A Second Avenue knishery

the digestive system with the inevitability of a depth charge, they are perhaps the one item of eastern European cuisine that most justifies the complaint, "I love Jewish food, but when you eat it, seventy-two hours later you're hungry again."

Although knishes are sold in such unlikely places as the bleachers of Yankee Stadium, they are more commonly had from a few remaining street vendors on the Lower East Side and the great temple of knishery, Yonah Shimmel's, on Houston Street. This spartan establishment, founded in 1910 by Shimmel, then the *shames* of the nearby Rumanian synagogue, is now owned and run by his grandchildren.

A Klog Tsu Kolombusn The Yiddish language is, of course, rich in curses, expressive maledictions for every purpose. The catchall for those who found their new lives in America less than they had hoped was *a klog tsu Kolombusn,* or "a curse on Columbus." It wasn't very kindly, but surely it had less sting than other, more personal epithets, such as "May you have a house, and this house have a thousand rooms, and those rooms have a thousand beds, and those beds each have a bed bug, and may cholera throw you from bed to bed." Or, a particularly potent one cited by Maurice Samuel, "May you turn into a blintz and he into a cat, and may he eat you up and choke to death on you, so that we would be rid of both of you."

Knish Knishes are pastries stuffed variously with cheese, mashed potatoes, buckwheat groats, even chopped liver. Extremely heavy if properly made, descending through

Kobrin, Leon (1872–1946) Born in the same town of Vitebsk, Russia, as Marc Chagall, Kobrin was, like the painter, as influenced by Russian as he was by Yiddish culture. He emigrated in 1892 and worked at a variety of jobs while he dedicated himself to writing. He was a realist, concerned with the life he and other Jews lived, and although he wrote with wit and humor, he eschewed the heavy sentimentality that characterized so much other Yiddish writing of the time.

The work that established Kobrin's reputation and was in some ways his most enduring creation was the novel *Yankl Boyle, or the Village Youth.* Kobrin later adapted the book as a play, and it became one of the longest-lived staples of the Yiddish stage. He also wrote many stories and plays about New York Yiddish life, concerned primarily with the gaps between generations. For instance, "Riverside Drive," written in the 1930s, tells of a man who marries an American-born Jewish woman and raises a family that his aged parents find completely alien to their traditional way of life. Kobrin wrote for *The Day* for twenty-five years, and was also a translator of note, rendering with his wife, Pauline, the works of Chekhov, de Maupassant, Gorki, and others into Yiddish. His own writings were translated into Russian, German, French, and English.

Kokhaleyn The *kokhaleyn*—"cook by yourself"—was a Catskill commonplace, a convenient way to enjoy a country vacation

without spending limited funds on hotel meals. One brought one's own food, kitchen utensils, even bed linens and towels, sharing a kitchen with others in the same boardinghouse. The *kokhaleyn* required both sociability and a certain competitiveness: the first to get along with those who shared your kitchen, the second to get to the stove before they did.

Kovner, B. (1873–1975) Few writers leave words that become permanent parts of the language in which they write; one such was Kovner (born Jacob Adler, he was given his pen name—it means "one from Kovno, Lithuania"—by Abraham Cahan), who wrote a humor column for the *Forward* until his retirement in 1936. Kovner's eponymic creations were Yente Telebende, a big-

B. Kovner (Top, L) is joined here by (Top row, L to R) Joel Slonim, Jacob Marinoff, Joel Entin; (Bottom row, L to R) Yehoash, Elyokum Zunser, Morris Winchevsky

The front page of *Der Groyser Kundes*, 1919

mouthed, contumacious housewife, and Moyshe Kapoyer—literally, "Moses Upside-Down." Yente was the type of woman who would tell her husband that she was sick and had to go to the country. When he said, "All right, we'll go to the Catskills," she'd wail, "What, again to the mountains? Spend my vacation with those Brownsville *yakhnes?* They shouldn't live so long. I want to go to a farm near Pikeville." "All right, Pikeville." "What?" she'd cry. "You're trying to get rid of me so you can run around with that blonde from Sheriff Street? Just look at him—he wants to be a free bird!" Moyshe Kapoyer, for his part, was a nice enough man, but perplexingly eccentric, a man who could be counted upon to do exactly the opposite of what one would expect. Both names are so deeply rooted in the contemporary Yiddish-American vocabulary that many younger speakers are utterly unaware of their origins, the best possible tribute to the precision of Kovner's characterizations. Kovner also

wrote volumes of lyrical, nostalgic poetry, and from 1912 to 1919 published the weekly magazine *Brownsville and East New York Express.*

Kundes, Der It was inevitable that so word-loving a culture as that of the Lower East Side, and one endowed with such a characteristic sense of humor, would have its humor magazines. *Der Kundes* was probably the best of them. Founded by Jacob Marinov in 1909, it was at first a biweekly that in time became successful enough to justify weekly publication under the name *Der Groyser Kundes (The Big Stick).* Along with its competitor, *Der Groyser Kibitzer, Der Kundes* specialized in satirical articles and vivid caricatures of well-known Yiddish figures. Those whose likenesses were distorted in the pages of these magazines were, early on, dismayed at their treatment; once the feature became institutionalized, however, it was thought an insult not to be caricatured.

L

La Guardia, Fiorello H. (1882–1947)
This most beloved of New York's mayors
was the son of unlikely Italian immigrants,
his father a Protestant, his mother a Sephardic Jew from Venice. His politics were
equally singular, a combination of Socialist
and Republican. His practically unbeatable
campaign style was predicated on his physical qualities (he was a short, stubby man
with an improbably squeaky voice, employed at high decibels to make a point and
to elicit appreciative smiles from his listen-
ers) and his fluency in both Italian and
Yiddish (he learned the latter as an interpreter at Ellis Island). After graduating
from New York University Law School, he
became a lawyer for striking garment workers in 1912. Capitalizing on Italian and
Jewish suspicions of Tammany Hall, La
Guardia represented Harlem in
Congress as a Republican, and
once defeated a Jewish Democrat
whom he challenged to an all-
Yiddish debate, knowing full
well that his American-
born opponent did not
speak the language.

La Guardia was elect-
ed mayor of New York
three times on Fusion
tickets, winning the en-
dorsement not only of
the Republicans, but
of the union-dominated
American Labor Party
as well. Perhaps the
most peculiar aspect
of his career was
his early condem-
nation of Hitler—
which in 1937 led
to an official apol-

ogy from the State Department to the
German Embassy—and his simultaneously
tame reaction to Mussolini, who for years
remained popular among La Guardia's Italian constituents.

"My mother undoubtedly had Jewish
blood in her veins," he once said, "but I
never thought I had enough in mine to justify boasting about it." Still, to the New
York Jews of eastern European descent, he
was a *landsman* of the spirit.

Labor Temple In 1910 a Presbyterian

La Guardia at a Jewish Labor Committee meeting, 1935.
The short, smiling man behind La Guardia is
David Dubinsky; next to him, B. Charney Vladeck

In this 1919 Milwaukee Labor Zionist pageant, Miss Liberty was played by Golda Meir, half a century later the prime minister of Israel

The Wanderer finds Liberty in America

clergyman, Charles Stelzle, organized the Labor Temple at Second Avenue and Fourteenth Street on the northern rim of the Lower East Side. The Reverend Mr. Stelzle had a primarily Jewish "congregation," young people of various Socialist persuasions who came to hear attacks on organized religion. In this citadel of rationalism, theorists like John Dewey and Thorstein Veblen alternated on the podium with such modernists as sex psychologist Daniel Schmalhausen and radical economist Scott Nearing.

Labor Zionism This wing of the Zionist movement, which also embraced socialism, was established shortly after the turn of the century. Its first leader and ideologue was Nachman Syrkin (1868–1924), who was already working on linking the Zionist movement with the Socialist dream before he arrived in the United States in 1907. Although active in the labor movement, the group—also known as *Poale Zion*—often found itself at odds with those Socialists who condemned the "Jewish nationalism" implicit in support of a Jewish state.

Probably the most enduring product of the Labor Zionist movement was the Israeli Labor Party of David Ben-Gurion and the Milwaukee-bred Golda Meir, which guided the new nation for the first twenty-five years of its existence. For many of those years, the party was burdened by the conflicts it perceived between its two aims, socialism and Zionism, and by its own wars with those parts of the Zionist world it perceived as bourgeois.

In America, the Labor Zionists, through their fraternal order, the Farband, also published political and literary magazines, operated Yiddish and Hebrew day schools, and generally supported Yiddish culture.

Landsmanshaft

Organized by and for immigrants from the same town or *shtetl,* the *landsmanshaft* was a mutual self-help society designed to help the newcomer who got

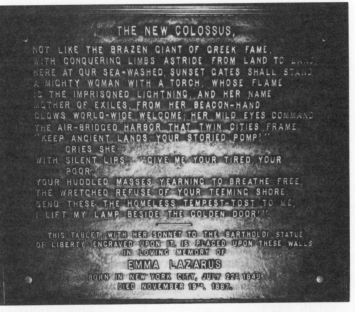

THE NEW COLOSSUS.

NOT LIKE THE BRAZEN GIANT OF GREEK FAME,
WITH CONQUERING LIMBS ASTRIDE FROM LAND TO LAND;
HERE AT OUR SEA-WASHED, SUNSET GATES SHALL STAND
A MIGHTY WOMAN WITH A TORCH, WHOSE FLAME
IS THE IMPRISONED LIGHTNING, AND HER NAME
MOTHER OF EXILES. FROM HER BEACON-HAND
GLOWS WORLD-WIDE WELCOME; HER MILD EYES COMMAND
THE AIR-BRIDGED HARBOR THAT TWIN CITIES FRAME.
"KEEP ANCIENT LANDS YOUR STORIED POMP!"
CRIES SHE
WITH SILENT LIPS. "GIVE ME YOUR TIRED, YOUR
POOR,
YOUR HUDDLED MASSES YEARNING TO BREATHE FREE,
THE WRETCHED REFUSE OF YOUR TEEMING SHORE.
SEND THESE, THE HOMELESS, TEMPEST-TOST TO ME,
I LIFT MY LAMP BESIDE THE GOLDEN DOOR!"

THIS TABLET, WITH HER SONNET TO THE BARTHOLDI STATUE
OF LIBERTY ENGRAVED UPON IT, IS PLACED UPON THESE WALLS
IN LOVING MEMORY OF
EMMA LAZARUS
BORN IN NEW YORK CITY, JULY 22ᴰ 1849
DIED NOVEMBER 19ᵀᴴ, 1887.

The words of Emma Lazarus, on the Statue of Liberty base

ments, the log-books of history, that are the papers of the *landsman-shaftn,* material often provided by the aged offspring of the last survivors of some of these groups. YIVO estimates there are fifteen hundred to two thousand *landsmanshaftn* still operating, at levels ranging from mere

sick, lost his job, needed burial, or simply longed for the company of his own sort. Although the first *landsmanshaftn* here were German, started before the Civil War, by the 1880s they were proliferating in the Yiddish-speaking community. By the 1940s more than five thousand such societies were meeting in New York halls and homes, oblivious to extraneous factors such as religion or politics, but embracing all who hailed from Bialystok, or Latichev, or whichever village or enclave they represented.

The theater benefit, that peculiar hybrid of show-going and social reunion, received its first major support from the *landsmanshaftn,* who used these shows as fund-raising events to support the sick and aged of their town of origin. As the members of the *landsmanshaftn* became Americanized, so did their social events: formal affairs involving the use of special regalia, balls, the kinds of events common to less parochial fraternal organizations.

Although the *landsmanshaft* is now in decline, it is nowhere near dead. At the YIVO Institute for Jewish Research, scholars are gathering and preserving the docu-

existence to robust activity. Among the contributions of YIVO's research among the *landsmanshaftn* has been the creation of records of what happened, during the Holocaust, in the course of their home communities' disappearance from the earth.

Lazarus, Emma (1849–1887) Emma Lazarus was a Sephardic Jew, but sixteen years after her death her words became the symbol of her Yiddish-speaking brethren. She grew up in a well-to-do, assimilationist environment—her father was one of the founders of the aristocratic Knickerbocker Club—but was from her earliest adulthood extremely conscious of her Jewishness. At age eighteen she wrote the poem "In the Jewish Synagogue at Newport"; in her late twenties, her *Songs of a Semite* included a poem about the persecution of Jews in Germany in the Middle Ages, and later still she translated the works of Heinrich Heine. When the immigration of Russian Jews quickened after the death of Czar Alexander II, she immediately embraced their cause, both as poet and as activist. "By virtue of our racial and religious connection with these hapless victims of anti-Jewish cruelty," she wrote, "we feel that it devolves upon us to exert our utmost strength toward securing for them permanent protection."

In 1883, solicited along with other prominent American writers to make a literary contribution to the fund-raising campaign for the Statue of Liberty (her work had been praised by Emerson and Whitman, among others), she wrote her sonnet "The New Colossus," the manuscript of which brought the fund-raisers $1,500 at auction. Although the poem was forgotten by the time Lazarus died of cancer just five years later, not even mentioned in her obituary in the *New York Times*, it was found in a bookstore portfolio in 1903 by artist Georgiana Schuyler, who had it engraved on a bronze plaque and placed at the base of the statue. Although she was separated by wealth, social status, and place of origin from the Yiddish-speaking Jews, Lazarus's words would nonetheless become the symbol of their immigration, and that

of every other ethnic group that would enter our country.

Leivick, H. (1886–1962) A towering figure in the Yiddish literature of this century, its very conscience in an era that stretched from czarist oppression to Hitlerite extermination, H. Leivick spent a lifetime probing the nature of man, of Jews, of existence. Irving Howe, writing about the theme of suffering that pervaded Leivick's work, said, "All his life, Leivick aspired toward pain, both as a way of sharing the ordeal of his people and in an effort to gain a kind of anonymous sanctity."

H. Leivick, arrested in Moscow and on his way to Siberia

Leivick Halper was born, the eldest of nine children, to impoverished parents in Byelorussia (he later changed his name to avoid confusion with fellow poet M. L. Halpern). Still in his teens, he joined the Jewish Socialist Bund and was twice arrested, the second time sentenced to a long term after he defiantly told the judge, "All that I have done, I did with an unflinching will to help destroy the autocratic regime." He was sent to Siberia, escaped in 1913, and came to

Mrs. Leiner and her son, Benny Leonard

New York, where he worked in a sweat-shop and as a paperhanger (the latter an occupation he would continue for most of his life).

Writing late at night after hours of backbreaking labor by day, Leivick was associated in his early years with *Di Yunge*, the poets who turned their backs on "social" poetry in favor of more personal forms of expression. Although he was never a wholehearted proponent of that school, he nonetheless wrote with a powerful lyricism that relentlessly examined the choices an individual man must make and scorned those choices that seemed easy ways out. His themes in prose, drama, and poetry were Messianic even in his early works, such as *The Messiah in Chains*, written while he was imprisoned in Minsk in 1908. This play, about a revolt by the angel Ariel against God's orders to chain the Messiah, emphasizes the need for Jews to continue calling for the Messiah and, eventually, to free Him to usher in a new age.

Among Leivick's other well-known plays was his adaptation of the folk tale *The Golem*, written in 1920, performed in 1925 by the Habimah in Moscow, and later produced in English both as drama and as opera. It was more than a story, this play; it told of how Rabbi Loewe of Prague in desperation breathed life into the inert clay monster he had fashioned only to learn that he had created a being that really did not want to kill, not even the enemies of the Jews. Yet the rabbi knew that a *golem* was needed, for the Messiah was too gentle to be called upon to inflict violence.

Leivick continued to write prolifically, even after contracting tuberculosis in the early 1930s and enduring a lengthy recuperation in a sanitarium in Denver. He returned to New York in 1936, becoming a writer for *The Day* and at last giving up his trade as a paperhanger. When he learned that his sister and brothers had perished in Nazi crematoria, he wrote such guilt-filled poems as "In Treblinka I Never Was," and wondered whether God could ever be forgiven for having loosed the Nazi murderers. In his last years, Leivick wrote an autobiographical account of his youth, *In the Czar's Prison*.

Leonard, Benny (1896–1947) Of all the Jewish ghetto kids who used athletics to rise from the slums to lives of respectability and comfort, Benny Leonard was the prize example. He first fought with gloves on at age eleven, and worked out in makeshift rings until he was fifteen, when he caught the eye of a manager who began getting him matches (his first professional fight earned him four dollars). Born Benjamin Leiner, he fought under the name Leonard lest his parents learn what he was up to. In 1917 he won the world's lightweight championship, a title he retained until his retirement in 1924. During his tenure as champion, some synagogues offered a *gomel benshen*—a prayer of thanksgiving—on the Sabbath following each of Leonard's successful fights.

A musical rendering of a sociological rift

What finally defeated Leonard was the stock market crash of 1929, which took away the nearly $1 million he had made in the ring and left him broke. Thus did he return to fighting in 1931 as a welterweight, a comeback he abandoned when he was knocked out a year later. He became a referee, owned a restaurant, and served as a lieutenant commander in the United States Maritime Service during World War II. Leonard died of a cerebral hemorrhage while refereeing a bout at St. Nicholas Arena.

Levin, Meyer (1905–1981) Although best known for *Compulsion*, his novel about the Leopold-Loeb murder case, Levin first attained public notice for *The Old Bunch*, his grittily realistic novel about the passage to adulthood of a group of poor Chicago Jews. It is a heavily populated novel, similar in many ways to James T. Farrell's *Studs Lonigan*, teeming with every imaginable "representative" character the ghetto could produce. Levin remained a productive and relatively popular novelist until his death, but seemed always to be at war with his critics, and even his readers. Daniel Fuchs, who emerged into the world of American letters with his own realistic ghetto novels just before Levin did, wrote in 1981 that Levin "believed he was the victim of a conspiracy of silence; that hostile, left-wing critics unfairly dismissed his work as 'too Jewish,' as sentimental; that he was systematically persecuted and then ridiculed because he was persecuted . . ." Inflamed by reaction to one of his books, Levin wrote a wild *cri de coeur* about the criticism, finally declaring in bitterness, "I ask only that others, particularly members of my family (incurable Jewish sentiment) should not be blamed for my errors. I acted alone."

Liessen, Abraham (1872–1938) Liessen was the pen name of Abraham Walt, the scion of a family of rabbis, a disillusioned yeshiva student himself, a Socialist rebel. He escaped czarist repression in 1897, arriving in New York and soon taking up Yiddish Socialist journalism. In 1913 he began a quarter-century's tenure as editor of *Di Tsukunft*, shaping it as a leading literary monthly of decidedly leftist politics. He was a poet himself; his roots were divided between his strong religious upbringing and his ardent social utopianism.

Liessen's magazine—*tsukunft* means "future"—has been published continuously since 1892, when it first appeared as the organ of the Yiddish-speaking membership of the Socialist Workers Party. When Liessen took command, it was under the sponsorship of the Forward Association.

Litvaks and Galitsyaners Of the infinite strains borne by the Yiddish-speaking Jews in the New World, not the least (though certainly not nearly the worst) was the sense of mutual disregard and mistrust between Jews from the northern part of the Pale of Settlement and those from the south. The former area, which included Lithuania, produced Litvaks; the latter, centered in Galicia in the western Ukraine, sent forth Galitsyaners. Although in later years and generations the Litvak-Galitsyaner conflict became a good-natured cultural rivalry, the source of innumerable jokes, it was not always thus. Meeting in America, sharing the same Lower East Side geography, the groups began their rivalry in intense mutual contempt, carried over intact from Europe. The Litvaks, who made up the largest contingent of immigrants in the 1880s, believed more or less in the Enlightenment, the knowledge of

Meyer London is welcomed to Congress. The headline reads, "Pleased to meet you!"; the caption, "A truly new sort of Jew." From *Der Groyser Kundes*, 1914

modern civilization as well as their own Jewish heritage. They published the first Yiddish newspapers, opposed the mystic ways of the Chassidim, and represented a legalistic, scholarly Judaism. The Galitsyaners, who came later, harbored hundreds of thousands of Chassidim among themselves, and in broad generalization held religious views closer to those of their mystic brethren.

The Litvaks believed themselves something of a cultural elite, and would say *"Besser a goy vi a Galitsyaner"* ("Better gentile than Galitsyaner"); the Galitsyaners maintained every Litvak hid a cross beneath his beard and was an apostate.

It was a rift rarely accorded recognition even in the Yiddish press, but the organization of the Yiddish community in this country into *landsmanshaftn* helped maintain the segregation. There were Litvak-only medical groups, Galitsyaner-only theater benefits, and vice versa. Delancey Street was almost a national frontier, the Russian and Litvak settlements arrayed to the south, the Galician (and others from

portions of the Austro-Hungarian Empire) to the north. And both the Litvaks and Galitsyaners had firm niches in a sort of social pecking order that ranged through all the various subgroups of Yiddish culture: the Hungarians regarded themselves as the cream of the East Side; the Russians looked down on the Litvaks; they, in turn, scorned the Polish Jews who, for their part, had no regard for the Rumanians. These last considered the Galitsyaners beneath contempt, yet all the Yiddish-speakers united in their dislike of the German Jews, and the feeling was, thank you, mutual.

London, Meyer (1871–1926) Meyer London was the first Socialist Party member to be elected to office in New York, and the first Jew of Russian birth to serve in the House of Representatives, to which he was elected by his Lower East Side constituents in 1915. He arrived in America at nineteen, became a lawyer, involved himself in the trade union movement, and gained fame for his advocacy of the cloakmakers during their historic strikes. London was a Socialist, but more a pragmatist than a revolutionary. In Congress, he opposed America's entry into World War I, suffering the brickbats of those who felt it the American Jew's obligation to be more patriotic than anyone; once American involvement in the war became fact, however, he was assailed by radical Socialists for voting in favor of the military appropriations necessary to support the AEF.

Los Angeles In 1850 Los Angeles numbered but eight Jews in its population of sixteen hundred; four years later, the city had a Jewish cemetery, four years after that a temple, and by 1950 more than half a million Jews, making it the second-largest Jewish city in the world, after New York. Los Angeles Jews first clustered in the city's downtown, where eastern European Jews whose health had deteriorated in the warrens of New York and other Atlantic coast cities congregated, having come to the city in search of the cure of a beneficent climate (more than two thousand came under the auspices of the Industrial Removal Office). Still, the community was small, and the few German Jews in Los Angeles who in 1912 worried about an influx of immigrants via the Panama Canal were needlessly concerned. Jewish Los Angeles would be settled not by European immigrants, but by their children.

As the movie industry grew, dominated almost from the beginning by eastern European Jews, so did the city's Yiddish-raised (if not European-born) population, both in the executive suites of the big studios and in the various service businesses created to cater to the Hollywood crowd. Boyle Heights in East Los Angeles, the city's first large Jewish neighborhood, acquired the familiar patina of Yiddish-language signs over *shuls* and bakeries and delicatessens. The most famous among these institutions was no doubt Canter's Deli, which had moved from Jackson Avenue

Jersey City to Brooklyn Avenue in Boyle in Heights. It caught on with the motion picture colony so swiftly that Ben Canter, the Minsk-born impresario behind the counter, brought his three brothers from the East to help run the booming business. Canter's fortunes grew as the city's Jewish community prospered; both relocated after World War II to Fairfax Avenue, the heart of the Beverly-Fairfax area. This five-square-mile neighborhood was seventy-five percent Jewish, an area of middle-class families who wanted to live near mass transportation (such as it was in car-centered L.A.) that would get them to the movie studios and to the garment industry that had, predictably, emerged in the city as its Jewish population grew.

Magnes, Judah Leon (1877–1948) Like Louis Marshall or, on good days, Jacob Schiff, Judah Magnes was a member of the uptown *Yahudim* who was nonetheless celebrated and honored in the tenements of the immigrants. He was born in Oakland, California, of a German-Jewish family, and became, successively, a Reform rabbi, head of the New York Kehillah, a Conservative rabbi, a pacifist activist, and, eventually, the first president of Hebrew University in Jerusalem. He preached traditionalism to the Reform, learned Yiddish, and was an ardent Zionist in unreceptive uptown circles.

Magnes as a young man attended Hebrew Union College, and was ordained a rabbi in 1900. He studied in Berlin and Heidelberg, traveled to eastern Europe (where he first sensed the stirrings of Zionism), and attended the 1905 Zionist Congress in Basel as a member of the United States delegation. After returning to America, he was appointed assistant rabbi of Temple Emanu-El, the citadel of Reform Jews in America. There, he urged his unreceptive congregants to pursue a more traditional Judaism. Though he failed in that effort, Magnes did serve as a bridge between uptown and downtown when he founded Kehillah, the representative body that was intended to speak for all New York Jews. In 1910, spending more and more time among the Yiddish-speaking Jews and less among his Emanu-El congregants, he assumed the pulpit of the city's leading Con-

servative synagogue, B'nai Jeshurun. In one of his last sermons, he told the congregation, "A prominent Christian lawyer of another city has told me that he entered this building at the beginning of a service on Sunday morning and did not discover that he was in a synagogue until a chance remark of the preacher betrayed it." Eventually, Magnes's effectiveness uptown was undercut when he embraced an antiwar position at the outset of World War I.

Magnes emigrated to Palestine in 1922, helping to establish the Hebrew University and serving as its chancellor and then president until his death twenty-six years later. Although Magnes's pacifism receded in the face of the Nazi menace, it remained evident in his constant advocacy of amity between Jew and Arab in a binational state, a sentiment that he voiced with particular force immediately after such upheavals as the Hebron massacre of Jews in 1929 and the Arab riots of 1936. He opposed partition of the Holy Land throughout his life, feeling it both worthy and necessary for Jews and Arabs to live together.

Mandelbaum, Frederika
(1860?–1933) She was known as "Mother" or, more commonly, "Marm" Mandelbaum to those who worked with her. By 1890 she had become one of the nation's leading dealers in stolen goods, a "fence" built of 250 blubbery pounds and blessed with a genial smile and a most sentimental manner.

Mandelbaum ran a gang that featured the notorious

Judah Magnes

Mani Leib

Monk Eastman, a highly visible East Side hoodlum. For her own part, she maintained the public image of a widow with four children, running a dry goods store at the corner of Rivington and Clinton streets. Her two-floor apartment atop the store, however, reflected the tastes of the finest homes in New York, whence much of the furniture and objets d'art had come. She dealt with burglars and pickpockets, and entertained this element with fancy dinners. Mandelbaum paid the law firm Howe & Hummel $5,000 a year for legal services, and it was said by law enforcement officials that her gang was involved in eighty percent of the bank robberies in the United States. When an incorruptible district attorney brought an indictment against her, Mandelbaum and her son jumped bail and went to Canada, where she spent the rest of her life.

Mani Leib (1883–1953) He was the purist of poetry, the slave of style, but somehow this devotion to technique enhanced rather than subverted the essential thoughts of Mani-Leib Brahinsky, immigrant to New York after a stint as rebel in the first, unsuccessful Russian Revolution. Mani Leib was one of the founders of *Di Yunge*, the poetic dissidents who rebelled against the prevailing school of the "sweatshop poets." A leatherworker by trade, he was fluent only in Yiddish, but in that language he was caught in a love of words, a passion Irving Howe attributes to two influences: the devotion of the eastern European intelligentsia to Russian poetry, and the Jewish "tradition of *edelkeit*, a term signifying both delicacy and nobility."

In his poem "I Am," Mani Leib writes about how the Muse tapped him, a cobbler, and made him not a cobbler "who writes,

Thank Heaven, but a poet who makes shoes." In his "To a Gentile Poet," he expressed both the fears and pride of a man writing in a language that is not that of his nation, remarking on the good fortune of "heirs of Shakespeare, whose words walk the world" while he, "unneeded, a poet among Jews, growing like wild grass, from soil not ours," sings of the cares "of men in a desert, beneath alien stars."

The gentle Mani Leib was the agent, in a way, of a bit of raucous unpleasantness that erupted on the East Side during the 1920s. The Russian poet Yesenin, who was married to Isadora Duncan, visited New York and spent much of his time in the company of Yiddish poets, with whom he spent hours discussing Slavic poetry. At a reception for him at Mani Leib's home, however, Yesenin became violently drunk, threatening and assaulting with vicious anti-Semitic curses all those about him. Placed in a straitjacket and taken away in an ambulance, he later attempted apology, but Mani Leib and his companions shunned him. The memory of the pogroms, of Russian townsmen with whom one did business by day but feared in the drunken night, was too close at hand.

Marshall, Louis (1856–1929) Born in Syracuse, New York, this son of German-Jewish immigrants became one of the leading champions of the Lower East Side Jews from whom he differed so greatly. An attorney of substantial success, Marshall was the second president of the American Jewish Committee and one of its founders. But it was his personal, particular acts that distinguished him: he was instrumental in persuading President Taft to abrogate in 1911 a treaty with Russia, on the grounds that the Russians discriminated against Jews and Catholics; he fought continually, and until the post–World War I backlash successfully, for the easing of immigration limits, many of which were championed by the restrictionist American Federation of Labor; he was personally responsible for the statement of apology Henry Ford made to American Jews for his anit-Semitic agitation

Louis Marshall (L)
and Cyrus Adler,
his successor as
president of the
AJC

of the 1920s; he performed a major role in establishing the Jewish Agency in behalf of Jews in Palestine, although he was not himself a Zionist; and he was an influential player in the peace conferences that followed World War I, arguing effectively for the formal recognition of the rights of minorities in the peace documents.

Almost alone among the uptown Jews—Judah Magnes, who would eventually desert that community, was another exception—Marshall actually studied Yiddish, and became fluent in it. But one of the consequences of his mastery of the language was the ease with which he became familiar with the Yiddish press. Deploring the sensationalism (and, not less, the radicalism) that characterized many of the successful Yiddish papers of the day, he raised the money to launch *Di Yidishe Velt—The Jewish World*—a newspaper that avoided socialism, Zionism, orthodoxy, and sensationalism, and that would, Marshall hoped, set a new standard of journalism for Yiddish readers. Designed fundamentally to serve as a downtown vehicle for uptown ideas, it lasted for two years before folding.

Montreal The Jews of Montreal are, after the French and the Anglo-Celtic Canadians, the third-largest ethnic group in Canada's largest city. From 811 Jews in 1881 to more than 45,000 in 1921, Montreal's Yiddish-speaking population kept rising, unhampered by the immigration restrictions that settled over American ports in the early 1920s. By 1961 Montreal's Jewish population would pass 100,000.

Unlike most American cities, Montreal did not have an entrenched German-Jewish community, nor was it unused to the multilingualism that sudden immigration created. Still, there were problems: Montreal

Montreal's eastern European Jews, from *The Apprenticeship of Duddy Kravitz*

has always had two parallel, government-supported educational systems, one French-speaking and Catholic, one English-speaking and Protestant. The Jews generally attended the Protestant schools, which paid less attention to religious matters than did the Catholic, but fought unavailingly for sixty-five years to have schools of their own, or nondenominational schools, established by the government. Finally, in 1968, five Jewish seats were created on the Protestant school board, and the board also recognized Jewish voluntary schools that complied with its standards. Among the latter, the particularly strong schools operated by the Labor Zionists helped Yiddish culture maintain a prominence in Montreal virtually unique in North America.

The heart of the Yiddish-speaking district in Montreal was concentrated in an area just to the east and slightly northeast of Mount Royal; though Baron Byng High School was nominally under the aegis of the Protestant school board, it was a de facto Jewish school, so dense was the area's Jewish population. The two streets that most embodied the flavor of the Jewish quarter were Boulevard St. Laurent, known as "The Main," and St. Urbain Street. It was along The Main that one was (and especially at Schwartz's, still is) most likely to find the delicacy native to Yiddish Montreal, the celebrated smoked-meat sandwich, universally pronounced "smookmit."

Montreal was rich in Yiddish institutions, including a thriving Yiddish theater; its own daily newspaper, the *Kanader Adler* (*Canadian Eagle*), which initiated a much-followed "policy for the Jewish voter," endorsing candidates for municipal, provincial, and national office whose interests matched those of the community as perceived by the paper's editors; and the Jewish Public Library, the largest of its kind in

North America, established in the early 1920s.

Probably the most visible products of Montreal's immigrant community were the distiller Samuel Bronfman, whose fortune was solidified by his enormous success producing liquor for the American bootleg market during Prohibition, and the novelist Mordecai Richler. In such books as *The Apprenticeship of Duddy Kravitz*, *St. Urbain's Horseman*, and *Joshua Then and Now*, Richler has provided an astonishing chronicle of the progress of the children of immigrant Jews as they strive to escape St. Urbain Street for the palmier heights of Westmount.

Moskowitz and Lupowitz The "2 + 2" emblazoned on the menus of Moskowitz and Lupowitz signified this restaurant's location at the intersection of

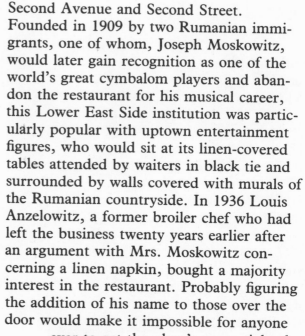

Second Avenue and Second Street. Founded in 1909 by two Rumanian immigrants, one of whom, Joseph Moskowitz, would later gain recognition as one of the world's great cymbalom players and abandon the restaurant for his musical career, this Lower East Side institution was particularly popular with uptown entertainment figures, who would sit at its linen-covered tables attended by waiters in black tie and surrounded by walls covered with murals of the Rumanian countryside. In 1936 Louis Anzelowitz, a former broiler chef who had left the business twenty years earlier after an argument with Mrs. Moskowitz concerning a linen napkin, bought a majority interest in the restaurant. Probably figuring the addition of his name to those over the door would make it impossible for anyone ever to get the place's name right, he chose instead simply to identify himself as "Director" on every menu.

Artie Shaw (R) at Moskowitz and Lupowitz, with proprietor Louis Anzelowitz

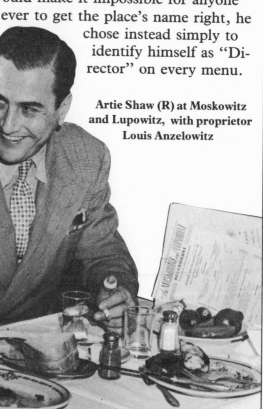

Movies, Yiddish Influence in the Unlike the case of movies performed in Yiddish, the story of movies written, produced, directed, financed, distributed, and, often enough, featuring American Jews of Yiddish descent is not nearly over. Almost as much as the garment trade, it remains an industry dominated to a great degree by the children and grandchildren of immigrants from eastern Europe.

It may be that immigrant Jews were attracted to the movie business because it was a medium of mass entertainment, in which area many immigrants had already scored notable success. Or perhaps it was an attractive field because it was a new one, an industry in which they would not have to compete with long-entrenched interests that might try, as they did in so many other businesses, to keep them out.

Whatever the sociological reasons, the specific cases were varied. Carl Laemmle, who would become president of Universal Studios, was managing a shoestore when he noticed on his first visit to a movie theater how small an inventory the owner carried— a few reels of film, which he didn't even own and which the customers would leave behind when they left, a screen, and a projector. Samuel Goldfish (he'd become famous as Goldwyn, a name taken from a corporate acronym) was a glove salesman who hooked up with his brother-in-law, vaudeville producer Jesse Lasky, to produce his first movie in 1913, an epic called *The Squaw Man,* directed by a young man named Cecil B. De Mille. Some, operating small retail businesses, gave over their shop space to nickelodeons, within months moved into distribution, then to production. Once Thomas Alva Edison's motion picture trust was broken by Adolph Zukor and William Fox, the industry rapidly took on a Yiddish inflection: in the 1930s Columbia, Warner Bros., Paramount, Twentieth Century–Fox, Universal, Metro-Goldwyn-Mayer, and the Goldwyn Studios were all owned and run by immigrant Jews. From this pantheon of moguls issued the films America grew up on— good ones and bad ones—and from it, too, issued a continuing murmur from "out there" that this was not quite right. Describing the dominant tone of "one of the most prolific sub-genres in twentieth-century American literature, the Hollywood novel," Robert Sklar wrote: "One did not have to join the ranks of conservative clergy

Louis B. Mayer

LUDWIG SATZ IN
HIS WIFE'S LOVER

זײַן װײַב'ס ליובאָוניק

Yiddish movies.
(L) Comedy, with Ludwig
Satz (white hat); (below)
Tragedy, with Berta Gersten
(seated) in *Mirele Efros*;
(facing page) Musical,
with Moyshe Oysher (at R)
in *The Singing Blacksmith*.

guardians of culture to feel outrage that immigrant Jews had developed and held control over the nation's newest and largest medium of mass commercial entertainment." These novels also made much of the cutthroat atmosphere rampant in Hollywood among the moguls. But, as Sklar says of one of the most vivid of these books, Budd Schulberg's *What Makes Sammy Run?*, "In his rise from the Lower East Side, Sammy, Schulberg makes clear, cuts himself off from the values of his religious and ethnic origins."

Movies in Yiddish The legendary contribution to Hollywood of Jews from Yiddish-speaking backgrounds has been noted so extensively that it overshadows the shorter and less momentous life of the Yiddish movie. Yiddish theater, however diminished, may still exist, but Yiddish filmmaking is dead. The heyday of the Yiddish film was in the 1920s and 1930s. One of the first such ventures was made by Joseph Green, who had performed in an Italian silent film, *Joseph in Egypt*. He received the Polish distribution rights to the movie, and added a Yiddish sound track and title cards. Meeting success with this fairly effortless translation, Green went on to produce four films in Poland, among them *Yidl Mitn Fidl* (1935), with Molly Picon, and *A Brivele Der Mamen* (1937). In America, the major Yiddish filmmaker was Joseph Seiden, who started as a projectionist and became a cameraman for

such as William Fox and Harry Cohn, eventual heads, respectively, of the firms that would become Twentieth Century–Fox and Columbia Pictures. Seiden, however, remaining in New York and working only in Yiddish, produced and directed some thirteen films in one decade. He later operated a Yiddish film rental agency, and a collection of thirty pictures he distributed are now preserved as the Ruttenberg and Everett Film Library, owned by the Jewish Historical Society in Waltham, Massachusetts.

Among the more notable products of the short-lived American Yiddish film industry are the 1939 production *Tevye*, starring Maurice Schwartz in the role of Sholem Aleichem's milkman, with music

by Sholem Secunda, and such other adaptations from stage works and fiction as Hirshbein's *Green Fields*, Ansky's *The Dybbuk*, and Gordin's *Mirele Efros*. More typical, however, might be such mass-market entertainments as *Where Is My Child?*, starring Celia Adler, and *Two Sisters*, with Jennie Goldstein. They were films that featured, wrote Nahma Sandrow, "both ladies rolling their eyes and staggering with emotion in an exaggeration of the style of American films made a decade or two earlier." Yet more dismaying to contemplate is the 1930s musical filled with Borscht Belt *shtik* and called—no translation required—*Ketskil Honimun*.

**Paul Muni, with mandolin (below)
and with swagger (facing page)**

Muni, Paul (1895–1967) This powerful actor was an intuitive performer who nurtured his craft in the Yiddish theater and saw it flower in an immensely successful English-language film career, in which he played a succession of noble, heroic figures with great distinction. At the peak of his career, his employers at Warner Bros. thought so much of him that they made sure the ads for his pictures identified him as "Mr. Paul Muni"— with the emphasis on the "Mr."

Muni Weisenfreund was born in Lemberg, in what was then Austria-Hungary, in a Yiddish theatrical trunk. His parents were strolling players who traveled from settlement to settlement, eventually departing for London and, in 1902, New York. His parents continued on the road, and their son traveled with them, playing everything from lowest burlesque to the most refined Ibsen and Strindberg. In 1918 Maurice Schwartz hired him for his Yiddish Art Theater at forty-five dollars a week, and Muni became one of the Schwartz company's stars. Part of one theatrical family, he joined another when he married Bella Finkel, a niece of Boris Thomashevsky.

It was in 1926 that Muni ventured uptown to Broadway, playing first an elderly, Orthodox father (he was thirty-one at the time) in *We Americans*. In 1930, by then known as Paul Muni, he attained stardom in Elmer Rice's *Counsellor-at-Law*, and soon thereafter went to Hollywood, playing the Al Capone role in *Scarface*. It was his last bad-guy part; from then on, Muni began stringing together heroic roles in films ranging from *I Am a Fugitive from a Chain Gang* to *The Louis Pasteur Story*, *The Life of Emile Zola*, and *The Good Earth*. He made periodic returns to Broadway over the rest of his career, but apart from his participation in the formation of *Mir Shikager*, the Yiddish actors' benevolent association in Chicago, he was never again involved in the Yiddish theater.

Murder, Inc. This was the title bestowed by the press on the killer squad of Brooklyn thugs organized by Louis "Lepke" Buchalter (1897–1944) to operate as an enforcement unit for the Syndicate, the national crime confederation that kept the peace, allotted territories, and determined the future prospects of its various members. Although it was Lepke who actually suggested that such a squad was necessary to keep uncooperative hoodlums in line or out of business, Murder, Inc., was actually run by Albert Anastasia, and its enforcers were a mix of Brooklyn Jewish and Italian killers.

The man who conceived the group was born on the Lower East Side, where his parents had arrived from Russia in 1890. There were eleven children, and only

$25,000 REWARD
DEAD OR ALIVE

TWENTY-FIVE THOUSAND DOLLARS will be paid by the City of New York for Information leading to the capture of "LEPKE" BUCHALTER, aliases LOUIS BUCHALTER, LOUIS BUCKHOUSE, LOUIS KAWAR, LOUIS KAUVAR, LOUIS COHEN, LOUIS SAFFER, LOUIS BRODSKY.

WANTED FOR CONSPIRACY AND EXTORTION

The Person or Persons who give Information Leading to the Arrest of "LEPKE" will be fully protected, his or her identity will never be revealed. The information will be received in absolute confidence.

RIGHT HAND

LEFT HAND

DESCRIPTION — Age, 42 years; white; Jewish; height, 5 feet, 5½ inches; weight, 170 pounds; build, medium; black hair; brown eyes; complexion dark; married, one son Harold, age about 18 years.

PECULARITIES—Eyes, piercing and shifting; nose, large, somewhat blunt at nostrils; ears, prominent and close to head; mouth, large, slight dimple left side; right-handed; suffering from kidney ailment.

Frequents baseball games.

Is wealthy; has connections with all important mobs in the United States. Involved in racketeering in Unions and Fur Industry, uses Strong-arm methods. Influential.

This Department holds indictment warrant charging Conspiracy and Extortion, issued by the Supreme Court, Extraordinary Special and Trial Terms, New York County.

Kindly search your Prison Records as this man may be serving a Prison sentence for some minor offense.

If located, arrest and hold as a fugitive and advise the THE DETECTIVE DIVISION, POLICE DEPARTMENT, NEW YORK CITY, by wire.

Information may be communicated in Person or by Telephone or Telegraph, Collect to the undersigned, or may be forwarded direct to the DETECTIVE DIVISION, POLICE DEPARTMENT, NEW YORK CITY.

118

Lepke went astray; he numbered among his sisters and brothers a rabbi, a druggist, and a variety of respectable citizens. When his father died, Lepke, in his teens, was left behind to live with a sister in Brooklyn while the rest of the family moved to California. Missing the Lower East Side, he returned there, joining a gang of small-time miscreants, among them Jake "Gurrah" Shapiro, who was to become his longtime partner in crime. After serving a prison

Three months after a wanted "dead or alive" circular was distributed by New York police, Murder, Inc., kingpin Lepke Buchalter was photographed as he prepared to face trial on narcotics charges.

term, Lepke embarked on what would be his notorious specialty, labor racketeering. He was a coarse strong-arm, setting fire to noncooperative businesses, supplying the muscle to terrorize unions and management alike, and frequently controlling both. FBI Director J. Edgar Hoover was direct in his appraisal of Buchalter: he was, Hoover said, "the most dangerous criminal in the United States." Having achieved this preeminence, largely through his successful infiltration and corruption of the garment, trucking, and motion picture operator industries, Lepke, with Shapiro, joined the Syndicate's board of directors and conceived the Murder, Inc., execution squads.

Under the leadership of Anastasia, who himself would die at the hands of other mobsters, Murder, Inc., disposed of more than two dozen uncooperative criminals. But Anastasia's Jewish right hand, Abe "Kid Twist" Reles, who had himself been involved in fourteen of those killings, turned state's evidence when finally charged with homicide in 1940. He told prosecutors of one thousand murders nationwide, eighty-five in Brooklyn alone, and implicated members of every Syndicate constituency. Held in "protective custody" by New York police in the Half Moon Hotel at Coney Island, Reles somehow fell to his death before his interviews with the prosecution were through, and the investigation of the Syndicate came to an end. That same year Lepke, long removed from the actual strong-arm work himself, was arrested for the murder of a trucker he had put out of business. He surrendered to columnist Walter Winchell, who turned him over to Hoover in person. Tried and convicted, in 1944 he was executed at Sing Sing, the only top-rank criminal of his era to meet such an end.

Nadir, Moyshe (1885–1943) If ever there was in the world of Yiddish letters a Jewish Pagliacci, it surely was Isaac Reis, who wrote under the name Moyshe Nadir. This witty man's prose could draw laughter, but it could also, when barbed, exact blood. A poet, one of *Di Yunge*, he strove to eliminate sentimentality, sometimes innocently drawing the reader on only to dash his feelings on the rocks of his bitter humor. He was a lonely man who once said, "When God had nothing to do, He created a world. When I have nothing to do, I destroy it." It was a deprecating self-appraisal; Nadir created much of value, including poems, criticism, journalism, translations from French and German, and an intricate use of the language that dazzled with its puns, jokes, neologisms, and other feats of wordplay.

In 1922 Nadir joined the Communist Party, remaining a fervent member until the Hitler-Stalin pact seventeen years later. He tirelessly espoused the party line as he attacked old friends and literary colleagues, going to Moscow and receiving a hero's

welcome in 1926, taking a pro-Arab line after the Hebron massacre of 1929. His party orthodoxy was so anathematic to others that his work in his Communist years was rarely reviewed outside party journals. The last four years of his life passed in self-recrimination for his sins of commission. He wrote, "For every drop of blood that I drew with my pen, I paid with two drops from my heart's blood. This is no excuse for all those I attacked with such blind fanaticism, and my heart weeps because of my deeds."

Name-Changing

"Of all the immigrant peoples in the United States, the Jews seem to be the most willing to change their names," wrote H. L. Mencken in *The American Language* in 1937. "Once they have lost the faith of their fathers, a phenomenon almost inevitable in the first native-born generation, they shrink from all the disadvantages that go with their foreignness and their Jewishness and seek to conceal their origin, or, at all events, to avoid making it unnecessarily noticeable." Of course, Mencken also noted that even among

Moyshe Nadir, 1926

(L to R) Name-changers Issur Demsky, Emmanuel Goldberg, Bernard Schwartz

those who, at the height of the eastern European immigration, "remained true to the synagogue," name-changing proceeded apace. Wolfson became Wilson, Davidovich became Davis, Rabinowitz became Robbins, Hillkowitz became Hillquit, Shapiro became Shepard.

In fact, name-changing was so common among immigrant Jewry that it lost any significance relating to identity or non-identity. Often it began at Ellis Island, where admitting officers who did not understand what a Jew was saying would give him an "American" name that approximated his real name, perhaps "Wallace" for "Wallenchinsky." Later name changes would occur because American-born offspring found long Slavic names too difficult to cope with; sometimes, Jews felt their names kept them out of jobs. In any event, surnames hung loosely on Yiddish-speaking Jews, who as a rule did not even have them in the old country until census requirements were imposed in the 1800s. Then, those who could afford to often paid officials for the right to take pleasant names, such as the -*stein*s and -*blum*s ("stones" and

"flowers," as in Goldstein and Rosenblum). Names based on geography were common, too—Warschauer, Berliner, Moscowitz. But when the name-changing took place in America, the geography was substantially more local. Numerous Lower East Siders took their new names from the streets around them—Clinton, Rutgers, Stanton, Ludlow. The classic name-changing joke concerns the fellow who encounters an old classmate who shouts, "Shmuel Rabinowitz! Haven't seen you for years!" "*Shah*," he admonishes, "that's not my name anymore. Too old-country. Now I'm C. D. Rivington." "How'd you think of that?" "You know I used to *shlep* fruit on Rivington Street." "Then what's the C. D.?" "Corner Delancey."

Perhaps the best name-changing story is a true one. A Bostonian named Cohen switched to Cabot, engaging the rancor of—and a lawsuit from—a genuine Yankee Cabot. The episode led one wag to paraphrase the old Boston rhyme: "Boston, land of the bean and the cod, where the Lowells speak only to Cabots, and the Cabots speak only Yiddish."

Nathan's The rise of Coney Island as playground to America's largest city brought with it Jewish residents, show people, subway-shuttling sun worshippers—and Nathan's. Nathan Handwerker had been a counterman at Feltman's, whose founder, Charles Feltman, had introduced the frankfurter in a roll, with mustard and sauerkraut, to Coney Island just before the turn of the century (it was dubbed the "hot dog" by cartoonist Tad Dorgan around 1906).

Going into business for himself in 1916, Handwerker set up a stand on Surf Avenue, on the direct route from the subway terminal to the boardwalk, and sold his franks for five cents each while Feltman was charging a dime. Handwerker's business prospered mightily, and soon on particularly busy days police had to be called to keep the hungry crowd at bay. Nathan expanded his line to include knishes, french fries, soft drinks, beer, corn on the cob, and, eventually, oysters and clams; a kosher establishment it wasn't. In 1958 Nelson Rockefeller, running for the governorship, was photographed munching a Nathan's hot dog and was quoted as saying that Nathan's was an indispensable stop for any candidate. Since then, it has been.

Although Nathan's has hung its shingle in a variety of other locations in the New York area, traditionalists insist only Nathan's in Coney Island smacks of the real *ta'am*.

Newspapers If ever the saying "two Jews, three opinions" had validity, it was proven in the heyday of America's Yiddish press. Beginning with *Di Yidishe Tseitung* in 1870, and through the great heyday of Yiddish journalism in the first third of this century, the newspaper industry expressed the vibrance and the variety of Yiddish life in America. The publications ranged from the brawny *Forward*, with a peak circulation of 250,000 in the 1920s, to short-lived efforts like *Di Yidishe Velt—The Jewish World*—founded by uptowner Louis Marshall to provide an alternative to the socialism rampant in most of the leading Yiddish papers of the day. Political philosophies were represented over the entire spectrum (although admittedly heavy on the left), from the Communist *Freiheit* to the *Tageblatt* (*Daily News*), a decidedly anti-Socialist paper that was the mouthpiece of the proletarian Orthodox community. This paper later merged with the *Morgen Zhurnal* (*Morning Journal*), which in its heyday concentrated on a straight, sobersided presentation of the news, supported the Republican Party, and spoke to and for a slightly higher "class" among the Orthodox than did the *Tageblatt*. The *American Mercury* characterized one of the *Morgen Zhurnal*'s editors thus: "Had his parents come over to America on the Mayflower, he might have been today the

Above: The original Nathan (holding his son, Murray, the current president of the company) at the Original Nathan's

editor of the *Boston Transcript* or the *Christian Science Monitor*."

Though many of the Yiddish papers, and especially *The Day*, which did not succumb until 1971, had admirable literary standards, it would be less than accurate to portray them, as a whole, as journalistic paragons. Ture, they together published the work of the community's great poets and novelists and thinkers, but if one paper liked a given book, say, its rivals would automatically trounce it. Columns in every paper were devoted to sniping at the competition and, in general, one found in the Yiddish press the same sensationalizing, the same pandering to lowest common denominators, that one found in the English-language press. Even Abraham Cahan, surely the most influential of the Yiddish editors, was not above the muck of charge and countercharge: when the *Tageblatt*, for which Cahan had an especial animosity, condemned a play of Jacob Gordin's as "sacrilegious," Cahan, even though he had been feuding with Gordin, decided to have the *Forward* sponsor a production of the work. What's more, he used the paper's columns to blast "the pigs and piglins of the 'sewer rag' " who had presided over the play's earlier demise. The Garden Cafeteria, on East Broadway, was a popular hangout for the reporters and editors of the Yiddish papers, and often resounded with the shouts of competition and animosity that these men so readily engaged in. They were, all of them, even down to the writers for the basest scandal sheet, in intense competition for the Jewish reader, and more, for his mind.

This science wasn't confined to New York, by any means; Yiddish papers, many of them dailies, operated from Montreal to Denver. All told, circulation at the industry's peak exceeded half a million, and the tradition of passing a paper on to one's fellow workers or neighbors was so prevalent that total readership was easily triple that, but in time, as the language disappeared from everyday use, as the political and doctrinal battles in the community were replaced by the less parochial concerns of an Americanized public, the Yiddish press withered and died. Today, only the *Forward* remains as a daily newspaper.

Niger, Samuel (1883–1955) Samuel Niger, born Samuel Charney (a Slavic surname that means "black," and may be related to the name he later adopted), was the most eminent, articulate, and feared literary critic in the world of Yiddish letters in the twentieth century. Irving Howe wrote,

The Yiddish newspaper in the Yiddish home

"His great strength was that he simply took for granted the viability of Yiddish, as critics in other languages take for granted the viability of their languages." Never did Niger worry whether Yiddish was "dignified" enough to merit the attention he lavished upon it, or whether it was destined to survive or not: it was what it was, and that was more than satisfactory.

Niger had already established a substantial critical reputation in various eastern European publications before he arrived in New York from Vilna in 1920. Early on, in 1907, Niger had written a major essay on Sholem Asch, and in a short time, his reputation overshadowed that of Ba'al-Makhshoves, the father of Yiddish criticism. In

Samuel Niger (R) with S. Ansky

New York, he became literary critic of *The Day*, and for thirty-five years the Yiddish literati hung—or fell—on his words. His interest was literature, his judgments based always in art, never in ideology. When the Jewish community was in a state of high agitation over Asch's popular novel about Christ, *The Nazarene*, with such powerful voices as Abraham Cahan assailing it as "a major crime against the Jewish people," Niger called it "Asch's highest achievement."

Niger was fundamentally a lonely man, his voice sought from many quarters, his company from few. He was the brother of Daniel Charney, a poet, and B. Charney Vladeck, the political leader.

-Nik Leo Rosten, in *The Joys of Yiddish*, calls it "the stalwart suffix," able to transpose virtually any part of speech into "a word for an ardent practitioner, believer, lover, cultist or devotee of something." It was used extensively by the immigrants as a means of incorporating an English term into Yiddish—alrightnik, nogoodnik, and so on—and is one of the two basic forms used to adapt Yiddish to America: this one employs a Yiddish tail on an English dog, whereas the other technique doesn't bother with the tail (thus the Yiddish word *sobvey*, for the hole in the ground in which New Yorkers ride, a word which, notes Maurice Samuel, appears in *The Modern English-Yiddish Yiddish-English Dictionary*).

Of course, it's a two-way street: if the Jews can take "no good" and put it in front of *-nik*, there's no reason to bar gentile America from taking *-nik* and tacking it onto "peace." And if one can ride the *sobvey*, the other is surely entitled to call the onlooker at a poker game a *kibitzer*. It's all called "cultural interchange."

Odets, Clifford (1906–1963) During the 1930s Clifford Odets emerged as one of the Jewish writers who, writing in English, mixed lyricism with realism to tell about the class struggle and man's aspirations, frequently in Jewish working-class settings. In 1935 two of his best-known plays, *Waiting for Lefty* and *Awake and Sing!*, were performed by the Group Theater, the theatrical company that staged so many plays of protest and social analysis during that period.

Waiting for Lefty, about a strike in the taxi industry, starred a young Greek-American actor, Elia Kazan, whose appeal for a strike was so impassioned he virtually swept audiences out to the picket lines. *Awake and Sing!*, concerning a Jewish working-class family in the Bronx, featured a cast that included Morris Carnovsky, Stella and Luther Adler (both children of the great Jacob), John Garfield, and J. Edward Bromberg, and was directed by Harold Clurman. A melo-

dramatic play, confident in the goodness of the little people who daily confronted the cataclysms of a failing society, it was a virtual transposition of the style, pace, and substance of the Yiddish theater to the English stage. The play was perhaps summarized in a speech by the old *zeyde*, who tells his grandson, "*Boychik*, wake up! Be something! Make your life something good. For the love of an old man who sees in your young days his new life, for such love take the world in your own two hands and make it like new. Go and fight so life shouldn't be printed on dollar bills." In their time, the clichés of Odets's work were original on the American stage. As Howard Taubman wrote in *The Making of the American Theater*, "A spirit of hope, which paradoxically flamed more brightly in the somber thirties than in the later decades of affluence, sang through this play."

Born in Philadelphia, raised in New York, Odets was, as an actor, one

Morris Carnovsky (L) and Luther Adler, in Odets's *Awake and Sing*

Orchard Street at Rivington, c. 1910

of the founders of the Group Theater. Soon turning exclusively to writing, he wrote, in addition to the plays mentioned above, *Paradise Lost, Rocket to the Moon, Night by Music, Clash by Night,* and perhaps his greatest success, *Golden Boy,* about a violinist who becomes a prizefighter. Even though Odets made the hero an Italian, it was certainly a theme that struck home with his Jewish audience.

Odets, like so many of his theatrical comrades, moved to Hollywood, living in Beverly Hills and writing for the screen. In 1950, however, he returned to Broadway with *The Country Girl,* about an alcoholic actor, and again in 1954 with *The Flowering Peach,* a treatment of the story of Noah and the ark. Although recommended for a Pulitzer by the prize jury, *The Flowering Peach* was rejected by the Pulitzer board.

Opatashu, Joseph (1887–1954) Already a writer when he arrived in New York at age twenty-one, Opatashu was immediately caught up in the literary energy around him. "Yiddish literature in America is still a multi-branched tree that sheds its withered leaves and grows new ones, fresh ones," he wrote shortly after his arrival in America. Although he would earn an engineering degree, Opatashu was ever a writer, producing short fiction and novels about

Jewish life both in Poland and in America, the latter at the suggestion of Sholem Aleichem. His work was naturalistic, never romantic, telling of horse thieves and smugglers and the darker sides of Lower East Side life. For forty years he was a regular contributor to *The Day*, providing an enormous collection of sketches and lengthier stories for its pages. His most successful work was *In Polish Woods* (1938), the initial volume of his trilogy about Chassidic life in Poland. Opatashu's son, David (born 1914), attained his own success as an actor, first on the Yiddish stage, then in English-language media.

Orchard Street Today the best-preserved remnant of Yiddish life on the Lower East Side, Orchard Street, as it has been for nearly a century, is a narrow, crowded thoroughfare known for the throngs who jam it in search of bargains. "It was that kind of street—a basement on another surface; an enchanted mountain of goods, voices, harangues, anger, stealth, heart, charity, nobility, at its lowest, or highest, for the poor," remembered Harry Roskolenko in his memoir *The Time That Was Then*. "It was a pious place, too, and efficiently human; a street of many strident banners. . . . The street confused everybody, for it was impossible to know who was the teacher of economics and who was the pupil."

Oysher, Moishe (1908–1958) This golden-voiced cantor from Bessarabia, a teenager when his family settled in Coney Island, enjoyed parallel careers in the liturgical realm and the secular territory of show business. "I keep so busy from Friday to Sunday, by Monday, look! I'm on a stretcher," he told an interviewer from *The*

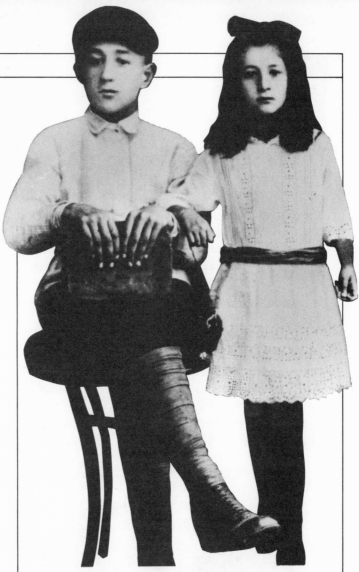

Moishe Oysher, at twelve, with his sister, Fraydele

New Yorker. "I sing in the synagogue, I sing at weddings, I sing at funerals, I sing at club dinners, I sing at benefits. For the High Holidays alone, I earn a figure in five figures. Once, when I told my grandmother that, she shook her head and said, 'Moishe! Your grandfather sang for a sack of potatoes.' Maybe I'd do the same in Bessarabia."

With his sister Fraydele, Oysher was an entertainer from the time he was a child, and made his first secular success when he took over the title role of *Yeshive Bokher* from Boris Thomashevsky in 1927. In 1938 he costarred with Herschel Bernardi in the film *The Singing Blacksmith*, based on the David Pinski play. Throughout his career as an entertainer, he remained cantor of the First Rumanian American Congregation on Rivington Street.

Pastor, Rose (1879–1933) She was the inspiration for Anzia Yezierska's novel *Salome of the Tenements,* and Yezierska's title just about did her justice. Born in Poland, she came to Cleveland with her family as a young child, and went to work in their behalf in a cigar factory at age eleven. Matured and radicalized by her working experience, Pastor moved to New York and became a writer and labor organizer while still in her teens. But the event that made her famous was her marriage to Graham Phelps Stokes, the leftist scion of an aristocratic gentile family (Yezierska had him reading a copy of *The Atlantic Monthly* on their honeymoon while his wife smoldered). As Rose Pastor Stokes, she led a strike of hotel workers in 1912, and in 1914 published her English translation of Morris Rosenfeld's *Songs of Labor*. In 1918 she was indicted and sentenced to a ten-year term on charges arising from her opposition to World War I. She remained a dedicated radical after her release, and in 1929, while demonstrating in New York against the oppression of the Haitian people, she was clubbed by a policeman, sustaining injuries that contributed to her death four years later.

Patryotn "Patriots" in this usage refers to Yiddish theater fans who were wildly impassioned partisans of particular performers. Jacob Adler's *patryotn* physically assaulted the adherents of David Kessler when he had the audacity to perform the role of Uriel Acosta, a part long associated with Adler. According to Lulu Rosenfeld's *Bright Star of Exile,* when an unknowing publicity man cheered Bertha Kalish at her curtain call after a performance in Keni Liptzin's theater, he was admonished by the latter's *patryotn,* "In this theater, only Liptzin is cheered." Some *patryotn* were more than admirers—they were nuisances. One such was the man who saw Adler's every performance of *The Jewish King Lear*. When the actor delivered the line "Will no one here give me even a piece of bread?," the man, with stunning regularity, would run into the aisle, offering bread and crying, "Mr. Adler, come with me! Children are no good!"

Peddlers and Pushcarts The peddler tradition was an ancient one in the European Jewish world. Even the aristocratic German

Rose Pastor

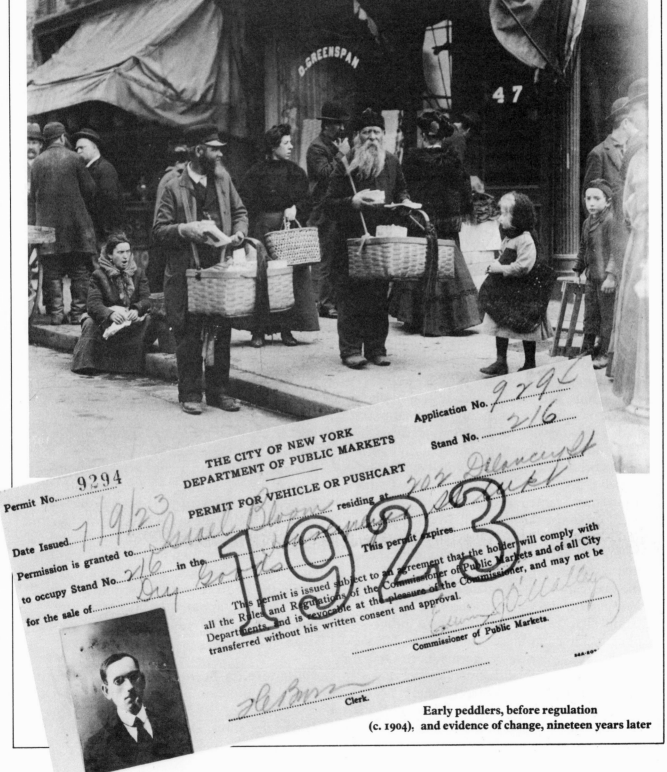

THE CITY OF NEW YORK
DEPARTMENT OF PUBLIC MARKETS

PERMIT FOR VEHICLE OR PUSHCART

Application No. 9294

Stand No. 216

Permit No. 9294

Date Issued 7/9/23

Permission is granted to _Samuel Bloom_ residing at _202 Delancey St._

to occupy Stand No. 216 in the _Dry Goods_ Market

This permit expires

This permit is issued subject to an agreement that the holder will comply with all the Rules and Regulations of the Commissioner of Public Markets and of all City Departments, and is revocable at the pleasure of the Commissioner, and may not be transferred without his written consent and approval.

Commissioner of Public Markets.

Clerk.

1923

Early peddlers, before regulation
(c. 1904), and evidence of change, nineteen years later

A Hester Street bread peddler; a cover protects his wares from the elements

Jews, who would later disdain the haggling that gave the Lower East Side its special aroma, had known peddling: great numbers of them, arriving in America after the German Revolution of 1848, toured the country with packs on their backs, selling stores of goods that would eventually become the basis for some of the most prosperous and stable retail businesses in the nation.

On the Lower East Side, though, and in the Jewish quarter of virtually every other American city with an immigrant population, business was small-scale. These were places where an immigrant might start with a few *shmattes* or some pots and pans, and find himself in fierce competition with others who had similarly homely collections of goods to offer. The peddler started with a pushcart (rented at eight to ten cents a day), or simply armed with a strong back and a stronger voice, wandered the city crying, "I cash clothes," pursuing garments that could perhaps be sold elsewhere. In the geographically specialized world of Manhattan, wedding dresses were sold on Grand Street, coats and furs were indigenous to Division Street, chickens to Hester Street, and, years later, garments to Orchard Street. Sexual distinctions prevailed on Chicago's Maxwell Street, where women, wrote Louis Wirth, "monopolize the fish, herring and poultry stalls."

The watchword of Jewish shopping in the land of the pushcarts and the storefronts that succeeded them was *metsiye,* the bargain that might really be one, or at the very least the purchase that gave the appearance of being one. Customers and merchants enjoyed the tortuous haggling that involved pleading, threats, innuendo, and final agreement; it was more a way of life than a means to an end, and as often as not a haggling bout would end with a customer stomping out, only to be intercepted at the door by the shopkeeper making his final offer. Louis Wirth again, on Chicago's pushcart district: "Everything has value on Maxwell Street, but the price is not fixed. It is the fixing of the price around which turns the whole plot of the drama enacted daily at the perpetual bazaar. . . . "

The pushcart businesses of New York went into decline when Mayor La Guardia conducted a slum clearance effort on the Lower East Side and formed the Municipal Enclosed Retail Market, forcing the street peddlers indoors. This might have been avoided had an effort to organize the peddlers succeeded a half-century earlier. In 1886 an officer of the nascent union appealed for the support of the Yiddish-speaking community: "It is true that peddlers are not wage-earners," he wrote, "but proletarians they are. The difference between a working man and a peddler is that the working man gets a starvation wage, while the peddler starves without a wage." The plea was apparently unconvincing; within a year and a half, the union was dead.

Philadelphia Between 1880 and 1915, the Jewish population of Philadelphia (which once included the Revolutionary War hero Haym Solomon) exploded from twelve

A Philadelphia ghetto scene (Gaskill Street) and a Philadelphia ghetto product (the Paley family's cigar brand)

thousand to two hundred thousand. These Jews crowded into the North Philadelphia area around Marshall Street, which was to its city as Maxwell Street was to Chicago and Orchard Street was to New York. Their welcome to Philadelphia, however, was rather warmer than that accorded their brethren in these other cities. In 1882 the steamship *Illinois* tied up to a Philadelphia pier and discharged 225 Jewish émigrés from Russia, who were greeted by a municipal reception and $20,000 to aid their settlement. Among the most remarkable products of the Marshall Street area (although he was himself of German extraction) was Judge Mayer Sulzberger. Rising to eminence in the legal profession, traveling in the nation's most elite Jewish social circles, Sulzberger nonetheless stayed rooted in immigrant Jewish Philadelphia, occupying a large brick house on the corner of Girard Avenue and Thirteenth Street. His home was a haven for eastern European immi-

Mike Thomashefsky's "only first class Jewish play house in Phila." Included in its company,
the young Maurice Schwartz (lower R)

grants, any of whom could enter upon presentation of a book to the judge—his was, at the time, the largest private Jewish library in the country. He was the first president of the American Jewish Committee, and instrumental as well in the founding of the Jewish Publication Society and Dropsie College, two noteworthy Philadelphia Jewish institutions. Another of the neighborhood's notable products was the La Palina cigar, the manufacture of which was brought to the city from Chicago by an immigrant named Samuel Paley. Profits from the La Palina would become the foundation of the fortune his son, William Paley, would construct as chairman of CBS.

Some venerable, still-standing rem-

nants of the teeming Girard Avenue neighborhood, which would later be abandoned for Oxford Circle and other neighborhoods to the northeast, include the Ambassador Dairy Restaurant and the building that housed the Girard Theater. Located in the heart of the area's "entertainment district" between Fifth and Eighth streets, the Girard Theater was a vaudeville house of long standing and occasional home of Yiddish theatrical productions. Today it is Klein's Spanish Food Market, a transformed relic of the distant Philadelphia past.

Picon, Molly (1898–   ) She was "the sweetheart of Second Avenue," this product of the North Philadelphia ghetto who made her first professional stage appearance when she was six. At twenty-one, trying to make her way in English-language vaudeville, she found herself out of work in Boston when the city's theaters were closed during the 1919 influenza epidemic. In need of carfare home, she went to the local Yiddish theater and met its manager, Jacob Kalich. They were married in 1919.

Kalich immediately took control of his young wife's career, first taking her to Europe to perfect her Yiddish, then writing for her the play *Yankele*, in which she played, Mary Pickford–like, a little boy. Its immediate success, derived from its star's gamine appeal and from the novelty of its light, comedic touch, inspired Kalich to continue writing Picon's material, usually with music by Joseph Rumshinsky. Among Picon's early hits were *Tzipke, Shmendrik*, and *Yiddle with His Fiddle* (which she also did as a Yiddish film in 1936). All told, Kalich wrote more than thirty shows for his wife (for her part, she wrote the lyrics to countless songs for those shows).

In 1929 Picon temporarily left Second Avenue for an extended vaudeville tour that took her all over America and to Europe, where she sang in English, Yiddish, German, and French. She appeared uptown in 1940, playing her first English-language dramatic role in *Morning Star*, and from that point on she shuttled back and forth between Second Avenue and Broadway. For more than two decades she also had her own radio show, in both Yiddish and English, and when she premiered as mistress of ceremonies of the *American Jewish Caravan of Stars* in 1951, *Variety* complained that the show contained "too little of the bean-sized Bernhardt."

Pinski, David (1872–1959) Through the first half of this century, no Yiddish writer was so widely translated as David Pinski, a Russian-born disciple of the great Yiddishist Y. L. Peretz. He was one of the first Yiddish writers to explore and propound Socialist themes in his work, even before his emigration in 1899. Although Pinski detoured somewhat from his intention to write when he studied medicine—as well as literature—at Columbia University, he still, even in those years, wrote prolifically, producing work for both the stage and the printed page.

One of his notable earlier works was *The Family Tsvi* (1904), a melodramatic treatment of the destruction of Jewish life inspired by the Kishinev massacre. Other works were variously concerned with themes of sexual passion, such as *Better Not to Be Born*, which dealt with the desire of a young man to rape a young girl of twelve, and *Yankel the Blacksmith,* made into a film starring Moishe Oysher and Herschel Bernardi. But Pinski's crowning achievement was undoubtedly *The Treasure,* produced in Yiddish at the Garrick Theater, in English by the Theater Guild, and in German by the famous company of Max Reinhardt—all within two years of its writing. Harvard drama professor George Baker called *The Treasure* one of the best comedies of the 1920s. A sort of Yiddish *Finian's Rainbow,* the play coincidentally appeared at almost precisely the same time as Sholem Aleichem's work of the same name and similar subject matter.

Pinski's fiction treated many of the same themes explored in his theater work, although one novel, *Arnold Levenberg,* was a rather daring experiment for a Yiddish writer. It concerned a wealthy German-Jewish family in New York, assimilated in every way, retaining their Jewish identity only through their exclusion from certain gentile clubs. It is a seriously flawed work, but inflamed with the writer's political and ethnic passions. Throughout his life Pinski remained a Socialist, aligned particularly with the Labor Zionist movement. He spent the last ten years of his life in Israel.

Protocol of Peace This was the historic document that recognized the rights of the needle trade unions in New York, bringing to an end the bitter Cloakmakers' Strike of 1910. It was a Jewish affair, this strike, Jewish workers going to war with Jewish manufacturers, and Jewish mediators brought in to end it. It was Louis Brandeis, enlisted by Jacob Schiff and Louis Marshall, who mediated the settlement of the dispute. As critical as were the terms of the eventual settlement was the name by which

Pushke **bearers for the Central Relief Committee, 1919**

it would be called: neither side could abide acknowledging a victory by the other. Marshall thus dubbed it "a protocol of peace," invoking biblical terminology in a nicely impartial phrase. Although the protocol was severely jostled in later years, it remained the pattern for all future agreements in the trade.

Pushke The *pushke* was as much a fixture as any piece of furniture in the immigrant Jewish home, and equally familiar by the cash register in Jewish businesses. It was a can into which people threw their loose change in behalf of various good causes, each *pushke* representing a different charity.

The most familiar *pushke* was the little blue-and-white receptacle of the Keren Kayemet L'Yisroel, the Jewish National Fund, devoted to purchasing land in Palestine; others were stationed to collect coins for old age homes, for yeshivas, for *landsmanshaftn*, for needy Jewish children. Charities were so varied that Leo Rosten could cite, only partly tongue-in-cheek, a *pushke* "For the Jewish Chicken Raisers in Kankakee Recently Bankrupted by the Ravages of Red Tick among Rhode Island Roosters."

The *pushke* was the household agent of *zedekah*, the biblical injunction to give to help others. During hard times, a family might draw from a *pushke* in the kitchen when cash suddenly ran short, but these loans were conscientiously replaced when times got better.

R

Ratner's One of the high temples of New York's dairy restaurant world, Ratner's first opened on Pitt Street in 1905, moving with its success to Delancey Street between Suffolk and Norfolk (it also had an "uptown" location, way up on Second Avenue near Sixth Street). It sported a capacious room for bar mitzvahs and wedding receptions upstairs, had the usual complement of celebrities from the entertainment world downstairs (it was just a few doors down the street from Loew's Delancey, a popular vaudeville theater), and its extensive menu ranged the entire breadth of the nonmeat Jewish cuisine, from blintzes to gefilte fish to those inventive concoctions, "vegetable liver" (heavily dependent on eggplant, treated to resemble in texture, if not taste, chopped chicken livers) and "protose steak"—if a "steak" could be made from vegetable protein, it would no doubt taste like this.

For all of Ratner's varied appeal, two things—one culinary, one not—stood out. The first were the extraordinary products of the restaurant's bakers, marvelous onion rolls and black bread offered in well-stocked baskets with every meal; the second, Ratner's world-weary waiters. Although the legend of the Jewish waiter gained force from hundreds of practitioners in scores of restaurants, Ratner's seemed to employ the quintessential specimens of the breed. Serving ten thousand meals a week—they still do, too—Ratner's waiters had the endearing (or, to some, annoying) habits of telling the diner who wanted

Nelson Rockefeller—with New York Attorney General Louis Lefkowitz—indulges in election-eve "good luck" blintzes at Ratner's

borscht that he really wanted *kreplach*, gently (or not so gently) mothering customers through meals that ran to uncounted courses, or—when unpredictable swings of mood set them off on another tack—thrilling visiting diners from uptown or the suburbs with their somehow appealing rudeness. The classic story of a Ratner's waiter concerns the diner who was worried that he would be late for the theater. Waving at a passing waiter, the customer asked, "Excuse me, do you have the time?" Lifting his eyebrows ever so slightly, the waiter replied, "Not my table."

Reisen, Abraham (1876–1953) and **Zalman** (1887–1941) The Reisen brothers were dedicated Yiddishists, scholars, and writers. It ran in the family: Kalman, their father, was a merchant in Kaidanovo, near Minsk, who wrote poetry in Hebrew and Yiddish on the side, and their sister, Sarah, was also an accomplished Yiddish poet.

The elder of the Reisen brothers, Abraham, was a poet and storyteller who, with Sholem Asch and H. D. Nomberg, formed a trio of disciples to the great Y. L. Peretz in Warsaw. A prolific writer, Reisen produced at least one poem and one story a week for the Yiddish dailies in America, to which he had emigrated in 1914. His work, said the critics, elevated Yiddish verse from folk poetry to something artistic and refined. He was not an ideologue, writing instead with poignancy about the individual. He was also one of the prime movers of the First Yiddish Language Conference in Czernowitz in 1908.

Abraham's younger brother, Zalman, never lived in America, but his work had a profound influence on American Yiddish writers. A philologist and literary historian, he was the author of textbooks on Yiddish that helped standardize the grammar. His *Leksikon fun der Yidisher Literatur un Prese,* as edited by S. Niger, appeared in 1914 and became the basis for his monumental bibliographic work, *Leksikon fun der Yidisher Literatur, Prese un Filologi,* published in four volumes from 1926 to 1929. Zalman lived most of his adult life in Vilna, a leader in Jewish literary life and Yiddish education. He was arrested by Soviet troops in 1939 and shot in Russia two years later for reasons that have never been made known.

Riis, Jacob (1849–1914) "Hardly less aggressive than the Italian," wrote Jacob Riis in 1890, "the Russian and Polish Jew, having overrun the district between Rivington and Division Streets, east of the Bowery, to the point of suffocation, is filling the tenements of the Old Seventh Ward to the river front, and disputing with the Italian every foot of available space in the back alleys of Mulberry Street. The two races, differing hopelessly in much, have this in common: they carry their slums with them wherever they go, if allowed to do it."

The Danish-born Riis wrote not with bigotry, but in anger at a system that imposed hopelessness and penury on new immigrants. His book, *How the Other Half*

Lives, not only lent a phrase to the American idiom, but served as well to draw attention to the conditions of the Lower East Side. His reformer's zeal found its outlet in the New York *Commercial Advertiser,* where he worked with Lincoln Steffens, Abraham Cahan, and Hutchins Hapgood. If Hapgood's *The Spirit of the Ghetto* unearthed the interior talents and potentials of the area's residents, Riis lay bare the conditions that conspired against those attributes. Riis was also a photographer whose pictures of tenement life are the best visual chronicle we have of that distant day.

Jacob Riis, 1904

Al Jolson and May McAvoy conjure with the reputation of Yossele Rosenblatt, in *The Jazz Singer*

Roosevelt, Theodore (1858–1919) The man whom Richard Hofstadter called "the master therapist of the middle classes" was not unmindful of the lower ones, either. Although he was a proponent of immigration restrictions that would bar anarchists and other radicals from America and was notably timid about sending an official condemnation of the Kishinev massacre to the Russian czar, Roosevelt was genuinely popular on the Lower East Side. A Republican and a reformer, his appeal to the anti-Tammany feelings among the immigrants was demonstrated in their support of his gubernatorial and presidential races. Campaigning after his return from the Spanish-American War, Roosevelt made one particularly ingenious pitch to Jewish voters, an appeal that was quite apart from matters of political reform: a Yiddish circular distributed in his behalf on the Lower East Side credited Roosevelt with helping to realize "the long felt Jewish desire to see Spain fall. . . . Every vote for Roosevelt's opponent is a vote for Spain!"

Rosenblatt, Josef (1882–1933) A musical prodigy, Josef—known widely as "Yossele"—Rosenblatt was an accomplished cantor in his Russian hometown of Belaya Tserkov while still in his teens. In 1912 he was induced to emigrate to New York to serve as cantor of Congregation Ohab Zadek, which paid him the exceedingly handsome salary of $2,400 a year. He served as cantor while pursuing a secular career in the concert hall and as a composer of songs, liturgical and otherwise.

Rosenblatt was a deeply religious man who not only frequently found his beliefs in conflict with his ambitions and desires, but who also complicated his life greatly because of them. He was persuaded to invest heavily in a Yiddish newspaper that was intended to be even more Orthodox than the already established Orthodox papers, but it failed; he also put a great deal of money into a "luxury" *mikva*, a ritual bath with such extraordinary features it would attract the Jewish women who were, more and more, giving up such Orthodox practices (it too failed). To recoup from such ventures, Rosenblatt entered vaudeville, but he would not compromise his religious beliefs and refused to perform with women, or accompanied by an organ. He also turned down a $1,000-a-performance offer to sing in Halevy's *La Juive* with the Chicago Opera. He did make one lasting impression in show business, however, when his voice was used in *The Jazz Singer*, the first talking motion picture.

Rosenfeld, Morris (1862–1923) In his day Morris Rosenfeld was the best-known and most popular Yiddish-American poet. His anguished verse sang of the despair of the sweatshops and found an enthusiastic audience not only in his own community, but also, in translation, among American intellectuals and radical activists. Born into a family of fishermen in Poland, Rosenfeld found his way to New York via Amsterdam

Morris Rosenfeld, c. 1886

and London. The good life he anticipated eluded him, and for ten years he toiled in the oppressive gloom of the sweatshops every day, days whose only illumination came from the moments he could steal to write his poems.

Rosenfeld's verses found quick favor among the Yiddish masses, but he was not able to escape the sweatshops until he was "discovered" by Leo Weiner, a Harvard professor of Slavic languages. In 1898 Weiner published a translation of Rosenfeld's work entitled *Songs of the Ghetto*, and its success led to selections appearing in prominent English-language newspapers. Noting this, members of the German-Jewish community raised money to help finance the poet's way out of his life of deadening labor; Jacob Schiff alone contributed six hundred dollars, and Rosenfeld was able to set up in business as a candy-store proprietor and newspaper distributor. His life as businessman proved uncongenial, and Rosenfeld soon became a journalist, writing for the *Forward* and other papers. Intensely proud, he railed against his "pen slavery" as a *Forward* staff writer and severed his ties with that source of sustenance. Similarly, although eager to publish poetry in English, in which he was not quite fluent, he would not accept the assistance of the poet Louis Untermeyer, whom he considered unsympathetic and, in his approach to poetry, "decadent." As with so many other artists in the rapidly changing society of the Yiddish-Americans, Rosenfeld outlived his fame, enduring a failure all the more burdensome because of his early success. He turned his energy and his heart to Zionism in his later years, spurned by both the English community that had once embraced him, and by *Di Yunge* and the other Yiddish poets who were blazing new literary trails.

Perhaps Rosenfeld's best-known poem was "Mayn Yingele," about the small child he rarely saw because of his sweat-shop existence. Its last verse, in Aaron Kramer's translation, could as well depict Rosenfeld's feelings about the community in which he once was celebrated:

I watch him, wounded and depressed
By thoughts I cannot bear:
"One morning, when you wake—my child—
You'll find that I'm not here."

Henry Roth

Roth, Henry (1906–   ) He wrote only one book, and it was nearly thirty years before it earned the success it deserved, but with that work alone Henry Roth placed himself at the forefront of novelists who wrote in English of the immigrant experience. The book was *Call It Sleep*, and it could well have been the book F. Scott Fitzgerald in 1926 had predicted would come out of "the Jewish tenement block, festooned with wreaths out of Ulysses and the later Gertrude Stein." It was surely a novel of those tenements, a story of the son of immigrants who, in his eighth and ninth years, emerges from an overlong infancy to confront the unkind aspects of slum life.

Call It Sleep was published in an edition of twenty-five hundred copies and reprinted soon thereafter in an equal quantity. Although it was reviewed respectfully on its publication, it soon disappeared from print and from the consciousness of even

the literary world. In 1960 a new edition, with introductions by Harold U. Ribalow, Maxwell Geismar, and Meyer Levin, was issued. Then, in 1964, Avon Books published a paperbound edition that became an enormous success, eventually reprinted twenty-five times and selling more than a million copies.

The author of *Call It Sleep* was born in New York, a graduate of City College who undertook the novel at the urging of the poet and teacher Edith Walton. Roth contracted to write a second novel after the publication of *Call It Sleep*, but never completed it. Instead, he lived a singularly unliterary life, teaching high school in the Bronx, operating a precision metal grinder in a machine shop in Massachusetts, and working as a hospital orderly and supervisor in Maine, finally abandoning that to raise ducks and geese near Augusta.

Writing in the *New York Times* in 1971, Roth used the third person to answer those who wondered why he had stopped writing: "Continuity was destroyed when his family moved from smug, orthodox Ninth Street, from the homogenous East Side to rowdy, heterogeneous Harlem. . . . It would have to follow that the personality became amorphous, ambiguous, at once mystical and soiled, at once unbridled, inquisitive, shrinking. No longer at home. I guess that's the word, after this smother of words. NO LONGER AT HOME." To Harold Ribalow, who was in large part responsible for the reissue of *Call It Sleep*, Roth was not to be questioned. After visiting the writer in Maine, Ribalow wrote, "The man appeared to be at peace with himself, and who was to say that obscurity on a byroad in Maine cannot lead to happiness?"

Rothstein, Arnold (1882–1928) In 1926, when the Communists in the ILGWU were attempting to settle their strike with the garment manufacturers, they turned to someone on the manufacturers' side whom they felt they could trust, a retired cloth merchant named Abraham Rothstein who was a philanthropist, chairman of the board of Beth Israel Hospital, a Hebrew scholar, a man called by Governor Al Smith "Abe the Just." He also happened to be the father of a boy named Arnold, one of the most powerful Jewish gangsters of that gang-ridden era. David Dubinsky maintained that when the elder Rothstein proved unable to help, the union turned to Arnold, who engineered a settlement that brought peace to the industry. The episode extended into the needle trades the influence of one of the most adept criminals of his time, the mobster Damon Runyon called "The Brain."

Rothstein *fils* began his career in petty gambling on the Lower East Side and quickly became a wealthy bookmaker, managing the gambling concession at the Hotel Metropole on Forty-third Street. He progressed through mob life until he became the keystone of organized crime in New York, the archmediator and arbitrator and clearinghouse of the burgeoning industry, going beyond gambling into bootlegging, narcotics, and various other criminal activities. At one time or another Rothstein had in his employ such star thugs as Waxey Gordon, Legs Diamond, Frank Costello,

Arnold Rothstein

Albert Anastasia, and Lepke Buchalter.

Undoubtedly Rothstein's reputation was enhanced by one of the biggest coups of his career—the fixing of the 1919 World Series, the famous "Black Sox" scandal. F. Scott Fitzgerald, in *The Great Gatsby*, rendered Rothstein as "Meyer Wolfsheim." In the words of Fitzgerald's Nick Carraway, "It never occurred to me that one man could start to play with the faith of fifty million people—with the single-mindedness of a burglar blowing a safe." Nick asks Gatsby why Wolfsheim was not in jail. "They can't get him, old sport," Gatsby replies. "He's a smart man." In fact, Rothstein was smart enough never to serve a single day in jail, yet not so smart that he could avoid a gangster's death. Fatally wounded by a gunman in New York's Park Central Hotel, he died refusing to say who had done him in. He was given an Orthodox funeral.

S

Schapiro's Wine "The wine so thick you can almost cut it with a knife" may not sound terribly appealing to those who know chablis from chianti, but it is a slogan that has worked for years for the oldest kosher winemaker in America, Schapiro's House of Kosher and Sacramental Wines on Rivington Street. Samuel Schapiro, the founder, arrived from Poland in 1899, opened a restaurant, added a small winery as a sideline, and soon saw the wine business eclipse the restaurant. In time Schapiro's winemaking facilities would occupy a city block of cellars and caverns beneath Rivington Street, between Essex and Norfolk.

For its entire history, Schapiro's has made its wines from grapes touched only by Orthodox Jews and trucked from the Finger Lakes to the city. During Prohibition the firm was allowed to continue production, as the wines were, indeed, designed for sacramental use. Today, still making its wines on the Lower East Side, Schapiro's has been dwarfed by its national competitors—Mogen David, which is based in Chicago, and Monarch Wine Company of New York, marketed under the Manischewitz name through a license agreement with the matzo-making firm.

Schiff, Jacob H. (1847–1920) If there was one man whose pocketbook, whose prestige, whose organizational abilities were brought to bear in behalf of the Lower East Side Jews,

it was the German-Jewish financier Jacob H. Schiff. For three decades, his endorsement of one charity or another—from institutions as large as the Educational Alliance, to the freedom from the sweatshop so desperately wished by the poet Morris Rosenfeld—inevitably attracted the money of his uptown brethren. He took it upon himself to argue the brief of the immigrant Jews in the culture at large, and he did it to great and enduring effect.

Schiff was himself an immigrant, a well-born Jew from Frankfurt who arrived in New York at eighteen and by thirty-eight had become the head of the investment banking firm of Kuhn, Loeb & Company, second in size and influence only to J. P. Morgan's bank. He assimilated easily, becoming a figure not only of wealth but of influence, yet always retaining a strong sense of his religion; his was a kosher house, and Schiff observed the Sabbath in spirit if not precisely to the letter. Because Schiff considered himself a "faith" Jew, not a "race" Jew, he initially lacked a feeling of community with the Russians and Lithuanians and Poles trying desperately to enter the golden door. In fact, in 1891 Schiff was one of a committee of German Jews who urged President Benjamin Harrison to try to influence the Russian government not to "force groups of . . . its people to seek refuge in another country, and that country our own."

Jacob Schiff (L) urges the immigrant Jew to go west; William Randolph Hearst advises him to stay in New York, where (said the caption) "In numbers is strength." From *Der Kundes*, 1909

Soon enough, however, Schiff felt the suffering of the Jews in eastern Europe and understood the pain of the new Americans on the Lower East Side. He visited there frequently, to listen and to learn, and was almost universally regarded as a sort of American Rothschild. Requests for assistance came from all over the East Side. In *Poor Cousins*, Ande Manners tells of the immigrant woman who encountered Schiff while he was visiting the Henry Street Settlement (which he helped establish). The woman wanted Schiff to buy a piano for her daughter. A Schiff aide asked if the girl was talented. "How would I know?" the woman answered. "She doesn't have a piano."

In addition to domestic charities and his efforts to help mediate labor conflicts in the needle trades, Schiff was active in the fight against anti-Semitic policies in eastern Europe. In 1903 he raised $1.5 million to aid victims of the Kishinev massacre, and in 1905 expressed his detestation of czarist repression by floating a $50 million loan to the Japanese for their war with Russia.

Schildkraut, Rudolph
(1862–1930) This versatile star of the Yiddish theater came from rather different roots from most: he was born in Constantinople and refined his craft in Vienna and Berlin, where he was a member of the celebrated Max Reinhardt company. Schildkraut first appeared in New York in 1911 with a German troupe, but worked to perfect his Yiddish and joined Boris Thomashevsky's company at the Bowery Theater. Still, he was allowed certain latitude: while the rest of the actors declaimed in Yiddish, Schildkraut performed his two most famous roles, Shylock and King Lear, in German. In 1922 Schildkraut made his debut on the English-language stage, in the Provincetown Players' production of Sholem Asch's *God of Vengeance*. He had done the play in Yiddish without perceptible official response, but when the English production was staged, it was raided by police and Schildkraut and the other actors were convicted of staging an "immoral drama," convictions later overturned on appeal. (Asch's play was pretty spicy material. It concerned a man who ran a whorehouse and was married to a former prostitute; their daughter, whom the father wished to protect from the seaminess belowstairs, nonetheless became involved in a lesbian relationship with one of the whores.)

In 1926 Schildkraut opened a theater under his own name in the Bronx, where he presented Yiddish productions of plays by Ibsen, Strindberg, and Shakespeare until he moved west and devoted his last few years to acting in films. His son Joseph (1895–1964) became a film actor of substantial renown, appearing in more than fifty movies over a forty-year period, usually in roles requiring a villainous mien and an exotic accent.

Schneiderman, Rose (1882–1972) In her autobiography, *All for One,* the labor leader Rose Schneiderman recalled a woman in a garment factory complaining that the owner was prone to pinching the women when he passed by their work stations. When Schneiderman confronted the man, he said, "Why, Miss Schneiderman, these women are like my children." She replied, "We would rather be orphans."

It was a small but telling episode from the life of this remarkable figure. A tiny woman, born in Poland, immigrant at six, working girl at thirteen (her father had died and her mother had lost her job), still earning only $2.75 a week at seventeen, Schneiderman was a self-educated tactician and a born leader who for more than half a century was a major actor in the American labor movement. She organized the first women's local in the garment industry—she herself worked in a shop that made cap linings—in 1903, and by 1906 was a vice-president of the Women's Trade Union League. She was able to give up her factory job and become an organizer for the league two years later when she became the beneficiary of an anonymously donated "scholarship" intended by the benefactor to enable her to attend school part-time, but which she used to give over her life to the movement.

Rose Schneiderman

In succeeding years Schneiderman would become general organizer for the ILGWU, an advisor to Al Smith (she engineered for Smith the successful 1923 campaign to create the eight-hour day for working women), a member of Franklin Roosevelt's Labor Advisory Board under the NRA, for twenty-four years president of the Women's Trade Union League, and for six of those secretary of the New York Department of Labor. But Schneiderman's finest moments came in the years 1909–1913, when she played critical roles in the series of strikes that redrew the lines between capital and labor in the garment industry. In the aftermath of the Triangle Fire in 1911, she told a memorial audience, "The old Inquisition had its rack and its thumbscrews and its instruments of torture with iron teeth. We know what these things are today: the iron teeth are our necessities, the thumbscrews are the high-powered and swift machinery close to which we must work, and the rack is here in the firetrap structures that will destroy us the minute they catch on fire. . . . I can't talk fellowship to you who are gathered here. Too much blood has been spilled."

Schwartz, I. J. (1885–1971) This Lithuanian immigrant came to America in 1906, in 1918 escaped the sweatshops, and found his way to Kentucky twelve years later. His few years' stay there served not only to broaden his view of America, but also to provide the experience that would enable him to produce his major work, an epic poem called *Kentucky*, published in 1925. This extraordinary work relates the story of a Jewish peddler who settles there, opens a store, brings his family over from Europe, and sees the town and its Jewish community grow. The peddlers become prosperous, their shops become department stores, and in the process their children intermarry and follow new ways. When the poem's protagonist dies a wealthy man, he expires surrounded by younger generations, with the strains of Dixieland music and the Psalms of David in his head.

In addition to another long poem, *Young Years,* which recalled Schwartz's European boyhood, he was probably best known for his translations of Whitman into Yiddish.

Schwartz, Maurice (1888–1960) He was, by his own claim, the Yiddish theater incarnate—or at least that portion of the Yiddish theater with aspirations to art. Schwartz encapsulated in his own career all that was great about the Yiddish stage in the golden years that stretched from the 1920s through the 1940s, even as the mother tongue was in decline. His influence on the English-language stage was equally large; Harold Clurman said the movement led by Schwartz "introduced intelligence to

Maurice Schwartz, in a production of Sholem Aleichem's play about the Yiddish theater, *Vagabond Stars*

the American stage." Schwartz was not modest about his achievements, at one time insisting that "any writing about the Yiddish art theater movement is about Maurice Schwartz, because Yiddish art theater is Maurice Schwartz, and Maurice Schwartz is Yiddish art theater."

Schwartz was born in the Ukraine, and left with his family for England when he was ten. His parents went on to New York without him, and the precocious Schwartz became involved in the Yiddish theater in London. Two years later he arrived in New York, became involved in various amateur productions, and was turned down for membership in the Hebrew Actors Union, a rejection reversed only through the intervention of Abraham Cahan of the *Forward*.

In 1918 Schwartz organized his own company, which in 1921 would become the Yiddish Art Theater on Irving Place. During its thirty years of existence, Schwartz's company produced 150 plays, ranging from the introduction of *The Dybbuk* to Yiddish adaptations of Gogol, Strindberg, and Chekhov (Schwartz's production of *Uncle Vanya* in 1922 was the first American presentation of Chekhov's work in any language). Alumni of Schwartz's company included Paul Muni, Luther and Stella Adler, Ludwig Satz, and Jacob Ben-Ami.

Schwartz's was a large and unforgettable personality, both on the stage and off. His acting style was so forceful, involving a blend of his utter theatricality and his con-

siderable ego, that Brooks Atkinson once wrote of the experience of watching a Schwartz performance, "You always know that you are not in a library." Over the years, he worked on the English-language stage and occasionally in films (he once played a Polynesian chieftain in a Hollywood B-picture) to help support his theater. Finally, in 1949, Schwartz announced a competition with a thousand-dollar prize for the best new Yiddish play; no one entered, and the next year his theater closed its doors. Schwartz continued acting wherever he could after his theater folded, finally succumbing in 1960. Actor Nathan Goldberg said, "Schwartz did not die five weeks ago; he died slowly over the years as the Yiddish theater slowly died."

Second Avenue "Knish Alley," "The Yiddish Rialto," successor to the Bowery as the Broadway of the Lower East Side, Second Avenue was a broad, open thoroughfare with its roots in the narrow streets of the ghetto and its treetops in the uptown to which so many of the immigrants aspired. In its heyday it featured fifteen Yiddish theaters; such landmark eating places as the Cafe Royale, Ratner's, Rappoport's, and Moskowitz and Lupowitz; newsstands and candy stores stocked with all the Yiddish newspapers; music stores and law offices, English schools and union halls. It was, said David Lifson, "the cultural center of world Jewry," a street for the *shpatsir* ("stroll") and the *kibitz*, a street along

YIDDISH ART THEATRE

SECOND AVENUE AND FOURTH STREET • NEW YORK

The first contribution of Maurice Schwartz's Yiddish Art Theatre for the benefit of the British War Relief Society, Inc.

MAURICE SCHWARTZ
in his
stupendous
production
of
I. J. Singer's
YOSHE KALB

MAURICE SCHWARTZ AS THE NYESHEVE RABBI

which the Yiddish-speaking could savor the way of life they had created.

Secunda, Sholem (1894–1974) A musician and composer who was music director of Yiddish radio station WEVD, a songwriter for the Yiddish theater and vaudeville circuits, and a composer of liturgical music, Secunda stumbled into one of the great popular song successes of the 1930s. With lyricist Jacob Jacobs, Secunda wrote "Bei Mir Bist Du Schon" for the Yiddish musical *I Would If I Could*. He sold the rights to the song to a New York music publisher for thirty dollars, which he split with Jacobs, and saw Sammy Cahn add English lyrics, give it to three young girls called the Andrews Sisters, and watch it become an immense hit, selling seventy-five thousand records in one month alone. Threat of lawsuit finally got Secunda and Jacobs a share of future royalties from a song whose title—the original was retained in Cahn's version—was so alien to American ears that many referred to it as "Buy a Beer, Mr. Shane."

Secunda was also instrumental in founding the Society of Jewish Composers, Publishers and Songwriters, an ethnic equivalent of ASCAP.

Segal's Cafe Segal's was distinctive among Second Avenue cafes: it didn't attract the theatrical trade, uptown visitors were few, and one can be certain that earnest discussions of the works of Sholem Asch, or of the merits of Jewish nationalism versus international socialism, were not heard within its walls. Segal's was a hangout for the underworld, criminals big and small gathering to discuss whatever it is that criminals discuss in social situations. In *The Rise and Fall of the Jewish Gangster in America*, Albert Fried

Sholem Secunda and the Andrews Sisters

quotes a list of the cafe's regulars that was compiled in 1912 by Abe Shoenfeld, chief investigator for the New York Kehillah: "Sadie Chink, ex-prostitute, owner disorderly house; Dopey Benny, gorilla, life taker; Little Mikie Newman, gangster; Sam Boston, gambler, owner, former fagin, fence, commission better [*sic*]; his wife, a pickpocket; Crazy Jake, gun (pickpocket); Little Natie (not the one from Broome St.), gun, right family name is Lubin being related to Lubin the Philadelphia Moving Film Company; Jennie Morris, alias Jennie the Factory, former prostitute and at present disorderly house owner, her mack is Henry Morris, owner 249 Broome Street; Tillie Finkelstein, gun-mol [*sic*] from Bessie London's School, married to Candy Kid Phil, do not know his family name."

Seltzer "Jewish champagne," some called it, and if seltzer were merely carbonated water, blessed with all the bubbles and none of the taste of champagne, its drinkers still got a kick from it. Seltzer was also *grepsvasser*, for when its consumers had loaded up on heavy, fat-laden eastern European food, a glass of seltzer would quickly produce a relieving *greps,* or belch.

The beverage attained prominence not least because of the kosher stricture prohibiting consumption of milk with meat. Although it could be found in food stores, it was more usually supplied by delivery men who carted the familiar bottles (for some reason, the blue ones were rated highest) around Jewish neighborhoods by horse and wagon. At the candy store, it was called "two-cents-plain," a reference to its price in those preinflation days. Seltzer also gained importance as a main ingredient in the egg cream, along with chocolate syrup and milk (there were no eggs in an egg cream, though some liked to think they were incorporated in the syrup). The limousine of soft drinks, the egg cream was usually consumed at the candystore counter.

Shadkhn In 1900 a Hester Street matchmaker, or *shadkhn,* told the *New York Tribune,* "I would starve to death in a month if I depended on matchmaking for a living. Once I lived on the fat of the land, and most of the marriageable young men and women in the quarter depended on me to make them happy for life. Now they believe in love and all that rot. . . . The love which they have learned to put so much faith in dribbles out in trips to Coney and walks around the parks before marriage. In a month or so they are figuring out ways of getting rid of each other."

Born, it is said, of Talmudic teaching, the position of *shadkhn* was vastly different in the New World and in the Old, and though the ritual match continued to be part of their work, the *shadkhn*s were as likely to perform as letter writers, notaries, and interpreters as they were to make marriage matches. Still, there was work among the most recent immigrants or for the children of the most traditional parents. Earning a fee ranging from five to ten percent of the bride's dowry (or a prearranged sum in the case of a particularly poor—or particularly beautiful—woman), the *shadkhn* swore

Relics: a 1981 advertisement for a *shadkhn,* and a contemporary seltzer bottle

by his abilities. One New York practitioner, Louis Rubin, claimed to have made more than seven thousand matches ("very few of them cut-rate"); others advertised with such slogans as "Every match is a catch, after a year it becomes clear," or "It is never too late to marry or die."

Shlepper The literal meaning of *shlepn* is "to drag, to pull"; in practice, it is the root of so wide a variety of usages that it almost becomes like the Eskimo vocabulary for "snow"—it has so many meanings because there was an awful lot of *shlepping* in Yiddish-American life. A *shlepper* was a drifter, a bum, someone who *shlepped* only his own tired bones. But it also, in the garment industry, came to mean the men who toted bundles of material from jobber to sweatshop and bundles of finished clothing from sweatshop to wholesaler (today this form of *shlepping* is done with racks pushed through the heavy traffic of Seventh Avenue). On Canal Street the *shleppers* were barkers, men who pulled customers in from street to store. And in the restaurant business, waiters were called *shleppers* because of their tray-bearing virtuosity.

Garment *shlepper*, 1910

Sholem Aleichem (1859–1916) Born Sholem Rabinowitz in the Ukraine, correspondent of Tolstoy and Chekhov, renowned today more for inspiring a musical play featuring a robust Jewish milkman than for his own stories and plays, Sholem Aleichem (the name means "Peace be with you") was perhaps the greatest writer to use Yiddish as his artistic medium. Celebrated throughout the Yiddish-speaking world—and several other quarters besides—he emigrated to New York in 1906, appearing with Mark Twain on a platform at the Educational Alliance shortly after his arrival. The recognition he received that night was possibly the high point of his years in New York. Introduced as "the Jewish Mark Twain," Sholem Aleichem listened as Twain rejoined, "I am the American Sholem Aleichem."

In America, the esteem of the masses remained Sholem Aleichem's, as his stories and plays, drawn from the everyday life of street and *shtetl*, both New World and Old, were revered everywhere. Still, he expected financial reward that never came to him, and he was unprepared for the critical assaults of radicals who thought his work sentimental and inconsequential. Dismayed, he soon went back to Europe, finally returning to New York in 1914.

The great source of Sholem Aleichem's material was his open door—which he advertised in Yiddish newspapers—inviting in anyone who cared to speak with him. His daughter, Marie Waife-Goldberg, wrote that some of his visitors were bores, "but others had information to offer, what America was like, how people lived here, and the stories of their own experience in the land of Columbus. My father absorbed it all in amazement."

Sholem Aleichem's most successful works were the play *It's Hard to Be a Jew*,

Sholem Aleichem

which is still occasionally revived, and the stories based on the invented *shtetls* of Kasrilevka and Anatevka, towns he peopled with such as Tevye the milkman and his sharp-tongued wife, his five marriageable daughters, and an unceasing supply of problems. These became the basis for *Fiddler on the Roof*, which ran a then-record eight years on Broadway (and did remarkably well in such languages as Finnish and Japanese, too) nearly half a century after Sholem Aleichem's death. His will, enjoining his heirs to read his stories on the date of his death in any language they wish, is still complied with by his grandchildren, who invite a cross-section of Jewish life to their apartments to hear his stories—and the will itself—read by leading Yiddish performers. The reading is always followed—again as specified by the writer himself—by the serving of tea and cookies.

Shul In Europe, each *shtetl* had a rabbi and a *shul;* in the New World, emigrants from each *shtetl* would maintain their synagogues on the same basis as they did the *landsmanshaftn*, the social groups rooted in the members' towns of origin. As a result, the streets of most Yiddish-speaking communities in America had a *shul* on every block, storefront gathering places for the small congregations who had not let the voyage across the ocean buffet their faith too greatly. Too, while the tugs of socialism and assimilation may have diminished strict observance, the fact of nationalism was an effective lever in the maintenance of a religious community.

So the *shuls* persisted, both as anchors of a way of life, and as the cornerstones of that substantial part of the community that remained Orthodox in belief and in practice. There was, of course, no common the-ology in the Yiddish-speaking neighborhoods; the effort in the late 1880s to establish unanimity by importing a "Chief Rabbi," Jacob Joseph of Vilna, was an abject failure. Different congregations went their different ways, some sticking assiduously to the religious intent of the synagogue, others expanding the definition of the synagogue to become social organizations as well. Later, a phenomenon called "the mushroom synagogue" began to appear in the neighborhoods to which the immigrants' children had moved. These were *shuls* that would pop up each September in temporary quarters simply to accommodate Jews who had strayed from regular attendance but needed a synagogue to go to for the High Holidays.

Shund Literally, *shund* means "trash," and thus was the term contemptuously applied to those Yiddish theater productions that pandered to the lowest common denominator, the Yiddish John Q. Public known as Moishe. The *shund* plays put on for the

The flag proclaims "Long live *shund*"; the caption read, "Be merry, *shund* players, you work for the dollar as art takes a walk." From *Der Groyser Kibitzer*

masses earned the contempt of the intelligentsia, but were often as not the means by which even the most august theatrical companies stayed in business. They featured a bastard Yiddish, peppered with English street slang, and their plots were predicated on the most egregious coincidences, the most hackneyed situations, the playwrights could dream up. If there was one characteristic *shund* plot, it was the one that featured the second-act curtain falling immediately after the horrified old mother says of her beautiful, unwed daughter: *"Oy, zi shvangert"* —"She's pregnant!"

Shvitz On the Lower East Side, where filth and crowding were the rule, the bathhouse became a neighborhood institution. Certain cultural factors helped it along, too; "social" bathing, particularly on Friday, just before the Sabbath, is such a firmly rooted Jewish custom that in Spain, during the Inquisition, those who secretly pursued their Judaism were often found out when

caught in their Friday ablutions. Of course, women have always been required to attend the ritual bath, and even men do so on certain occasions. But the Russian *shvitzbod*—literally, "sweat bath"—was born of the customs of the Old World, combined with the needs of the New (in 1897 only eight percent of Lower East Side homes had baths).

The *shvitz* featured a bed of hot coals repeatedly doused with cold water, creating a haze of steam that turned complexions red and instilled, it was said, a feeling of well-being and relaxation (especially after one emerged from the bath for a cold shower). Men would play cards and maybe enjoy a bite of herring as the steam curled around them; some would submit to the

The big *shvitz*— Libby's Hotel and Baths, under construction at Delancey and Chrystie Streets, 1924

flagellations of attendants wielding bundled birch leaves in an approximation of a massage. Women were allowed their *shvitz*es, too—Molly Picon recalled going to the Ludlow Baths on Mondays and Wednesdays, ladies' nights. Moses Rischin reports that in 1880, only one or two of New York's twenty-two bathhouses were Jewish, but by 1897 more than half the city's sixty-two *shvitzbeder*—many of them in tenement flats converted from dwelling places, some in large, grand quarters—catered to the Yiddish immigrants. The *shvitz* still lives on in its modern incarnation as the sauna, but the classical version remains only in a few reliquaries, where old Jewish men and their muscular but aging Ukrainian attendants are steaming out of Jewish life like the last chuffing locomotives that ran north to the mountains.

Singer, Isaac Bashevis (1904–   ) Born to a rabbinical family in Poland, the younger brother of the novelist I. J. Singer became not only the most widely read Yiddish writer in the world, but also the winner of the Nobel Prize for literature in 1978. Singer was a journalist in Warsaw before he came to New York in 1935 and began to contribute to the *Forward* (for which he still writes) on the recommendation of his brother. He wrote occasional book reviews and human interest stories for the paper until 1944, when he joined the staff.

Singer's best-known works include *The Family Moskat, Satan in Goray,* and the celebrated short story "Gimpel the Fool," which appeared in English translated by Saul Bellow. Although Singer's stories, concerned with Jewish life in Poland and, of late, New York, appear with regularity in *The New Yorker,* they still make their initial appearance in the *Forward,* in the language in which he continues to write. Of that language, he said in 1963 in an interview in *Commentary,* "You don't feel very happy about writing in a language when you know it dies from day to day. . . . The only thing is, I don't have this feeling when I write. . . . In my case, writing Yiddish and thinking about the readers would really destroy the writer completely."

His brother, **Israel Joshua Singer** (1893–1944), was "discovered" for American readers in 1923 when Abraham Cahan

**I. B. Singer
(with the King of Sweden)
in Stockholm, 1978**

of the *Forward* happened upon the title story of *Pearls*, Singer's first collection of stories, published in Warsaw. Cahan hired Singer as the *Forward*'s Polish correspondent and continued to publish his work after Singer emigrated to the United States in 1933. The elder Singer's novels—sweeping, sagalike works of great breadth and ambition—included *Yoshe Kalb*, *The Family Carnovsky*, and the classic *The Brothers Ashkenazi;* all were adapted for the stage as well, and became integral parts of the Yiddish theater repertory.

Skulnik, Menashe (1892–1970) His tiny, five-foot four-inch body topped by a tight,

too-small, narrow-brimmed hat, Menashe Skulnik was a natural comedian in both Yiddish vaudeville and theater, where he spent most of his life, and on Broadway, where he became a star at sixty years of age. He was a sentimental clown who thought "the best laugh is when it comes with a tear," and he milked his audiences for both on Second Avenue, on Broadway (where he starred in Odets's *The Flowering Peach*), and on radio (he was the voice of Uncle David in "The Rise of the Goldbergs" for twenty-nine years). Skulnik's greatest theatrical successes came in those shows in which the script, he said, would be filled with lines for the other actors, but

Advertisement for 1937 Broadway production of I. J. Singer's *The Brothers Ashkenazi*

which merely said "Menashe enters" for him, followed by enough blank pages to accommodate his extemporizing.

Smith, Charles (18??–1914) "Silver Dollar" Smith was a politician, saloonkeeper, and cultural figure on the Lower East Side. A Republican assemblyman who switched to the Democrats in 1892 because, he said, of his opposition to the immigration curbs propounded by Republicans in Congress, Smith fit well with Tammany. Abraham Cahan, in his memoirs, recalled encountering Smith "making a campaign speech from the rear of a wagon parked diagonally across from his saloon. After talking for about five minutes, he growled, 'Boys, you know I deliver a better speech in my place than out here in the street. . . . ' The entire crowd followed him into his saloon. He set up drinks for everybody—on the house! That was the kind of speech he made."

Smith's bar, on Essex Street near Grand, opposite the Essex Market Courthouse, was decorated with a thousand silver dollars embedded in the floor, five hundred more on a chandelier, and still more fashioned into a crescent and star behind the bar. Smith was an unlikely figure, all the more so when one considers that his given name was, according to Irving Howe, either Charles Solomon or Solomon Finkelstein.

Socialism "To this hard-working people," wrote the historian David A. Shannon, "Socialism was more than just a political movement: it was a way of life. In some neighborhoods one grew up to be a Socialist, a reader of Abraham Cahan's *Jewish Daily Forward* . . . , and a member of one of the needle trade unions just as naturally as in some other parts of the country one grew up to be a Republican and a reader of the *Saturday Evening Post*."

The Jews of the Lower East Side came by their socialism naturally: if the revolutionary ferment that bubbled throughout Europe in the nineteenth century were to surface anywhere, it would be in the lands under the iron control of the czars; if it were to find sympathetic expression among any of the people who felt the czarist oppression, it would be among the Jews.

Menashe Skulnik

When they arrived in the world of the tenements and sweatshops, it was inevitable that the immigrants would rally around a political strategy, a way of thinking, that held the promise of a brighter future.

The labor unions, of course, were the primary vehicles of Socialist education and organization in the Yiddish-speaking community. As early in the settlement of the Lower East Side as 1887, two Jewish branches of the Socialist Labor Party were formed, and out of these came the men and women who would organize the garment industry. Ten years later, in Europe, the Jewish Workers' Union of Russia, Lithuania, and Poland—known as the Bund—

was formed, further underscoring the possibility of creating a radical system of belief that was compatible with Yiddish culture. At the turn of the century, Socialist debate raged throughout the East Side among the people Hutchins Hapgood identified as "the most educated, forcible and talented personalities of the quarter." Even the least skilled workers, Hapgood added, possessed "a certain familiarity with economic ideas."

And thus in this fertile ground, with the eloquent prompting of men like Abraham Cahan, Morris Hillquit, and Meyer London, did socialism, and scores of Socialist institutions—reading clubs, debate societies, day schools, even

Labor Day Parade in Washington Square, 1912

New York Socialist rally, 1916

synagogues—take root. Under the leadership of segments of the radical press and the Labor Zionists, socialism was made compatible with Jewish nationalism. Behind the flag carried by the shirtwaist makers, it brought historic victories in the factories and the sweatshops. By 1917, when Hillquit received twenty-two percent of the citywide vote in the mayoral election, New York Socialists—their leaders immigrant Jews, their masses largely composed of the same—sent ten Socialist assemblymen to Albany, seven Socialist aldermen to City Hall.

Eventually, with the unions organized, FDR at the head of the Democratic Party, and a marked increase in prosperity among the immigrants' children, socialism's hold would loosen. But in its time, a people raised in a messianic faith waited in enormous numbers for a savior to come cloaked in red, and among them ideology probably counted less than passion and instinct. At a lengthy meeting of shirtwaist workers in 1909 that became a tactical debate, teenaged worker Clara Lemlich took the platform and said, "I have listened to all the speakers. I would not have further patience for talk, as I am one of those who feels and suffers from the things pictured. I move that we go on a general strike!" Benjamin Feigenbaum, the antireligious Socialist who was chairing the meeting, asked the screaming crowd, "Do you mean faith? Will you take the old Jewish oath?" According to an account published in *McClure's Magazine*, "Thousands of right hands were held up and the whole audience repeated in Yiddish, 'If I turn traitor to the cause I now pledge, may this hand wither from the arm I now raise.' "

Steerage For all but a few of the almost thirteen million immigrants of all ethnic backgrounds who came to the United States between 1900 and 1914, as well as for the millions who arrived in the nineteenth century, steerage was their *Mayflower*. Steerage was the area below a vessel's decks, originally so named because it was near the steering apparatus at the stern, where the pitching and tossing of the ship were more keenly felt than in the relative equilibrium of amidships.

Steerage was also the bread and butter of the steamship companies, which provided little of either, or of other food or accommodation, for the human "freight," as it was called in the trade. For thirty-four dollars, an immigrant purchased the right to sleep in a cot stacked below one and above another (each passenger had a berth measuring 2' 6" by 6' 2"), separated from family (steerage was divided into male and female sections), subsisting on fetid rations if the immigrant did not honor the kosher laws, or whatever amount of black bread and herring could be brought on board if he did. Rarely were steerage quarters washed, except near voyage's end, when the ship had to pass inspection in the port. "Neighborliness, obedience, respect and status were valueless among the masses that struggled for space on the way," wrote Oscar Handlin. All the while, up above, a lordly class in fancy dress enjoyed the greatest luxury.

Many immigrants knew conditions varied according to the steamship lines, as did the length of the trip—anywhere from twelve to eighteen days. Too many, though, judged the seaworthiness and the stability of a liner by the number of smokestacks she carried, and many ships sported up to five stacks, at least two of them dummies, to lure immigrants. The first vessels to boast somewhat improved conditions were the German ones, which provided a little more space and even kosher kitchens; the food may have been gruel, but at least the Orthodox could eat it. Worst of all the ships may have been the *Staatendam*, on which steerage passengers had to steal drinking water from second class at night if they were to drink at all.

Given the horrors of the passage, it is somewhat surprising to learn that, because of the nature of the voyage if not its substance, many immigrants bore fond thoughts of the ships they traveled on. They realized that this trial was a necessary prelude to arrival in the land of their hopes, and they would ever

A *schiffscarte* for steerage passage; and, finally above decks, immigrants on the ferry to Manhattan from Ellis Island

remain grateful for the opportunity of passage. Abraham Cahan remembered with a certain warmth at least one aspect of his time aboard the *British Queen* in 1882, sailing from Liverpool to New York: on one of the steerage passengers' daily trips to the open decks, "as the wonderful colors sank with the sun, our hearts would fill with a terrible longing for home. Then we would draw together and sing our Russian folk songs filled with nostalgia and yearning." The Norwegians, the Swedes, and the few English aboard listened to Cahan and his fellow Russians singing, and then each group, in turn, sang their songs as the Russians listened. The horrible voyage, they all knew, would end.

Steffens, Lincoln (1866–1936) Steffens was the star reporter of his day, itself a long and critical one in the history of American journalism. Entranced by the social and cultural ferment of the ghetto, which was located near Newspaper Row on Nassau Street where most of the city's leading dailies were published, Steffens threw himself, and the papers he worked for, into the life of the Lower East Side. He met Abraham Cahan, whose novel *Yekl, A Tale of the Ghetto* he admired, and persuaded him first to write for the *New York Evening Post*, where Steffens was an editor, and later to join him on the staff of the *Commercial Advertiser*.

Perhaps Steffens's greatest contributions to Yiddish-American life were the journalistic training he gave Cahan, and the encouragement he gave gentile reporters such as Hutchins Hapgood and Jacob Riis in their own explorations of Lower East Side life. Steffens is best remembered today for his central role in the "muckraking" school of American journalism, but he later remembered his own life at the turn of the century in different terms: "At that time," he wrote, "I was almost a Jew. I had become as infatuated with the Ghetto as eastern boys were with the wilds of the west, and. nailed a mezuzah to my office door."

Street Gangs The street gang was, and is, an urban social phenomenon that springs up whenever people from more stable, less industrialized societies find themselves crowded into the alien precincts of the city slum. On the Lower East Side, in the North End of Boston, around Detroit's Hastings Street—in every American city with an immigrant ghetto—these gangs were the block associations, as it were, of immigrant youths. Although the breeding grounds from which professional gangsters would develop, the gangs themselves were not necessarily criminal. In fact gang morals had real, if misplaced, force. A Chrystie Street boy would very carefully venture onto Forsyth Street, and boys from neither of those sectors of the Jewish zone dared stray onto the Italian blocks west of the Bowery. Eric Hoffer wrote, "The ghetto was a fortress as much as it was a prison."

One East Sider classified gangs into three different categories, the three similar only in the youth of their members and their universal use of the corner candy store as clubhouse, shrine, and stage (the memoirs of entertainers who emerged from the ghetto are replete with tales of trying out routines on captive audiences enjoying egg creams at candy-store soda fountains). First there was the social gang, very sports-minded, organized around playing stickball or stoopball. Then there was the gang that occupied a particular corner each evening, flirting with girls and otherwise annoying passersby. Finally there was the tough gang, the troublemakers who took money from strange kids, spent idle hours gambling, and were antisocial in scores of other ways. Members of such a gang ranged in age from six to about twenty, hung out in poolrooms and outside saloons, and supported themselves through picking pockets. The booty was divided among members, with the older boys, Faginlike, teaching the tricks of the trade to the younger through an apprentice system that would leave the latter with only a pittance—but also with a hierarchy to move up as the seniors moved on to large-scale criminality. Such passage wasn't inevitable, though; Eddie Cantor spent much of his boyhood in "Pork-Faced Sam's" gang, which specialized in selling back to shopkeepers goods just stolen from them, and working as scabs during strikes. Cantor knew enough to give it up.

Stuss This variant of the casino game of faro was the drug of gambling Jews in the Yiddish-speaking ghettos. It was cheap to

East Side crapshooters, 1910

3512

establish a *stuss* house, for the game merely required a table on which one could paint cards representing the thirteen denominations that make up one suit of the deck. Players put their money on the cards of their choice and waited for the dealer to turn up a card from the deck in front of him. Those who bet on the first card turned over lost, those who bet on the second won. It was as straightforward a way to risk money as it sounds, except, inevitably, when the operators managed to cut their risks by cheating.

The prevalence of the *stuss* houses, which often had the protection of corrupt police, drew the attention of the New York Kehillah, whose investigators became so adept at infiltrating East Side gambling that they could tell the police of a new *stuss* house as it was being readied for opening by carpenters and painters.

Sweatshops "To begin with," Sholem Aleichem's Berl-Isaac told his fellow villagers in Kasrilevka after returning from a trip to America, "the country itself, a land flowing with milk and honey! People make plenty of money; you dig into money with both hands, you pick up gold by the shovelful! And as for 'business,' as they call it in

New York sweatshop, 1908

America, there is so much of it that it just makes your head spin. You want a factory—so you have a factory; you want to, you push a pushcart; and if you don't, you peddle or go to work in a shop—it's a free country! You may starve or drop to death of hunger right in the street—there's nothing to prevent you, nobody will object."

Berl-Isaac was right about two things: you could go to work in a shop—a sweatshop—or you could starve to death in the street. Sometimes, you could do both in this most brutal arena of labor, the product of a step-by-step manufacturing process that presaged the assembly line. German-Jewish cloth merchants would assign bolts of fabric to individual contractors, who would in turn hire unskilled and semi-skilled immigrants to convert the cloth into garments. Workers—many of them women and children—would buy their own thread, cutting knives, and needles (usually from the contractor, at a five hundred percent markup), and be paid for each piece they produced. Being a "sweater"—the name for the contractors—was a low-investment business; often as not, the shop was a tenement flat, and the labor force was eminently available and exploitable.

In 1900 more than 150,000 Jews were employed in the Lower East Side garment trade. They worked at jobs that required speed, deftness, and a capacity for dull, monotonous repetition of the same task: one worker cut, one stitched, the next made buttonholes. Labor began at daybreak, continued beyond the dinner hour, and persisted into the night, workers taking their pieces home in hope of extracting a further handful of change from their toil—at, according to Jacob Riis describing boys' jackets, eight cents for sewing, three for

ironing, five for finishing. Half of a cloakmaker's life was said to be spent looking for work, the other half trying desperately to manage a living from it. Complaint was futile—the contractors (who usually earned double what their most skilled worker made) would blame the suppliers, and the workers never knew who the suppliers were.

The thirteen thousand living quarters in New York licensed for sweating in 1911 were dank, crowded, stiflingly uncomfortable places, breeding grounds for tuberculosis; the wages—in 1900 a child working in a sweatshop averaged $2.94 a week—a contributor to malnutrition. Eventually the sweatshops gave way to factories, and factories bred union organizing, and that in turn led to an easing of the hardships of the garment workers. But images preserved by those who wrote of sweatshop life remain enduring reminders of this cruelest form of labor. Riis described the scene in one tenement sweatshop occupied by five men, one woman, two young girls, and a boy: "The floor is littered ankle-deep with half-sewn garments. In the alcove, on a couch of many dozens of 'pants' ready for the finisher, a bare-legged baby with pinched face is asleep. A fence of piled-up clothing keeps him from rolling off on the floor. The faces, hands, and arms to the elbows of everyone in the room are black with the color of the cloth on which they are working. The boy and the woman alone look up at our entrance. The girls shoot sidelong glances, but at a warning look from the man with the bundle they tread their machines more energetically than ever. . . . [The shop] turns out one hundred and twenty "knee-pants' a week, for which the manufacturer pays seventy cents a dozen."

Tenements In 1879 the "dumbbell" tenement was introduced, a six- or seven-story structure pinched in the middle to create airshafts; within years such buildings covered the Lower East Side and the other poor neighborhoods of New York. Four apartments occupied each floor of the building, light and air entering directly into only one room in each flat. Maurice Hindus wrote, "You couldn't get to love a tenement flat; it was not home. We never stayed long enough in one flat anyway. That was the way it was in the big city. People moved from house to house, from one neighborhood to another, never missing the old place, glad perhaps never to have to see it again." By the end of the 1880s a million New Yorkers, most of them immigrants, lived in more than thirty thousand tenement buildings that the *New York Times* would some years later call "the filthiest places in the western continent."

Large families crowded into the small rooms, escaping to the streets and roofs for fresh air. Mothers lowered lunches and schoolbooks to their children in an "elevator"—a box raised and lowered on a long rope. The private toilet was unknown, queues forming outside the common bathroom on each floor—or, in the worst of the tenements, in the lot behind the building. Baths didn't exist at all, tenement residents relying on public baths scattered through the neighborhood or a tub in the kitchen.

In 1887 Dr. Felix Adler, son of the rabbi of Temple Emanu-El and himself the founder of the Ethical Culture Society, started the Tenement House Building Company, erecting six model tenements on Cherry Street. Other reformers also made

their contribution to improving housing on the Lower East Side, and new laws enacted in 1901 and periodically thereafter ensured that every tenement room had a window, even if only on an airshaft, and every building at least one indoor toilet.

The one positive contribution of the tenements was the vocabulary native to them: such resident ladies as the *dannstairske*, the *oppstairske*, and the *nextdoorke*. All these women were united not only by a common address, but also by a shared distrust of the *lendler*, or landlord, the man who came in person to collect his rents of nine or ten dollars a month.

Thomashevsky, Boris (1868–1939) This vain, flamboyant man, who called himself "America's Darling" and was known throughout the Yiddish theater community for unrelenting amorous advances toward

Boris Thomashevsky, 1928

any young woman who came within reach, symbolized both the best and the worst of the Yiddish theater. Not a notably great actor, he excelled in melodrama, and what was not melodrama he made into melodrama. He was actor, author, and impresario, outrageous in the first capacity, prolific in the second (he wrote more than one hundred plays), and distinguished in the third. Although often associated with the basest *shund* theater, he produced plays by such notable writers as Jacob Gordin and Ossip Dymov, and brought to the American Yiddish stage such actors as Ben-Ami and Schildkraut. When he had his own theater on Second Avenue, Thomashevsky had cigarettes embossed with his name sold in the lobby. Michael Tilson-Thomas, the contemporary conductor, is Thomashevsky's grandson.

Tin Pan Alley The cacophony of pianos and singers and song pluggers and agents that created such a din along New York's Twenty-eighth Street (and gave it, courtesy of the journalist and songwriter Monroe Rosenfeld, its descriptive name) was, in a number of ways, conspicuously Jewish. George Gershwin, Al Jolson, Eddie Cantor, and Harold Arlen all were sons of cantors; Irving Berlin, Vernon Duke, and others were immigrants, and scores more the sons of immigrants. Together, these men forged an invisible bond between Tin Pan Alley and Second Avenue. Although they didn't write or perform Yiddish songs as such, they certainly introduced eastern European inflections into American popular music. They and others also rode a crest of popular dialect-songs early in the century; on one day Irving Berlin could write a "Marie from Sunny Italy," on the next a "Goodbye, Becky Cohen." Al Dubin could write

the lyrics for "My Yiddisha Butterfly" ("Flutter, flutter, flutter / 'round your Abie Perlmutter / Oi, my Yiddisha Butterfly! / Ask your Fadder and your Mudder / If they want a clothing cutter / in the fam'ly by and by"), Wolfie Gilbert those for "Waiting for the Robert E. Lee" (forty years later Gilbert wrote his friend Harry Golden,"Harry, please let me know what is a levee"). There was little that was specifically Jewish about the work of these men, but ethnicity was marketable in music, and they had the talent to exploit this. Less appealing were the works of those who could produce such blatantly anti-Semitic songs as "The Sheeny Under-taker."

Concurrent with the burgeoning of Jewish influence— positive and nega-tive—in the popular song industry was the Yiddish-American musical tradition de-veloping in Yiddish theaters and vaudeville houses. Ronald Sanders considered Yiddish popular songs "pastiches," noting that "pastiche is the gift of peoples who live in culturally ambivalent situa-tions." This ambivalence em-braced everything from the lightheartedness of Sholem Secunda's "Bei Mir Bist Du Schon" to the classic "Eli, Eli," a heartrending lament of the miseries of the Jews in czarist Russia, a song heard for years at virtually every East Side wedding and bar

mitzvah, a reminder of sorrow at times of joy.

Tracy, Arthur (1903–   ) A Russian-born troubador who gained fame in the 1930s, Arthur Tracy began singing in a synagogue choir and made his way into the Yiddish theater as a teenager through the assistance of Paul Muni's mother (Tracy earned $2.50 a week for his first job, at Philadelphia's Girard Avenue Theater). At seventeen he was singing on Atlantic City's Boardwalk; soon, Mike Thoma-shevsky, brother of actor Boris, heard him on the vaudeville circuit and lured him to Second Avenue to ap-pear in the show *The Bar Mitzvah*. Tracy remained a popu-lar figure in Yid-dish theater and vaudeville for years, attaining success in the wider culture with his recording of "Marta," which sold literally millions of cop-ies, and on the CBS radio network. He sang in a variety of lan-guages, always equipped with an ac-cordion and dressed in a costume that fit his billing as "The Street Singer." In the Steve Martin film *Pennies from Heaven*, it is Tracy's ver-sion of the title song that is heard on the soundtrack.

Triangle Fire On Saturday after-noon, March 25, 1911, fire enveloped the Triangle Shirtwaist Company, which occupied the top three floors

Arthur Tracy, 1931

of the ten-story Asch Building near Washington Square. Although the fire depart-department was able to extinguish the blaze within half an hour, in those thirty horrible minutes 146 workers, most of them young Jewish and Italian girls, lost their lives. It was the most traumatic incident in New York's industrial history, and it inflicted grief and rage on the entire Lower East Side.

The conditions that led to the fire were dreadful: doors that should have opened onto a staircase were locked (to prevent pilferage, the company's owners later said); other doors that should have opened outward opened inward instead and were sealed shut by the weight of bodies straining to escape. No fire drills had ever been held, and many of the women who died leaped in panic through broken windows.

It was a galvanic moment in labor history, as the entire community—indeed, virtually the entire city of New York—rushed to stand by the workers in the shirtwaist industry. Rallies and parades and protest meetings enlisted wide support, but it was probably Rose Schneiderman's classic speech to an audience of uptown women at the Metropolitan Opera House that best expressed the sentiment of the Lower East Side, especially when she said, "I would be a traitor to these burned bodies if I came to talk of fellowship." The tragedy of the Triangle Fire strengthened the garment unions and brought about reforms in various industrial laws. But to the owners of the company, Max Blanck and Isaac Harris, who sold their

Triangle blouses wholesale for $1.50 each, the terrible story ended in acquittal on all counts of building code violations and thus the release of insurance monies to cover their losses.

Tsimes Revolt In the early 1880s, newly arrived Jewish immigrants were often taken to the Ward's Island Refuge run by the less-than-charitable Hebrew Emigrant Aid Society. Those who found themselves thus "sheltered" were expected to obey all commands without complaint (there was, in any event, no machinery to accommodate complaint). The food, questionable at best, was often filthy or laden with worms; occasionally, however, on holidays or other special occasions, the HEAS workers would serve *tsimes*, a sort of carrot and potato pudding. When one waiter refused to ladle out a portion to an

Aftermath of the Triangle Fire

importunate immigrant, a brawl resulted, ending with the arrival of club-swinging police from the Harlem precinct. The so-called Tsimes Revolt led to an investigation, reforms, and a shake-up in the management of the refuge, which closed for good in 1883.

Tucker, Sophie (1884–1966) The "last of the red hot mamas" was an attractive, *zaftig* singer with a powerful and throaty voice that mesmerized two generations of vaudeville fans. "I was born on the road," she wrote in her autobiography. "Not on the Orpheum, the Pantages, Keith, or any of the other circuits I've travelled on since. The road I mean is the long, rutted track that leads away from Russia across Poland to the Baltic." Her family arrived in Bos-

ton, then moved to Hartford, and in 1906 Sophie started her career at the Cafe Monopol. By 1915 she was one of the very top draws on the vaudeville circuit, and two songs became her trademarks: "Some of These Days," and "My Yiddisha Mama." The latter was a frankly sentimental tune that was guaranteed to turn an audience—whether gentile or Jewish—hopelessly weepy.

Tummler A *tummler* is one who makes noises, fun noises, a *tuml*—a joyous tumult, you might say. But the *tummler*, whatever he was in the old country, underwent a sea change (actually, a mountain change) when the species arrived on these shores. The *tummler* was known in America as the paid court jester/social director in the Catskills

Sophie Tucker and her band, 1918

hotel, the fellow who kept the customers laughing with his jokes and his impromptu, one-man skits in the dining room, in the lobby, on the porch.

In her memoirs, Jennie Grossinger recalled that Grossinger's in its earliest days could not afford to hire a *tummler*. But a waiter named Benny Kolodny turned out to be a natural, showing the lengths he would go to—for however feeble a laugh—when he took a live hen into the dining room and pulled two eggs from her backside, giving them to a diner who had insisted on fresh eggs. Another Grossinger retainer, chief bellboy Benny Rheingold, would have a stooge say, "Benny, give me a sentence with the word envy in it." Rheingold would reply, more times than regular guests cared to remember, "I vent to a vedding last night, envy had fish, envy had *kreplach*, envy had chicken, envy had strudel."

The art would later have more polished practitioners, ranging from Danny Kaye to a saxophone player named Sid Caesar. But perhaps the most polished of the *tummler*s was Moss Hart, later the immensely successful director and playwright colleague of George S. Kaufman. In his autobiography, *Act One*, Hart wrote a dirge about the life of a *tummler*: "Social directing provided me with a lifelong disdain and a lasting horror of people in the mass seeking pleasure and release in packaged doses. Perhaps the real triumph of these summers was the fact that I survived them at all; not so much in terms of emerging with whatever creative faculties I possess unimpaired, but in the sense that my physical constitution withstood the strain, for at the end of each camp season I was always fifteen to twenty pounds lighter and my outlook that much more heavily misanthropic."

Danny Kaye, still "tummling"

U

United Hebrew Trades

Founded in 1887 on the model of the United German Trades—which helped their fledgling Jewish counterpart with a ten-dollar donation, the UHT's first—the UHT was the outgrowth of the ethnically based organizing conducted at the time by the Socialist Labor Party. Morris Hillquit, who led the UHT in its primary struggle to organize the garment trades, employed Yiddish-language appeals predicated on Socialist doctrine. The UHT was an umbrella organization never intended to have a worker membership of its own, but rather to be the instigating force in the creation of other, independent unions. The group organized three unions in the needle trades within its first year, and also met success in fostering Jewish locals in the printing and bakery industries. The Hebrew Actors Union was among its earliest affiliates. Eventually, the UHT would be triumphant throughout the garment industry, numbering nearly a quarter of a million members in its various branches by World War I.

Uptown Jews

The conflict between the established German Jews—by and large living in fine comfort "uptown"—and the immigrant eastern European Jews colored almost every aspect of the American Jewish community's life. On the one hand, the uptown *Yahudim* were, over the years, generous—if condescending—in their charitable support of their downtown cousins; on the other, the resentment of the downtowners for the arrogance of the assimilated uptowners was pervasive. When Rabbi Isaac Mayer Wise, drawing the distinction be-

The very uptown Levy family, 1904

tween his Americanized community and the teeming masses downtown, intoned, "We are Israelites, they are Jews," not a few downtowners replied, "We are Jews, they are *goyim*."

The differences between the two groups were numerous. Uptown Jews were merchants, bankers, businessmen; downtown Jews were workers. Uptown Jews belonged to Reform temples; downtown Jews were, if religious, Orthodox, and if not, likely to be Socialist. Uptown Jews regarded German culture as the hallmark of civilized society; downtown Jews spoke Yiddish, a language thought barbarous and vulgar by the uptowners. Uptown Jews controlled the garment industry and detested unionism; downtown Jews labored in their shops and struggled mightily to organize them. Uptown Jews were Americanized and were able to dress and live in fine American style; downtown Jews were shabby, unbarbered, housed in tenements.

The association, all things considered, was not propitious.

The acrimony between the two groups—the one often dispensing its charity to avoid embarrassment in gentile culture, the other accepting it with suspicion and distrust—spawned a vitriolic literature in press and pulpit as each side deprecated the other. The uptown *Hebrew Standard* said, "The thoroughly acclimated German Jew . . . is closer to the Christian sentiment around him than to the Judaism of these miserable darkened Hebrews." Downtown, the Socialist *Die Tsukunft*, writing of uptown efforts to "further religion and morality" on the Lower East Side, sniped, "Don't they know that a Hester Street teamster is a scholar and savant and an utter saint compared to the president of a Fifth Avenue Temple?"

Even the pattern of uptown charity did not begin promisingly. At first, prominent German Jews attempted to stop the flow of Russian immigration; in Boston, a shipload of immigrants was turned back through the offices of that city's established Jewish community. But when those efforts failed, the thrust of uptown activities changed, in direction if not in spirit. Realizing the abominable anti-Semitism of the czarist regime, so virulent that even wealthy, manicured German Jews in America could not

An uptown wedding, c. 1910

The caption on this newspaper cartoon read, in part, "I don't recognize him, my frent,/ I ain't dot kind of Shoo;/ I own a shtore, un' bay my rent,/ Und make it bay me, too." The accent was grossly inaccurate, even if the portrayal of the sentiments was not.

enter Russia on business, the uptown community sought to make Americans of the new immigrants.

It was a fitful effort for years. The Hebrew Emigrant Aid Society ran an abominable shelter on Ward's Island, by some accounts as cruel as the streets outside Castle Garden. Steadfast in attempts to "Americanize," German-Jewish benefactors for more than a decade forbade Yiddish in the halls of the Educational Alliance, and kosher food was not served at the Clara de Hirsch Home for Girls until 1913. For years, no doctor of Yiddish-speaking heritage was on the staff of Mt. Sinai Hospital. There were exceptions to the condescension that emanated from uptown—people like Jacob Schiff, Alice and Irene Lew-

isohn (founders of the Neighborhood Playhouse), Lillian Wald, and Rabbi Judah Magnes seemed genuinely appreciative of Yiddish culture—but by and large, distaste issued forth from one side, distrust from the other.

In time, events and evolution changed the course of relations between the two groups. The horror of the Kishinev pogroms was a uniting factor, and the wars that rent the garment industry were so ghastly, and so embarrassing in the culture at large, that men and women from both sides came to realize that peace was a critical necessity. Later, as the children of the immigrants progressed economically and did indeed become Americanized, lineage—*yikhes*—became less important than other credentials. Finally, the dreadful specter of Hitlerism proved a truly uniting factor, and when the anti-Zionist feelings of the German Jews disappeared in the flames of the Holocaust, the American Jewish community was, for all practical purposes, united.

In her *Poor Cousins*, the best account of the relations over the years between the two groups, Ande Manners tells about an event that in some ways symbolized the end of the tensions. "In 1950," she writes, "Robert Sarnoff, grandson of a desperately poor Russian tailor, married Felicia Schiff Warburg, great-granddaughter of the richest, most important *Yahudi* of his time. In 1970 the Sarnoffs were divorced, and the ex-Mrs. Sarnoff married Franklin Delano Roosevelt, Jr. One wonders what their respective *zaydes*, Abraham Sarnoff and Jacob H. Schiff, and *bobbe*, Sara Delano Roosevelt, would have made of it all."

V

Vladeck, B. Charney (1886–1938)

Brother of the poet Daniel Charney and the literary critic S. Niger, Vladeck was a Socialist officeholder and, in a New York political system virtually established on a foundation of ethnicity, an eloquent exponent of a politics based on ideology instead of ethnic or religious background. A revolutionary Bundist in Russia, imprisoned several times, he escaped to America, studied the life of Abraham Lincoln, attended the University of Pennsylvania, and went to work for the *Daily Forward*, eventually becoming its general manager. He became a citizen in 1915, and two years later was elected Williamsburg's member of the New York City Board of Aldermen. In 1921 the Republican and Democratic parties mounted an anti-Socialist Fusion campaign in New York, and Vladeck was defeated. Remaining active in Socialist politics and labor activities, he returned to the city council in 1937 as a candidate of the American Labor Party. "For many years we have been telling our people that the real, the true bond of comradeship is not religion but kinship of aspirations and ideals," he said at the time. "Intelligent Jews . . . resent the idea of just voting as Jews in any election and not as citizens. They resent the idea of voting, not on the basis of principle, not on the basis of the common good, but on the basis of religious or racial affiliation." Years earlier, according to Deborah Dash Moore in *At Home in America*, Vladeck had outlined the issue in a homelier fashion: in 1920, she says, he "curtly reminded his fellow politicians . . . that he never considered the *tefillin* a political symbol."

Vladeck was also an energetic exponent of public housing, and is memorialized today by a project on the Lower East Side that bears his name.

B. Charney Vladeck is third from R in this 1937 gathering of dignitaries after a performance of Singer's *The Brothers Ashkenazi*. Others, reading L from Vladeck, include actor Isidore Cashier, Albert Einstein, Maurice Schwartz and Fiorello LaGuardia

Wald, Lillian (1867–1940) One of the sainted figures of the Lower East Side, Cincinnati-born Lillian Wald was a well-to-do German Jew whose dedication to the immigrants was so complete that she not only worked tirelessly in their behalf, but actually chose to keep her residence in their midst. After attending Miss Cruttenden's English-French Boarding and Day School for Young Ladies, Wald entered nursing school and found work at the New York Juvenile Asylum. Her ideas of nursing went beyond the narrow definition of the day; she believed that nursing also required education to a way of life that would assure family health. She brought her ideas to the East Side while teaching nursing to a group of immigrant women; asked to make an emergency house call, she immediately became aware of the need for a resident nursing service in the area. Moving into the

Top, Lillian Wald; bottom, one of the Henry Street nurses on house calls, 1914

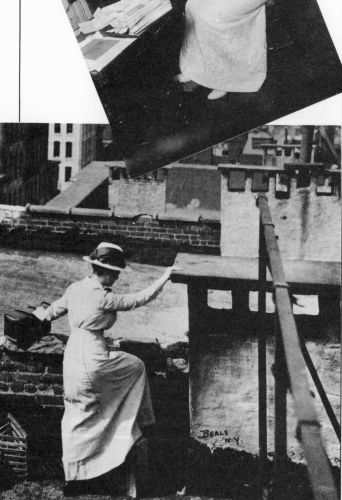

neighborhood, Wald joined with Mary Brewster in 1893 to found the first Visiting Nurse Service, and a year later established, with the backing of Jacob Schiff, the organization that would become the Henry Street Settlement.

Some of Wald's case notes, dated 1893, describe the conditions she found in the tenement blocks and what she did to alleviate them: "Case of Mrs. G., 183 Clinton Street, rear tenement, second floor. First found by Miss Brewster, July 1st, puerperal septicemia [a post-childbirth systemic infection of the blood], lying on vermin-infested bed without sheets or pillow cases. Husband, a peddler, had $40 saved at beginning of illness, 3 weeks before. All had gone and none coming in, for he had been obliged to remain home to care for five children and wife." The notes go on to report that she arranged to have the flat cleaned, obtained meat and wine from the United Hebrew Charities, gave the family three dollars weekly to hire a woman to wash the clothes and look after the children so the father could return to work, loaned the mother "all utensils necessary for good nursing," enrolled the children in a penny-saving program at the College Settlement, and provided regular care for the ailing mother. "This and proper food soon told," Wald wrote, "as the mother is convalescing."

The Henry Street Settlement, which grew out of such ministrations, provided a variety of services beyond medical care, including an ambitious arts program and various athletic activities. It remains an active presence on the Lower East Side today. Lillian Wald's proselytizing on the plight of immigrants, and especially their children, led directly to the formation of the Federal Children's Bureau in 1912.

Jerome Weidman sits on piano with Lillian Roth, flanked by conductor Lehman Engel (at piano) and composer Harold Rome, during rehearsals for the Broadway production of *I Can Get It For You Wholesale*, 1962

Weidman, Jerome (1913–   ) In 1937 the publication of *I Can Get It for You Wholesale*, by the twenty-four-year-old Jerome Weidman, was a bombshell. The novel was the story of Harry Bogen and how he rose from shipping clerk to wealthy garment manufacturer by double-crossing everyone he encountered on his way. It was a tautly written tale about a particularly ugly character, and the author wasted little effort indicating what he felt about Bogen. For many Jews it was an exceedingly uncomfortable book, and many branded it anti-Semitic. Its publisher, Simon and Schuster, even stopped printing its sequel, *What's in It for Me?*, despite its brisk sale. Years later, Weidman (a Lower East Side boy whose father was "the fastest pocket-maker on Allen Street") told an interviewer, "I have lived with Jewish people all my life and I have to paint them, warts and all. My beat is the beat that Sinclair Lewis took, life in America."

Weidman had his supporters in the literary world. F. Scott Fitzgerald called the book "a break-through into completely new and fresh literary terrain; a turning point in the American novel." Alfred Kazin, himself of a working-class Jewish family, wrote, "In the best sense of the word this book is a moral book; its morality is vivid because it is so dramatically abused by the narrator. . . . In one priceless scene, mostly crisp reprimand, Mr. Weidman has conveyed the atmosphere of a typical Jewish home with more fidelity and understanding than I have ever seen it conveyed before."

Weidman went on to write nearly forty more books, among them two dozen novels, most of which dealt with Jewish characters in conflict with themselves and the gentile world around them. He was also the author, with George Abbott, of the Broadway musical *Fiorello!*, and twenty-five years after the publication of *I Can Get It for You Wholesale*, of the musical based on the novel. It starred Elliott Gould as Harry Bogen, but was memorable mostly for the Broadway debut of Barbra Streisand as the secretary, Miss Marmelstein.

WEVD "The station that speaks your language" is what this New York FM radio broadcaster (it sold off its AM station in 1980 to a Christian evangelical group) calls itself, and it lives up to its billing by filling the air with music and talk in Yiddish, Hebrew, Turkish, Japanese, Portuguese, Spanish, Greek, German, and Italian— among other languages.

Yiddish, however, is the station's mother tongue, so to speak. WEVD was founded in 1926 by the Socialist organization that also published the *Daily Forward* (its call letters honor the memory of Eugene V. Debs, the Socialist leader). In 1943

Zvee Scooler, WEVD's gram-mayster

sixty percent of the station's air time was devoted to Yiddish-language programming, and its Yiddish commercials, with jingles and interspersed English phrases, became the material out of which emerged first humor and then nostalgia. The Yiddish-lilt jingle that hawked clothes for Joe & Paul, a Lower East Side garment house, was particularly popular.

WEVD has always been strong in the broadcast of programs dealing with Jewish culture, and in its later, less ideological years, even with those of a religious nature. Among its most enduring programs was the much-beloved "Yiddish Philosopher," filled with observations on the ways of life of Jews and other people. Still broadcast today, as it has been every Sunday morning since the station's founding, is the "Forward Hour." This variety show features a weekly editorial, in rhyme, by the *gram-mayster* ("master of rhymes"), the actor Zvee Scooler.

Williamsburg Perhaps only the Amish are comparable to the Chassidim in their religious devotion, their closed society, their serenity in exclusivity. However, the fact that the Chassidim of the Williamsburg section of Brooklyn (and nearby Crown Heights) maintain their separateness in the middle of a huge city makes them somewhat more remarkable; if not remarkable, it at least makes their neighborhood special. Williamsburg had a long Jewish history before the Chassidim arrived shortly after World War II. In the 1890s it was a neighborhood of middle-class German Jews; after the turn of the century, eastern European immigrants poured across the river from the Lower East Side, and by the middle 1930s it was almost exclusively Yiddish-speaking, with fully one-third of its Jewish population employed in garment factories nearby. As wealthier residents moved out toward the broader avenues of Flatbush, the neighborhood became more and more a haven of Orthodox Jews where, according to one report, "every second man wears a beard and [most of] the children on Lee Avenue . . . have a yarmulke and go to a Yeshiva."

At the end of the Second World War Williamsburg suddenly became the haven of thousands upon thousands of Chassidim, largely from Hungary, displaced by Hitler and the war. Even to the Orthodox then resident in the area, this sudden change was radical; Chaim Potok's excellent novel *The Chosen* chronicles the distance between

Williamsburg, 1980

the devout Jews who already occupied the neighborhood—"foreigners" by the standards of much of the Jewish community, let alone the American public as a whole—and the Chassidic Jews who soon dominated the area. Today, Yiddish is the lingua franca along Bedford Avenue, but the *Forward* isn't found on newsstands—secular publications are taboo. Stores close for the Sabbath on Friday afternoons, and television antennas—watching TV is a proscribed activity—are absent from the rooftops of Chassidic households. In the high-rise apartment houses occupied by the Chassidim, automatic elevators stop on each floor on the Sabbath so that those riding in the cars need not "work" by pressing the buttons. This all exists in a fortresslike setting, a densely populated neighborhood of fifteen thousand (the largest numbers of whom work either as clerks on Wall Street or in the midtown diamond trade) surrounded by some of the poorest blacks and Puerto Ricans in New York.

Although they may not be apparent to outsiders, there are strict social gradations in the Chassidic community, ranging from *rebbes* to *shtickel rebbes* (religiously educated and related to a rabbi), *talmidei hachamin* (learned, but no money), *sheine yidn* (literally "beautiful Jews," but colloquially Jews of rectitude and propriety), *balebatishe yidn* (wealthy donors to Chassidic activities), and *yidn*—Jews, but in this case members of Chassidic sects. Among the sects themselves there is some friction, particularly between the Satmar Chassidim (who oppose the state of Israel because it is a secular nation not ordained by God) and those who support the Zionist cause.

Winchevsky, Morris (1856–1932) Winchevsky was something of an anomaly

Morris Winchevsky

among the "sweatshop poets" with whom he was identified: he was an educated man, fluent in Russian, German, Hebrew, English, and Yiddish. He came to America in 1894 as a well-known figure in the Socialist movement, having lived nearly twenty years in England, where he had begun to write in English and had been a member of the literary Socialist circle that revolved around William Morris. When he arrived here, he was hailed as the *zayde*—the grandfather—of socialism, and used poetry as the means to his political end (just as he used Yiddish itself as a means to reach the Jewish masses). Despite his Socialist deprecations of it, Winchevsky was the only one of the sweatshop poets who brought a store of Jewish culture with him to America.

Wise, Stephen S. (1874–1949) This Budapest-born leader of the American Reform rabbinate earned his reputation as a freethinker in Portland, Oregon, and returned to New York spreading his gospel in the uptown and downtown communities alike. Wise announced that he had rejected Temple Emanu-El's offer of a position because that citadel of New York's German-Jewish aristocracy refused to assure him a "free pulpit," from which he could take whatever social and religious positions his conscience dictated; Louis Marshall maintained the job had never been offered. In any case, Wise founded the Free Synagogue, a Reform congregation with a free pulpit, no fixed dues, and—utterly new in the world of the German Jews—free pews. The Free Synagogue opened a branch downtown, at Lillian Wald's suggestion, and Wise in effect attempted a conversion movement among the children of the area's Orthodox Jews. It met with only limited success, but Wise, undeterred, earned some glory on the Lower East Side for his untiring support of the labor movement. He believed, as he said in an article in *The American Hebrew*, that "The synagogue may hope to speak to the workingman only if it first speaks for the workingman."

Workmen's Circle The oldest national Jewish fraternal order in the United States, the Workmen's Circle (in Yiddish, *Arbeter Ring*) was founded as a determinedly Socialist version of the benevolent societies founded by immigrants along synagogual, *landsmanshaft*, or other social lines. In its original incarnation, dating from 1892, it was dedicated to helping the sick and needy, and to the propagation of socialism and "scientific" thinking.

From those earliest days, the Workmen's Circle was staunchly antireligious, keeping its schools open on the High Holy Days, closing instead on May 1. As in

Stephen S. Wise (R), with Nathan Straus (L) and Louis D. Brandeis, members of the Jewish delegation to the Versailles Peace Conference, en route, 1919

many left-wing Jewish organizations, factionalism was common, and in 1926 Communist branches of the Circle split off to form the International Workers' Order, or the *Ordn*. The remaining Workmen's Circle was hardly tame, however; even during the heady days of the New Deal, portions of the Circle kept their staunchly leftist faith by persisting, at least until the outbreak of World War II, in their criticism of Roosevelt and his policies. Even so honored a figure as Supreme Court Justice Louis Brandeis came in for assault, as in this song from a play, *Five Out of Nine Have It*, published in the Workmen's Circle newspaper:

> . . . I am Louis Brandeis
> A liberal I'm supposed to be.
> It never does you any good,
> Because I'm in the minority.
> It makes a perfect set-up
> For Morgan and his minions,

> The Masses are demanding bread
> And they get dissenting opinions!

However, as the community changed, becoming more Americanized and less ideological, so did the Circle alter, growing more concerned with the disappearance of the Yiddish language and less with politics. It devoted great energies to the preservation of Yiddish culture and invested heavily in its secular Yiddish schools. It also sponsored a small network of Jewish day schools, the Folksbiene theater group, and a noteworthy choral project. The Workmen's Circle's past, however, is perhaps best represented in the names of those buried in its section of the Mount Carmel Cemetery, among them Sholem Aleichem, Abraham Cahan, B. Charney Vladeck, Meyer London, and Morris Rosenfeld.

Workmen's Circle leaders, 1915

Yehoash (1872–1927) His full name was Yehoash Solomon Bloomgarden, and among Yiddish poets and writers, he defied classification. Emigrating from Lithuania at age eighteen, he took for his themes a broad spectrum of subjects, but his innermost love was simply for the use of words, Yiddish words that both inspired and challenged his creativity. Influenced by English and American poets, and by Heinrich Heine, his poems were in many ways unique among Yiddish works, concerned as they were with the seasons, with nature, with the sea and the countryside. But Yehoash was not remote from the times: among his poems were those entitled "Broadway," "Lynching," and "Woolworth Building."

Still, for all his originality and undoubted gift, Yehoash was not a success—at least a material success—as a poet, nor as a bookkeeper, tailor, peddler, or other occupations he pursued. Stricken by tuberculosis, he spent ten years in a Denver sanitarium, and there he finally flourished as a translator and scholar. With his physician, Charles D. Spivak, he prepared a Yiddish dictionary in 1911, defining in the process more than four thousand Hebrew and Aramaic words expropriated by Yiddish. It was also in the sanitarium that he began the major literary effort of his life, a translation of the Hebrew Bible into Yiddish, a chore over which he agonized for years. This

Yehoash

monumental work was eventually serialized, over a five-year period, in *The Day*, and was a huge success when it was published between hard covers. Yehoash was also responsible for translations into Yiddish of such works as Longfellow's *Hiawatha*, *The Rubaiyat of Omar Khayyam*, and tales of Aesop, Fontaine, and Lessing.

Yezierska, Anzia (1885–1970) A novelist whose goal was to "build a bridge of understanding between the American-born and myself, to open up my life and the lives of my people to them," Anzia Yezierska initially found in America a world different from the one about which she had dreamed. Born into a large family in Plonsk, in Russian Poland, she emigrated as a teenager, hoping to discover in this country a Zion where women could unlock their hearts and minds and enjoy a freedom unthinkable in the old country. Instead she found a grueling, impoverished life, and had to battle single-mindedly to achieve her goals. While working in sweatshops, in laundries, and as a cook, she got her education at Columbia on a settlement-house scholarship. Setting out on her life as a writer, she took the unheard-of step of leaving her husband and child. She wrote short stories at first, stories about the Lower East Side that told of how poverty and narrow tradition stifled the human soul. In 1920 these stories were collected and published as *Hungry Hearts*.

When the book came to the attention of Samuel Goldwyn, he paid Yezierska $10,000 for the film rights and $200 a week to work in his studio.

The movie was completed in 1922, and Yezierska was a success, a well-off woman who nonetheless found neither fame nor relative fortune satisfying. She left Hollywood after a year, returning to New York to resume chronicling the adjustment of immigrants to American life. Between 1920 and 1932 she published six books, including what was probably her best novel, *Bread Givers*, and then lapsed into a nearly two-decade silence, finally publishing in

1950 a semiautobiographical memoir, *Red Ribbon on a White Horse*. The book, which featured an introduction by W. H. Auden, took its title from a Yiddish proverb her father uttered to Yezierska as he lay dying: "Poverty is an ornament on a Jew like a red ribbon on a white horse." The saying haunted her and made her reexamine the life her parents had embraced and which she had abandoned.

These were feelings that had lived with Yezierska for a quarter of a century. In 1925 she had written for *Cosmopolitan* an article titled "This Is What $10,000 Did to Me." In it, she spoke of how her head was turned by her new wealth, and yet how it left her feelingly terribly guilty. Wrought by turmoil, she traveled to Europe and attempted to atone by returning in steerage. After a day, however, she found she could not stand the conditions, having become used to comfort. She moved into a Fifth Avenue hotel on her return and discovered that she no longer hated the rich; that "they were not ogres, heartless oppressors of the poor. They were human as other folks." But in the last paragraph, Yezierska wrote, "I look back and see how happy I ought to have been when I was starving poor, but one of my own people. Now I am cut off by my own for acquiring the few things I have. And those new people with whom I dine and to whom I talk, I do not belong to them. I am alone because I left my own world."

Yiddish in English There is certainly irony in the fact that Yiddish, a language beleaguered by assimilation in America, should have made what is probably its longest-lasting impression, outside its own circles, on the English language spoken in the United States. This process began as

Anzia Yezierska,
from *Cosmopolitan*, 1925

The headline reads, "How Aunt Jemima helped Mother win the title 'Our Sweetheart?'" In the copy, what Jemima calls "pancakes," the family refers to as "latkes." From an advertisement in Yiddish newspapers, 1938

Yiddish-speaking immigrants and their children reacted to the American environment by practicing an everyday usage that has been alternatively dubbed "Yidlish," "Yinglish," or "Ameriddish." Despite recurring campaigns to purify Yiddish, the process of interaction was inexorable. Often the exchange seemed capricious: a young girl remained a *meydl* in American Yiddish, but a boy became a *boy* or *boychik*. A *bilet* became a "ticket," a *hun* became a "chicken." There was no pattern to the appropriation of English words into the Yiddish vocabulary; it just happened.

And so did the process work in the other direction. It began, of course, in New York, spreading through the usual means, and some less than usual (the heavy preponderance of eastern European Jews in the entertainment industry, for one), to the rest of the country. Though the stand-up comics popularized a variety of vulgarisms, more proper words spread into English as well. *Kosher* became an acceptable synonym for "clean" or "honest," and *kibitzer* became standard American first for the chatty onlookers at a game of chess or cards, then for anyone vocally critical, albeit good-naturedly, of other people's actions. *Mavens* are experts, *meshuge* means "crazy," and rare is the urban *goy* who doesn't know what the word means. One American dictionary lists *schmuck* as a "person of bad character," a definition that created a tiny scandal when it was accepted by the crossword puzzle editor of the *New York Times*, apparently unaware that the word is also a coarse vulgarism for "penis."

Not only words, but fractions of words found their way into English, most notably the suffix *-nik*, but also the ubiquitous *shm-* that begins so many Yiddish words. This latter was appropriated in such words as

183

Yiddish in English, pictorialized

"shmo," a coinage that means pretty much the same as "nebbish," and in expressions like "tired, shmired," or "big, shmig," a usage connoting a feeling that what is being discussed is not very urgent or important, a sort of verbal shrug that is eminently Yiddish in its expressive quality.

Yiddish also loaned its sentence structure to English: "He needs it like a hole in the head," and "You should drop dead," are rhythmically derived from the Yiddish (in fact, the first phrase is virtually a direct translation of a common Yiddish expression). Vocabulary, intonation, syntax, all gave to English in the same way American Yiddish took from its host country. It is, of course, what we expect in the meeting of two cultures—or, better, so what else is new?

Yiddishism Toward the end of the nineteenth century the Yiddish language was at a crossroads. Eastern European Jews were becoming a secular people dispersing along many roads—linguistically, politically, religiously, socially. The language represented a vibrant culture, an advanced literature, but more and more Jews were speaking Russian, German, or English in their respective territories. The German Jews scorned Yiddish as vulgar, cheap. Socialists saw it as a parochial language, and wished to integrate the Jewish masses into Socialist societies that ignored ethnicity. Zionists, who saw Yiddish as the tongue of servitude and repression, urged Jews to adopt Hebrew. Those who were less possessed by ideology, especially the immigrants, heard their children grow up speaking the language of the culture they had adopted. Yiddish was suffering the fate of a tongue that was, as Isaac Bashevis Singer pointed out decades later in his 1978 Nobel Prize

speech, "a language of exile, without a land, without frontiers, not supported by any government." Critical changes in the lives of Jews who knew Yiddish as their mother tongue swept away the thrust of the old homily "He who knows no Hebrew is an ignoramus, but he who knows no Yiddish is a gentile."

Before this onslaught against a language that had served its people for more than a thousand years stood the Yiddishists, men and women who saw the salvation—indeed, glorification—of the language as the cornerstone of Jewish identity and culture. Eight million of the world's fourteen million Jews spoke Yiddish, they argued, so Yiddish—a language whose very name means "Jewish"—was obviously the language of the Jewish people. As democratic aspirations became reality in the New World and dreams of nationalism were focusing on Palestine, men like Chaim Zhitlowsky, who was one of the organizers of the Czernowitz Conference, argued that Yiddish culture was flourishing and the language could be the vehicle of cultural awakening. These arguments helped win the allegiance of Socialists (who became persuaded that Yiddish was the only means of reaching the people) and of Zionists (who would by and large, at least until World War II, accept the nationalist argument). Among the growing Jewish middle class, however, the efforts of the intellectuals were more telling: when men like Sholem Aleichem and Y. L. Peretz began writing in Yiddish, the movement gained persuasive argument as well as advertisement.

The campaign for Yiddish was destined to survive for many decades, but the effects of assimilation and Nazi policies made its eventual decline inevitable. In Palestine, statehood only reinforced the pro-Hebrew attitudes of many Zionists, who established Hebrew as the nation's official tongue. Still, the language lingered; in the late 1950s, a common Israeli joke told of a mother on a bus berating her child in Yiddish, giving him a *klap* whenever he replied in Hebrew. When a stranger asked why she beat a child who spoke such good Hebrew, the mother answered, "I want him to know Yiddish, he shouldn't forget he's a Jew."

Di Yidishe Tsaytung The first entry in what would become a crowd of Yiddish newspapers in America, *Di Yidishe Tsaytung* first appeared on March 1, 1870, a self-described "weekly paper of politics, religion, history, science and art," with the English title, "The New York Hebrew Times," emblazoned above the Yiddish logotype. Its publisher was I. K. Buchner, like so many of the first Yiddish editors a Lithuanian Jew devoted to the subjects of the New Enlightenment. It took its editorial material from German and other European Jewish periodicals, and was quickly scorned by English-language Jewish publications. The uptown *Jewish Times* said, "Buchner's *Yidishe Tsaytung* is a weekly publication written in the Jewish and German-Polish jargon, and its

contents are as laughable as its language. It provides reading material entirely suited to the recently imported Russian Jews, and is a shining example of Middle Ages superstitions and naivete." The paper, produced by lithography, cost six cents, and loyally followed the party line of Tammany Hall. It finally expired in 1877.

YIVO Institute for Jewish Research
This remarkable institution is the world's great repository of documents and books dealing with the life and world of the Yiddish-speaking Jews ("YIVO" is an acronym for Yidisher Visnshaftlekher Institut, which

Current YIVO headquarters on Fifth Avenue.

Top, the Vilna staff of YIVO, before World War II;
bottom, YIVO Vilna archives returned from Germany after World War II

roughly means "Jewish Scientific Institute"). It was founded in Berlin in 1925, with Vilna—"the Jerusalem of Lithuania"—its headquarters. The institute's goal was not only to gather information on Yiddish and its culture, but also to disseminate knowledge of it. When Hitler's war began, YIVO's extensive archives were seized by the Nazis. A new headquarters was established in New York, where Dr. Max Weinreich, one of the institute's founders, had settled, and efforts to start anew began. When the war ended, much of the archive was discovered intact in boxes in Frankfurt and sent to New York.

Today YIVO occupies an unlikely building, the former home of Amy Vanderbilt, a Louis XIII–style mansion on Fifth Avenue in which it continues a vigorous program of collection, study, teaching, exhibition, and publishing. Among its many notable publications, perhaps the best known are Dr. Weinreich's monumental study of the Yiddish language, recently issued in English translation, and the Yiddish-English dictionary and Yiddish textbook written by Weinreich's son, Uriel, who was head of the linguistics department of Columbia University.

YKUF The Yidisher Kultur Farband was one of the organizations that appealed to those Jews who believed that the Bolshevik Revolution had succeeded not only in overthrowing the hated czar, but also in bringing a new messianic era to the world they had left behind in Russia. Founded in 1937, the YKUF carried the party line to the Yiddish-speaking community while actively involving itself in the preservation of Yiddish culture. Although many members, including its first chairman, writer A. Mukdoni, were not party members, it func-

tioned in close liaison with Soviet policy, which cost it much support when the Soviet Union concluded its nonaggression pact with Nazi Germany in 1939. Nonetheless, YKUF was able to contribute much to the promotion of Yiddish poetry and prose in America, publishing over the years more than 250 books dealing with all aspects of Yiddish life and literature.

Yom Kippur Balls In the last decade of the nineteenth century, Jewish anarchists and other radicals sought to underscore their break with what they deemed the "superstition" of religion. One particularly effective means of making the point was the so-called Yom Kippur Ball staged annually on Kol Nidre night. Parades preceded the ball, and though it is likely that in the process the anarchists offended some of those who might have been inclined toward their cause, the point was more solidarity than recruitment. Merriment replaced atonement and reflection as the order of the night, and the menu invariably featured ham sandwiches accompanied by tea with milk. Much as they tried to shake the grip of their religious pasts, however, more than a few of the Yom Kippur Ball celebrants gagged on the unfamiliar, long-proscribed taste of pork.

Di Yunge They were the young immigrant poets who rebelled against the propagandistic themes of their poetic elders, eschewing the metrical cries of pain and politics that characterized the work of the "sweatshop poets." *Di Yunge* took shape in 1907, taking their name—"the young ones"—from their journal, *Yognt*, or "Youth." Their opponents sneeringly dismissed them, but *Di Yunge* forged ahead, throwing off the old themes of social significance, socialism, and

Jewish nationalism, and plunged instead into art for the sake of art. They retained traditional verse forms, but experimented with words as much as with ideas, betraying the same impulses succumbed to by others in the modern movement then sweeping through all of western poetry. *Di Yunge* were not as a rule well-educated bohemians, but they greedily lapped up the poetry of modernists writing in other languages, identifying with artistic goals far removed from their own community.

Still, they were indisputably part of the Yiddish community, not simply by virtue of the language in which they wrote, but because of the clear influence of Jewish themes upon their work. Writing of *Di Yunge*—of M. L. Halpern, Mani Leib, Moshe Nadir, I. J. Schwartz—Irving Howe said, "*Di Yunge* were modern poets, but, more important, modern Yiddish poets. More than they knew or could suppose, they shared in the experience against which they rebelled."

Di Yunge. **Top row (second from L), H. Leivick; bottom row (C) Abraham Reisen, (R) M.L. Halpern**

Zangwill, Israel (1864–1926) This lively man of letters was an English Jew, London born, who first came to prominence with the publication in 1892 of a volume of stories called *Children of the Ghetto*, in which he introduced the English public to the Jews of London's East End. He wrote about tragicomic lives in which generations, dogmas, cultures, and ideologies were in constant conflict. One of the first expositions of the lives in exile of Jewish emigrants from Russia, this work was commissioned by Mayer Sulzberger of Philadelphia, driving force in the nascent Jewish Publication Society. It was in America, especially after the New York production of his play *The Melting Pot*, that Zangwill achieved his greatest fame. Presented in 1908, the play—which was dedicated to Theodore Roosevelt—preached assimilation, the divine creation of a new American species from the many varieties of immigrants who were streaming into the country. One critic questioned whether "this foreigner" was not presumptuous in offering us "this sentimentalism and 'patriotism.' "

Zangwill was a Zionist, later becoming a territorialist, espousing the establishment of Jewish colonies wherever land could be bought for them. He was an outspoken critic of America's isolationism in the years after World War I, and also assailed the materialism of Jewish life in New York. His books, in addition to *Children of the Ghetto*, included *Ghetto Tragedies*, *Ghetto Comedies*, and *King of the Schnorrers*, the latter recently adapted as a Broadway musical. He also wrote poetry, and his studies of Heine, LaSalle, Spinoza, and other

Jewish thinkers were collected in the volume, *Dreamers of the Ghetto*.

Zeydes and Bobes Grandfathers and grandmothers, women and men leaving a land where they were oppressed for another where they were in many ways unwelcome. Many would find privation, poverty, early death; others would thrive, finding just the freedom and opportunity they had sought. They all spoke Yiddish when they came. Their sons and daughters spoke less, their grandchildren almost none at all. When we were young, they were familiar figures, men and women we loved, but somehow peculiar; they spoke in accents barely moderated by decades in America, they ate strange foods, perhaps read newspapers filled with unfamiliar letters. If we turned our backs on their "foreign-ness" then, today we embrace what we can retrieve of their lives.

Zeydes, the Hebrew Home for the Aged, Dorchester, Mass. All of these men are over 100 years old

Adams, Joey, with Henry Tobias. *The Borscht Belt*. New York: Bobbs-Merrill, 1966.

Antin, Mary. *The Promised Land*. Boston: Houghton Mifflin, 1912 and 1940.

Ausubel, Nathan. *Pictorial History of the Jewish People*. New York: Crown, 1964.

Baum, Charlotte, Phyllis Hyman, and Sonia Michel. *The Jewish Woman in America*. New York: Dial Press, 1976.

Berkow, Ira. *Maxwell Street*. Garden City, N.Y.: Doubleday, 1977.

Bernard, Jacqueline. *The Children You Gave Us*. New York: Bloch Publishing Co., 1972.

Bernardi, Jack. *My Father, the Actor*. New York: W.W. Norton, 1971.

Bregstone, Philip. *Chicago and Its Jews*. Chicago: Privately published, 1933.

Burns, George. *Living It Up*. New York: Putnam, 1976.

Cahan, Abraham. *The Education of Abraham Cahan*, trans. Leon Stein, Abraham P. Conan, and Lynn Davidson. Philadelphia: The Jewish Publication Society of America, 1969.

———. *The Rise of David Levinsky*. New York: Harper & Row, 1960.

Cantor, Eddie. *As I Remember Them*. New York: Duell, Sloan & Pearce, 1963.

———. *Take My Life*. Garden City, N.Y.: Doubleday, 1963.

Dimont, Max I. *The Jews in America*. New York: Simon and Schuster, 1978.

Dinsky, Lazar. *Days in Shop*. New York: Posy-Shoulson Press, 1936.

Eisenberg, Dennis, Uri Dan, and Eli Landau. *Meyer Lansky, Mogul of the Mob*. New York: Paddington Press, 1979.

Fein, Isaac M. *Boston—Where It All Began*. Boston: Boston Jewish Bicentennial Committee, 1976.

Feingold, Henry L. *Zion in America*. New York: Twayne, 1974.

Feinsilver, Lillian Miriam. *The Taste of Yiddish*. South Brunswick, N.J.: Yoseloff, 1970.

Feldstein, Stanley. *The Land That I Show You*. Garden City, N.Y.: Anchor, 1978.

Gethers, Judith, and Elizabeth Lefft. *The World Famous Ratner's Meatless Cookbook*. New York: Bantam, 1975.

Gittleman, Sol. *From Shtetl to Suburbia*. Boston: Beacon, 1978.

Gold, Michael. *Jews Without Money*. New York: International Publishers, 1930.

Golden, Harry, with Richard Goldhurst. *Travels Through Jewish America*. Garden City, N.Y.: Doubleday, 1973.

Goldsmith, Emanuel S. *Architects of Yiddishism at the Beginning of the Twentieth Century*. Rutherford, N.J.: Fairleigh Dickinson University Press, 1976.

Goren, Arther. *New York Jews and the Quest for Community*. New York: Columbia University Press, 1970.

Hapgood, Hutchins. *The Spirit of the Ghetto*. New York: Funk and Wagnalls, 1965.

Hindus, Milton, ed. *The Old East Side: An Anthology*. Philadelphia: The Jewish Publication Society of America, 1969.

Howe, Irving. *How We Lived*. New York: Marek, 1980.

———. *World of Our Fathers*. Harcourt Brace Jovanovich, 1976.

Jessel, George. *The World I Lived In*. Chicago: Regnery, 1975.

Kahn, Yitzhak. *Portraits of Yiddish Writers*. New York: Vantage, 1979.

Karp, Abraham. *Golden Door to America*. New York: Viking, 1976.

Katzman, Jacob. *Commitment*. New York: Labor Zionist Letters, 1975.

Lee, Albert. *Henry Ford and the Jews*. New York: Stein and Day, 1980.

Levin, Nora. *While Messiah Tarried: Jewish Socialist Movements, 1871-1917*. New York: Schocken, 1977.

Levitan, Tina. *The Firsts of American Jewish History*. Brooklyn, N.Y.: Charuth Press, 1957.

Lifson, David. *The Yiddish Theatre in America*. New York: Yoseloff, 1965.

Liptzin, Sol. *The Maturing of Yiddish Literature*. New York: Jonathan David, 1970.

Madison, Charles. *Yiddish Literature*. New York: Ungar, 1968.

Manners, Ande. *Poor Cousins*. New York: Coward, McCann & Geoghegan, 1972.

Marx, Arthur. *Goldwyn: A Biography of the Man Behind the Myth*. New York: Norton, 1976.

Meltzer, Milton. *Taking Root*. New York: Dell, 1976.

Metzker, Isaac. *A Bintel Brief: Sixty Years of Letters from the Lower East Side to the Jewish Daily Forward*. Garden City, N.Y.: Doubleday, 1971.

Miller, James. *The Detroit Jewish Theatre, 1920-1937*. Detroit: Wayne State University Press, 1967.

Moore, Deborah Dash. *At Home in America: Second Generation New York Jews*. New York: Columbia University Press, 1981.

Novotny, Ann. *Strangers at the Door: Ellis Island, Castle Garden and the Great Migration to America*. Riverside, Conn.: Chatham Press, 1971.

Pomerantz, Joel. *Jennie and the Story of the Grossingers*. New York: Grosset & Dunlap, 1970.

Postal, Bernard, and Lionel Koppman. *American Jewish Landmarks*. New York: Fleet Press, 1977.

———, and David H. White. *The Best of Ten Years in the Jewish Digest*. Houston: D.H. White, 1965.

Reisner, Neil. *Jewish Los Angeles: A Guide*. Los Angeles: The Jewish Federation Council of Greater Los Angeles, n.d.

Riis, Jacob. *How the Other Half Lives*. New York: Hill & Wang, 1957.

Rischin, Moses. *The Promised City*. Cambridge: Harvard University Press, 1954.

Rockland, Mae Shafter, with Michael Aaron Rockland. *The Jewish Yellow Pages*. New York: Schocken, 1976.

Rosenfeld, Lulla. *Bright Star of Exile*. New York: Crowell, 1977.

Roskolenko, Harry. *The Time That Was*

Then. New York: Dial, 1971.

Rosten, Leo. *The Education of H★Y★M★A★N K★A★P★L★A★N*. New York: Harcourt, Brace, 1937.

———. *The Joys of Yiddish*. New York: McGraw-Hill, 1968.

Roth, Cecil. *The Concise Jewish Encyclopedia*. New York: New American Library, 1980.

Samuel, Maurice. *In Praise of Yiddish*. New York: Cowles, 1971.

Sanders, Ronald. *The Downtown Jews*. New York: Harper & Row, 1969.

———, and Edmond Gillon, Jr. *The Lower East Side*. New York: Dover, 1979.

Sandrow, Nahma. *Vagabond Stars: A World History of Yiddish Theatre*. New York: Harper & Row, 1977.

Schappes, Morris U. *The Jews in the United States: A Pictorial History, 1654 to the Present*. New York: Citadel, 1958.

Schoener, Allon. *Portal to America: The Lower East Side 1870–1925*. New York: Holt, Rinehart and Winston, 1967.

Schwartz, J.B. *Orchard Street*. New York: Comet Press, 1960.

Secunda, Victoria. *Bei Mir Bist Du Schön: The Life of Sholem Secunda*. Weston, Conn.: Magic Circle Press, 1982.

Shapiro, Judah J. *The Friendly Society: A History of the Workmen's Circle*. New York: Media Judaica, 1970.

Shulman, Abraham. *The New Country*. New York: Scribner, 1976.

Spalding, Henry D. *Encyclopedia of Jewish Humor*. New York: Jonathan David, 1969.

Teller, Judd L. *Strangers and Natives: The Evolution of the American Jew from 1921 to the Present*. New York: Delacorte, 1968.

Tucker, Sophie. *Some of These Days*. Garden City, N.Y.: Doubleday, Doran, 1945.

Wiernik, Peter. *History of Jewish America*. New York: Hermon Press, 1972.

Yezierska, Anzia. *Breadgivers*. New York: Persea Books, 1975.

———. *Red Ribbon on a White Horse*. New York: Persea Books, 1981.

Picture Credits